AF449148

This is a major study of the structure, sources, language, and position in literary tradition of the alliterative Old English poem, *Christ and Satan*. The author considers in detail the theme, dialects of origin and transmission, and probable date of composition.

The treatment of heroic and Christian diction and imagery is especially valuable: Sleeth uses it as a base to propose new conclusions about the thematic unity and structure of the entire manuscript (Bodleian ms Junius 11) of which *Christ and Satan* is the last part.

Through circumspect examination of individual words and phrases, Sleeth demonstrates a particular sensitivity to etymologies, ranges of meaning, and contextual fit. He concludes that this is the work of a single poet treating a powerful theme, central to the Christian religion, in terms of well conceived, rhetorically effective design.

This book, which includes in microfiche a considered text of the poem itself and a hitherto unavailable proposed line-by-line scansion, makes a significant contribution to the understanding of Old English poetry.

MCMASTER OLD ENGLISH STUDIES AND TEXTS 3

Alvin A. Lee *General Editor*
Laurel Braswell
Maureen Halsall
Prudence Tracy *University of Toronto Press*

CHARLES R. SLEETH

# Studies in *Christ and Satan*

UNIVERSITY OF TORONTO PRESS
Toronto Buffalo London

**Canadian Cataloguing in Publication Data**

Sleeth, Charles, R., 1914–
   Studies in Christ and Satan
   Includes text of the poem in Old English on
   accompanying microfiche.
   Bibliography: p.
   Includes index.
   ISBN 0-8020-5484-6
   1. Christ and Satan. 1. Christ and Satan. 11. Title.
   PS1634.S54        829.1        C80-094858-0

To the memory of my loving parents

the Reverend Waitman T. Willey Sleeth (1869–1942)
and
Pleasant Kendall Sleeth (1872–1965)

who did not exalt themselves

# Contents

**MICROFICHE**

**1
Sleeth's Text**

**2
Scansion for Sleeth's Text**

# Preface

The initial stages in the preparation of this book occurred in the early 1970s.
The work was undertaken in the belief that, although the time was past for a
grudging tolerance of Old English Christian poetry as a necessarily inferior
product to the heroic poetry, and although the Christian poetry's vigour
and subtlety were being increasingly recognized, *Christ and Satan* had not
yet received, as its share of this reappraisal, the focused attention
appropriate for it as the New Testament portion of the chief Old English
manuscript of poetry based centrally on Scripture, Manuscript Junius 11 in
the Bodleian Library. The large amount of work on *Christ and Satan* which
has been published between the start of work on this book and the writing
of this preface, including as its largest item a critical edition by R.E.
Finnegan which appeared in 1977, has been considered here to the best of
my ability, in the continuing belief that this book may fill a need which still
exists for a full-scale treatment of the poem under most or all of its major
aspects.

These aspects include the following: the unity of the poem, which
Finnegan treats ably from one point of view and I from another and
complementary one; its theme and structure; its possible date and place of
origin; the dialects of its origin and transmission; its sources; its place in the
heroic and Christian traditions of Old English poetry; and its manner of
fitting into the structure of MS Junius 11. Both early and recent scholarship
has been taken into account, with the object always in view of expressing
valid new conclusions where the evidence warrants them. This object may
have been attained (others must judge) to some degree in the treatment of
date and sources; to a more marked degree in the treatment of dialect; and
still more in the treatment of unity, theme, and structure, where the
conclusion is reached that in this work a single poet is treating a powerful

theme, central to the Christian religion, in terms of a well-conceived, rhetorically effective design, and in the treatment of its place in the heroic and Christian traditions of Old English poetry and its structural relation to MS Junius 11 as a whole.

Since this book was originally conceived as an edition, it includes a critical text of the poem itself (presented here in microfiche), prepared carefully and, it is hoped, on sound and well-considered principles of textual criticism. The detailed comparison of my text with Finnegan's which is included as the appendix should be useful, as should the microfiche on scansion. The reference value of both, I believe, is not entirely dependent on the rightness of the views expressed in them.

My indebtedness to M.D. Clubb's edition of 1925 has inevitably been great, in excess of the times I have referred to it.

My tutors and mentors, to whom I want to pay a well-earned tribute of thanks although many of them are unfortunately not alive to receive it, include the late P.C. McQuain, who introduced me to Old English poetry in translation in Nicholas County High School, Summersville, West Virginia; Louis W. Chappell, formerly of West Virginia University, who introduced me to the Old English language and literature there; and the late Professors C.L. Wrenn and J.R.R. Tolkien, who gave me the benefit of their learning and love of literature in my years at Oxford.

I thank the Bodleian Library, Oxford, for furnishing me with a photographic copy of pages 213–29 of Manuscript Junius 11, the sole manuscript of *Christ and Satan*; Princeton University, for access to the ample material in the open stacks of its library, which was indispensable for this work, and for generously affording me the opportunity to consult the work of Junius and Hickes in their locked collections; Drew University, Madison, New Jersey, for the use of its library facilities including Inter-Library Loan, which was provided by Mrs Dorothy Hulsart; and especially Brooklyn College of the City University of New York, not only for the use of its library facilities including Inter-Library Loan, which was provided by Mr James H. Gibson, but also for a one-semester sabbatical leave with full pay which enabled me to get off to a good start in the preparation of this work.

Finally, I thank my wife and family for considerable help in proofreading my typescript, and for unfailing interest, encouragement, and forbearance.

This book has been published with the assistance of grants from McMaster University and from the Subsidized Publications Fund of the University of Toronto Press.

CRS

Oxford, Bodleian Library, MS Junius 11 p 213

ꝺ[...]maꞃ heꞃꝺon ꝼoꞃg on ꞃꝝeᵹle·ꞃelꝩꝩin cꝩꝺum·þæꞃ nu ꝩꞇub·
ꝺone ecan æðele ꝼꞃonꝺað hæleꝺ ꝩn heh ꝼelꝺ·heꞃuᵹꝺ ꝺꞃⷝten·
ꝼoꞃꝺun ꝩꞃꝭcum·ꝩic ꝩnꝩꞃe ꞃceal biꝺan ꝝbenꝺum·⁊ ine ·æc
ꞇꞃan ꝼoꞃ ham ꝼoꞃ oꝝeꞃ hꝩᵹꝺum·æꝝꞃe ꝝⷝꝝene·ꝺa hꝝm ⁊
ꞃ[...]eꞃaꝺan azole ᵹaꝝꞃꝩꝝ ꝼꞃæꝝꞇe·ꝩꞃꝩꞃꞃ ꝝulle·ꝝuꝝle beꞃꞃoꝝeꝝe·
þu uꞃ ᵹeleꝝꝺeꞃ·ꝺuꞃꞀ lꝩᵹe ꝺꞃnne·þ ꝩe hælenꝺe·heꞃan ne ꞃceal
ꝺoꞃ·ꝺulce ꝝeaꝝum þ ꝺu aꞀcæꝝꞇ alleꞃ ᵹeꝝalꝺ·heoꝼꞃeꞃ ⁊ eoꞃþan
ꝝeꞃe haliᵹ ᵹoꝺ ꞃcꝩꝝenꝺ ꞃeolꝝa nu eꞃꝝc cu eꞃꞃꝝ ⁊ꞃceꝝꝺa·
[...] ꝝnꝼꝩꞃ locan ꝼꞃꞃe ᵹebunꝺen·ꝝꞃnꝺꞃ⸴ꝺu ꝺeꞃ ꝩul
ꝺoꞃ·ꝺꞇ þu ꝝoꝝuꝝꝺ ahcæꝝꞇ·alꝝuꞃ onꝝalꝺ·⁊ ꝝe enᵹlaꞃ ꝝnꝺ
ꝺec·Acol ꝩꞃ hꝝnon ꞃeon·habbað ꝝe alle ꝝꞃa ꝼoꞃ ꝺꝝnum
leahꞇꞃunᵹum·lꝩꝺne ᵹeꝼeꞃeꝺ·Sæᵹꝺeꞃ uꞃ ꞇoꞃoꝺe þ ꝺꞃꞃꝝꝝu
ꝝeꞃe·meoꞇoꝺ mon cꝝꝝꝝeꞃ·haꝝuꞃ cu nu maꞃe ꝝuꝝel·Sꝝa
ꝩꝝen ꝝulle·ꝼacnum ꝼoꞃꝺum·heoꞃa alꝺoꞃ ꝺæᵹn unꞃeoꞃꝺa
ꝺoꞃ·onceꞃꝝum eꝝꝺum·eꝝꝝ heo aꝝꝩꝺe·ꝺꞃeamum beꝺæꝝꝺe·
hæꝝꝺan ꝺꞃꝩhcneꞃ ꝝꞃc ꝼoꞃ oꝝꞃ hꝩᵹꝺum·uꝼan ꝼoꞃꝝcen·
hæꝝꝺon hꝩꝝ co hꝩhce·helle ꝼꞃoꝝaꞃ beoꞃnꝝꞃenꝺe bealo·blace
bꝩꞃꝝꞃoꞃ·ꝼeꞃꝝan ꝼoꞃ ꞃꝝeꝝene·ꞃceaꝺꝝꝝ hꝝeaꞃꝝꝺoꞇꞇ eꝝune
æᵹlecan ᵹeonꝺ þazole ꞃcꝝeꝼ ꝼoꞃ ꝺam medlan þe hie æꞃ
ꝺꞃuᵹon꞉                               ·11·

E ꝼꝝ ꞃeoꞃꝺaꝺe·oꝺꞃe ꞃꝝꝺe ꞃeonꝺa alꝺoꞃ·ꝝæꞃ þa ꝼoꞃ ꝝoꝝꞀc
aᵹen ꞃeꝝꝺꝺan he ꝺeꞃ ꝝcꝝ ꝼoꞃꝝᵹe ꞃelꝺe·he ꝝꝝeꝝꞇenꝺe·ꝺoꞃ
he ꝝꝝeoꝝan onᵹan ꝝꝝꝝe ꝝꝝꝝe·hebꝝꝺ ꝝꝝelc ꝝaᵹeꞃ·ꝺꞃeam
ꝺonne he ꝝꝝꝝꞇum·ꝝoꞃꝺ ꝝnꝺꞃaꝝ ꝝc ꝝæꞃ ꝩu ꝝnheoꞃꝝum·haliᵹ
ænᵹel ꝺꞃꝩhcenꝝeoꝝꝝe·heꞃꝺe me ꝺꞃeam mꝝꝺ ᵹoꝺe·mꝝcelne
ꝼoꞃ meoꞇoꝺe·⁊ ꝺeoꞃ meneᵹo ꝝꝝa ꞃome·þa ꝝc ꝝnmoꝺe mꝝnu
hoᵹaꝺe þ ꝝc ꝝolꝺe coꝝ ꝝꞃꝝan ꝝulꝝeꞃ leocꝝan·beaꞃn hælenꝺeꞃ·

Oxford, Bodleian Library, MS Junius 11 p 214

hpæt. dracan ꝼ neaddꝛan ꝼ þone dimman ham · ꝼoꞃ ðon mihte
ᵹe hepan · ꝼeðe æt hylle pæꝛ · tꝛelꝼ milum neh þ ðæꝛ pæꝛ toða
ᵹe haꞃ · lude ꝼ ᵹeomꞃe ᵹodeꝛ andꞃacan · hpeoꞃꝼen ᵹeond
helle haze on æleð · uꝼan ꝼ uzan him pæꝛ æᵹhpæꝛ ꝼ · pꞇcum
pepuᵹ · puldꝛeꝛ be ꝛcypede · dꞃeamum be dælde · heoꝼon ꝛeop
ᵹe hyᵹꝛ · þa heo on heoꝼonum ham ꝛtaðelodon þ hie poldon
be næman neꝛᵹende cꞃꞙꞇ · podeꞃa puceꞃ · ah he on pihtoᵹ
heold · lꞙned heoꝼona ꝼ þ haliᵹ ꝛeld · niꞙ næniᵹ ꝼpa ꝼnozoꞃ ·
ne ꝼpa cꞃæꝼtiᵹ · ne þæꞃ ꝼpa ᵹleap · nym þe ᵹod ꝛeolꝼa · þ aꞃeczan
mæᵹe · ꝼpeᵹleꝛ leoman · hu ꝛundu þæꝛ ꝛcineð ymb utan · meꞁodeꞃ
mihte ᵹeond þ mæꝛe cynn · þæꝛ habbað enᵹlaꝛ · eadiᵹne dꞃeam ·
ꝛanctaꝛ ꝛinᵹað · þiꞙ · ꝛeolꝼa ꝼoꝛ ᵹod · þonne beoð þa eadiᵹan ·
þe oꝼ eoꞃðan cumað · bꞃunᵹað to beaꝛme · bloꝛtman ꝛ tenceꝛ pꞙꞇe
pynꝛume þ ꝛꞙnd poꞃð ᵹodeꝛ · þonne hꞙe be ꝼædmeð ꝼædeꞃ man —
— cyn neꝛ ꝼ hie ᵹe ꝛeᵹnað miꞙ hiꝛ ꝼpꞙðꞃan hoꞃd · lædað to lihte ·
þæꝛ hi liꝼ aᵹon · azo aloꝼe · up licne ham · bꝩ phtcꞙe buꞙh
ꝛtyðe blæð bið æᵹhpæm · þæm ðe hælende hꞙꞃan þenceð ꝼ pel iꝛ
þanꝼe þæt mot :-

Pæꝛ þ enᵹel cyn æꞃ ᵹe nemneð · luciꝼeꝛ haten · leohte beꝛende · ·
ꝼoꞃ ᵹeaꞃdaᵹum · in ᵹodeꝛ pice · þa he in puldꝛe · ꝼꞃohꞇ on · ꝼalðe ·
þ he oꝼeꝛ hyða aᵹan polde · Satanuꝛ ꝛ peaꞃto ᵹe þohte þæt he
polde on heoꝼonum · he hꝛeð pyꝛcan · uppe miꞙ þam ecan ·
þæꝛ ealdoꝛ heoꞃa · yꝼeleꝛ oꞃð ꝼꞃuman · him þ eꝼꞇ ᵹe hꞃeap ·
þa he to helle · hnꞙᵹan ꝛceolde · ꝼ hiꝛ hꞙꞃeð miꞙ hine · into ᵹe ᵹlꞙðan ·
neꝛᵹendeꝛ nꞙð · ꝼ no ꝛeoððan þ hi moꝛten · in þone · ecan · anðꝛlꞙan
buzon ende · þa him eᵹꝛa be com · ðꞙne ꝼoꝛ deman · þa he dꞙꞃi
in helle · bꝛæc ꝼ beꝛᵹde · bliꝛ peaꞃð monnum · þa hi hælendeꝛ · heaꝼoð

Oxford, Bodleian Library, MS Junius 11 p 226

STUDIES IN 'CHRIST AND SATAN'

# 1

# The Work and the Question of Its Unity

The seventeen last pages of text (213–29 inclusive) in Manuscript Junius 11 in the Bodleian Library at Oxford comprise over seven hundred lines of alliterative Old English verse (728 by my count), whose subject matter consists of laments of Satan and his followers after their fall from heaven into hell, Christ's Harrowing of hell, his Resurrection, his post-Resurrection life on earth, his Ascension, his gift of the Holy Spirit at Pentecost, his enthronement at the right hand of God the Father, his judging of mankind at the Last Judgment, and his Temptation, during his life on earth, by Satan, in that order and with widely varying breadth of treatment of the several topics. Lacking a title in the manuscript, this work is now usually called *Christ and Satan*, a name conferred by Grein 1857a.[1]

In one form or another the question of unity has been mooted since the beginning of serious study of these last seventeen pages of MS Junius 11, which the scribe identifies at the end as Book Two. Conybeare 1826, while recognizing Book Two as 'an entirely distinct poem' and asserting that its principal subject is the Harrowing of hell, says that the introductory laments of Satan and his followers 'rather ... resemble an accumulation of detached fragments than any regular design';[2] and Thorpe 1832, even while arguing for Caedmon as the author of the whole manuscript, considers Book Two to have become so 'corrupt and mutilated' as to consist now of 'little else than a series of unconnected fragments.'[3] Thorpe, of course, attributes the state of the existing text to extremely bad transmission, and Conybeare apparently to faulty composition, rather than to diversity of authorship. Ludwig Ettmüller, *Handbuch der deutschen Litteraturge-schichte*, however, sees Book Two as several independent poems,[4] repeating less confidently in his partial edition of 1850 that he thinks they may be two or more in number.[5] Other scholars of the mid-nineteenth century, including Bouterwek and Grein in their editions, implicitly accept the unity of the work, with Grein conferring on it the name *Christ and Satan*, which has since been prevailingly used. Only Watson 1875, in this period, emphasizes what he calls its 'defective,' 'mutilated,' and 'confused' state, apparently attributing this, like Thorpe, to bad transmission but for his own part clearly implying that this involves much addition as well as fragmentation.[6] Rieger 1876 was the first to assert that one poem ends with line 365 and another begins with line 366.[7] In the following year, ten Brink 1877 divided the work as follows: ll. 1–365, a single poem on the fallen angels; ll. 366–662, a fragmentarily preserved poem on Christ's Harrowing of hell and Resurrection with other related topics; ll. 663–728, another much shorter fragment on Christ's Temptation.[8] His formulation raised the discussion to a new level by clearly delimiting the sections of text (hereafter to be called Parts I, II, and III) that any proponent of unity must reconcile with each other.

Since 1877, most of those who have denied the unity of *Christ and Satan* have accepted ten Brink's division of it into three works, at the points he indicated: the principal exceptions have been Groschopp and Abbetmeyer. Groschopp 1883 attempted to demonstrate that *Christ and Satan* in its existing form consists of remnants of a single larger poem patched together by a restorer, with some changes of order and some insertions, into what was intended as a unity.[9] Abbetmeyer 1903, on the other hand, while accepting ten Brink's second and third divisions, saw in ll. 1–365 no less than six distinct Plaints of Lucifer, considerably out of order in the existing work and in one instance broken up into four now discontinuous or transposed segments;[10] he viewed the entire work as 'a collection of poems describing mainly the sufferings of Satan after the descent of Christ.'[11] Neither Groschopp's nor Abbetmeyer's views on this matter have met with any acceptance, and this is not surprising, since in making detailed assertions about the textual prehistory of a piece of Old English poetry, both showed a degree of confidence for which no basis has ever been established.

Prominent among those who accepted ten Brink's division into three poems was Wülker (1885, 1896, and especially his edition of 1894). Kühn 1883 sought to marshal lexical and metrical evidence for the same view, but his results have not been found convincing.[12] More recently Bartlett 1935, in dealing with rhetorical formulas in Old English poetry, has listed each of ten Brink's three divisions of *Christ and Satan* as having an introductory formula and a concluding formula, thus implying that they may be three separate poems without saying so outright.[13] For the most part, however, those who deny unity have simply accepted ten Brink's view without themselves contributing much to the discussion. Presumably they have been influenced mainly by purely literary considerations: the lyric manner of ll. 1–365 as against the epic manner of ll. 366–728; the fact that the Temptation of Christ is out of chronological order; and especially the apparent lack of a single thematic focus for the three parts. This last argument has been particularly powerful, and its influence has remained effective down almost to the present day. Within the last thirty-odd years, for example, views ranging from outright rejection of unity to heavily qualified acceptance have been expressed by Anderson 1949 ('a group of stories [sic]'),[14] Kennedy 1952 ('probable that these ... are ... three separate poems'),[15] Schlauch 1956 ('three parts not closely connected'),[16] Shepherd 1966 ('a collection of related pieces' not 'organised or organisable into a luminous unity'),[17] Wrenn 1967 ('a triple group of poems'),[18] and Dubois 1962, who neatly and non-committally says what many must have been thinking in the words: 'Certains ont pu y voir une unité en triptyque.'[19]

After ten Brink's definitive formulation of the case against unity, the argument in favour of unity was for a long time conducted almost exclusively on metrical and linguistic grounds. Graz 1894, ascertaining the relative frequency of the different metrical types of half-line and also of the different alliterating sounds in the work, found such close agreement between ll. 1–365 and ll. 366–728 in both respects as to demonstrate clearly, in his view, that *Christ and Satan* is a single poem.[20] Barnouw 1902 was no less unequivocal in concluding that it is a single work on the basis of grammatical and syntactic criteria: frequency of the combinations article plus substantive, article plus weak adjective, article plus weak adjective plus substantive, and weak adjective plus substantive.[21] Frings 1913, investigating the phonology of *Christ and Satan* with exemplarily careful distinction of the work of the scribes (three in number) and their Corrector, all of whom show West Saxon spelling habits in varying degrees, demonstrated satisfactorily that what the scribes were copying from was an Anglian text with a set of very characteristic sound features which occur in all its parts, and concluded that from the linguistic point of view no argument could be brought forward against the unity of *Christ and Satan*.

It must be observed that metrical, syntactical, and phonological investigations, no matter how irrefutable the detailed conclusions they reach may be, can never prove that a given text is a single work of literature. Even to the most favourably disposed reader they can prove nothing more than identity of authorship of the parts of the text, which is not the same thing. To one more sceptically inclined, they may well appear capable of proving no more than such closeness in time and place of origin of the parts that identity of authorship is not precluded. Positive support for unity can only be furnished by evidence of focus or patterning in the substance of a text, that is, by an identifiable theme or structure. Graz and Barnouw do not appear to have taken this into account sufficiently. Frings, on the other hand, was careful to claim only that he had removed any possible linguistic objections to the unity of *Christ and Satan* by demonstrating the linguistically homogeneous character of the original text from which the scribes copied it into MS Junius 11.[22] For positive evidence in support of unity he appealed[23] to Brandl, who meanwhile (1908) had maintained that the work was a single poem, specifically an attempt to represent the work of Redemption in terms of the institution of the comitatus, with Satan and his followers portrayed in Part I as disloyal thanes who have rebelled against their liege lord and now lament their exile and their exclusion from the joys of the hall, and with the apostles and especially the souls liberated by Christ at the Harrowing of hell portrayed in Part II as loyal thanes who are now to enjoy eternal hall-jubilation in heaven, while Part III depicts the Temptation of Christ as the only meeting of Christ and Satan in single combat.[24]

Since the time of Brandl and Frings, fresh arguments for the unity of *Christ and Satan* have generally been based on considerations of theme and structure, the linguistic homogeneity of the work having been solidly established by Frings. The tendency with a few exceptions has been increasingly away from Brandl's emphasis on Germanic heroic motifs, on the tacit assumption that this approach stands a text like *Christ and Satan* on its head, fostering a dismissive attitude towards homiletic features which must in truth have been central. Thus Clubb 1925 still asserts that the most plausible defence of the unity of *Christ and Satan* is Brandl's,[25] but his own contributions to the topic are of a different order: besides a striking list of verbal parallels between the three parts,[26] many not found in any other poem, he points out that in all three parts Christ is set forth as Satan's chief adversary so that the work 'is built around the struggle between these two adversaries' (as suggested by the name Grein gave it in 1857), and moreover that 'the character of Satan and his relation to his followers are exactly the same in Part III as they were in Part I.'[27] Both observations are indeed just; in connection with the latter, one thinks particularly of how Satan is reviled by his followers in both these divisions.

Gollancz 1927 views the work as 'a unity with three divisions,' though his third division includes the Last Judgment as well as the Temptation of Christ since it begins not at line 663 but at line 597, where a large zoomorphic or rather diabolomorphic capital letter occurs in the manuscript; he bases his conclusion on the presence, in the various parts of the work, of 'the same type of mind ... and the same unusual theological knowledge and outlook.'[28] Krapp 1931 opts for the unity of the work, rather hesitantly, bolstered by his awareness that 'it is not primarily a narrative poem,' but 'better described as a set of lyric and dramatic amplifications of a number of Biblical and legendary themes of a familiar character,' a formulation which hardly sounds like a defence of unity at all.[29] Malone 1948 grounds his acceptance of the work's unity on the contrast between Christ and Satan, which in all parts of the work is repeatedly expressed in eschatological and moral terms: 'the punishments and rewards of the life to come [are] ... picture[d] ... over and over' and 'we should follow Christ, not Satan.'[30] Huppé 1959 argues for the unity of the work on the ground that it has a single theme, 'the incommensurate might of God,' stated in the opening lines, illustrated in various ways by the overthrow of the rebel angels, the Harrowing of hell, and the Temptation of Christ, and repeatedly given 'a direct moral application to man's situation.'[31] This reading has much to recommend it, but as Finnegan 1969 has pointed out, it does not take into account the work's conspicuous emphasis on the Second Person of the Trinity at the expense of the First Person.[32] Besides, as will be argued below,[33] it does not sufficiently recognize the thematic importance of a principal attribute of Christ, that of humbling himself, only briefly alluded to by Huppé.[34]

Isaacs 1968, arguing that 'the structural principle of *Christ and Satan* may be found in the pattern of the speeches by the seven separate voices, distinct from his own, which the narrator uses,'[35] which he calls 'the "one-man band" technique,'[36] seems to presuppose unity of *Christ and Satan* instead of trying to demonstrate it; nevertheless his implied argument for unity is a rather strong one, since nothing contradictory to it emerges from his stylistic analysis. Finnegan 1969 considers the work to be a unity and its theme to be the revelation of Christ's character and the implications of this revelation for the conduct of man's life,[37] and shows that a conspicuously recurring pattern in the work, consisting of a narrative-dramatic section followed by a homiletic-hortatory section that draws on it, is rooted in both the Latin and the Old English sermon tradition, where exempla were similarly yoked with following exhortations.[38] In emphasizing in his consideration of Part I those details which reveal the character of Christ, specifically his omnipotence, as demonstrated by 'the total defeat of the devils,'[39] Finnegan's argument runs the risk of denying the poet any adequate justification for making Satan the focus of so much attention in this half of the work; but in ranging the work firmly in the homiletic tradition he has done a service of permanent value. Furthermore, in his consideration of Part II he justly observes, and develops the observation, that its 'most affecting scenes ... are devoted not to a glorification of Christ's power ... but to a manifestation of His charity and love.'[40] He does so, however, without indicating that the self-abasement by which Christ expresses this charity and love is not only closely linked with his omnipotence in the structure of the work, but is also, as will be argued below,[41] one-half of the very motif which most indissolubly binds together Part I and Part II into a firm unity.

My own views on the unity of *Christ and Satan*, which have emerged fragmentarily in some of the comments above, must now be stated in full, together with the evidence which in my view supports them:

(1) There is no distinct scribal indication that pages 213–29 of MS Junius 11 contain more than a single poem. Line 663, the beginning of Part III, begins in the interior of a manuscript line which is composed entirely of minuscule letters and which like all the upper part of page 228 is remarkably crowded. To be sure, line 659 begins with a small capital, but this is also in the interior of a manuscript line, and furthermore the reference of ll. 659–62 is clearly to the life of the blessed souls with Christ in heaven, which is connected with the preceding sixty-odd lines on the Last Judgment rather than with the following sixty-odd on the Temptation of Christ, so that for Part III to begin at this point would not be a strong argument against unity. Part II, beginning at l. 366, does indeed begin at the left margin, but the same thing is true of every canto in this text, for example those that are numbered II, III, V, and VI, and the large capital wyn with which l. 366 begins is exceeded in size not only by the Ð at the beginning of l. 1 but also by the diabolomorphic H at the beginning of l. 597, which no one has suggested taking as the beginning of an independent poem. This wyn at the beginning of l. 366 is in turn measurably larger than the capitals at the beginning of the other cantos, but the difference is not striking and in the case of the E at the beginning of l. 75 can fairly be called slight.

(2) The metrical and linguistic homogeneity of the work as we have it has been fully established by Graz 1894, Barnouw 1902, and Frings 1913.[42] Considerations of this kind will be treated in more detail below, in the section on date and dialect.

(3) Part II arguably, and Part III indisputably, begin with transitional

lines linking them to Parts I and II respectively. At the close of Part II the poet is describing the rejoicing of the blessed in heaven after the Last Judgment, and the last words in this description are these (661–2): is sylf Cyning,/ ealra Aldor, in ðære ēcan gesceft 'the King himself, the Lord of all, is in that eternal kingdom (literally, creation).' The opening lines of Part III (663–4) follow with unmistakable reference: Þæt is se Drihten, se ðe dēað for ūs / geþrōwode, Þēoden engla 'That is the Lord who suffered death for us, the King of angels.' Line 665 continues with equally unambiguous pronoun reference, Swylce hē fæste fēowertig daga 'Also he fasted forty days,' telling of Christ's fast in the wilderness as a preliminary to the Temptation that came at the end of it. The beginning of Part II, namely ll, 366–8, Wæs þæt encgelcyn ær genemned / Lūcifer hāten, lēohtberende, / on geārdagum in Godes rīce 'That order of angels was formerly called Lucifer by name, "light-bearing," in days of old in God's kingdom,' cannot be directly connected with the closing lines of Part I, but does appear to make a general connection with Part I as a whole by giving the angelic name of its principal character, the chief of the rebel angels. (His diabolic name Sātānus or Sātān is then mentioned for the first time in l. 371.) If the dubiousness of calling Lucifer an order of angels should persuade us to accept the view of Thorpe 1832 and Gollancz 1927 that something is missing between l. 366 and l. 367, the reference of þæt encgelcyn would nevertheless continue to be more probably back than forward, and indeed ær genemned could then plausibly be interpreted as 'above-mentioned' rather than 'formerly called,' with reference to the æðele cyn of l. 20.[43] By either reading, ll. 366–8 serve as preliminary to a brief recapitulation in ll. 369–79a of the revolt and Fall of the angels, which was the theme of the repeated laments in Part I, after which the actual narrative of the Harrowing of hell begins with intentional abruptness at l. 379b.

(4) All three parts of the work show a strongly Christocentric point of view, allowing God the Father to recede into the background. As Clubb 1925 pointed out,[44] the depiction of Satan as directing his enmity particularly at Christ, so natural as to be almost inevitable in Parts II and III where the Harrowing of hell and the Temptation of Christ are treated, is also a striking feature of Part I, the laments of Satan and his followers after their Fall, where it is by no means a matter of course.[45] In Part II, as a matter of fact, the most conspicuous emotion of the devils at the Harrowing of hell is fear (egsa 379, 392, 405, mid egsan ealle afyrhte 384, egsan gryre 453, hinsīðgryre 455), and the hostility of Satan to Christ is made overt principally in terms of its reciprocation: thus in l. 377 the Saviour's enmity (Nergendes nīð) subjects Satan and the other rebel angels to the pains of

hell; in ll. 443–5 Christ at the Harrowing of hell has shoved the devils farther down into lower darkness, and in ll. 451–5, since one continuous passage is involved, the Drihten God who in his wrath has inflicted on the devils the dim dark shadow and terror of death is presumably Christ as well; in ll. 492–3, again, Christ relates that he had created the pain of hell in earlier time as a retribution, that is presumably as punishment for the rebel angels; only in ll. 484–7 is Satan's enmity to Christ represented in active form within this section, when Christ, instead of saying that Satan tempted Adam and Eve to disobey the Father's command by eating the forbidden fruit, unexpectedly identifies the command as his own (Hælendes word).

Part III in its turn consists almost exclusively of a direct contest between Christ and Satan, so that explicit brief statements of the enmity between the two are hardly needed and hardly to be found. In Part I, however, where the poet might be expected to represent the revolt of Satan and his followers as a rebellion against God the Father, as the author of *Genesis B* unequivocally does, he instead shows them rebelling against Christ and being punished by Christ. Thus in ll. 84–6 Satan recalls that in his pride he had intended to overthrow the Light of glory, the Son of God (Bearn Hēlendes). Similarly, in ll. 115–19 Satan laments that he and his followers cannot expect that the King of glory (Wuldorcyning) will ever grant them possession of heaven again, and immediately expands on this statement by saying that he, the Son of the Ruler (Waldendes Sunu), has power over everything, glory and punishments alike. Again, in ll. 173–6 Satan says that he is being punished because he wanted to drive the Lord (Drihten), the Son of God (Sunu Meotodes), from his throne. Yet again, in ll. 194–7 the poet in a homiletic passage urges that every man should be warned by Satan's example not to anger the Son of the Ruler (Bearn Waldendes). And finally, in ll. 344–8 the poet tells us that the devils in hell lamented the heinous plan they had formed in heaven to deprive the saving Christ (nergendne Crīst) of the rule of heaven. Besides the implications of several of the passages just mentioned, ll. 67–8, in which the poet tells us that Christ had expelled the rebel angels from heaven, clearly show him as their punisher. With such an array of evidence, even conceding that the word Hælend, literally 'Saviour,' was applied not exclusively to the Son but occasionally to the Father,[46] we may add one further passage in which the Hælend is the target of rebellion and one in which he is its punisher: respectively ll. 51–4, where Satan's followers reproach him for persuading them, by a lie, not to obey the Saviour (Hēlende hēran), and ll. 281–2, where the poet, commenting on the laments of the rebel angels in hell, says that the Saviour God (Hælend God) had become angry at them.

Not only do all three parts of the work thus celebrate Christ as the principal adversary of Satan, but Parts I and II glorify him also as the Creator of the universe.[47] (Part III contains no reference of any kind to the creation.) In the introductory and theme-stating section of Part I, with all due respect to the contrary opinion of Huppé 1959,[48] the person who is referred to in l. 2 as Meotod, in l. 3 as hē, in l. 4 as seolfa hē, and in l. 8 as Meotod again can hardly be other than the person referred to in l. 9 as hē selfa, and his latter reference is explicated by variation in l. 10 as Godes āgen Bearn 'God's own Son.' In effect, then, the whole of ll. 1–18 exalts the might of God the Son as the Creator of the physical universe, while ll. 19–21 specify that he is also the Creator of men and of angels. This latter specification is confirmed by l. 243 gāsta Scyppend 'Creator of spirits,' a variation of se dēora Sunu 'the dear Son' in l. 242. Similar statements abound in Part II. To be sure, Eve's statement in ll. 440–1 that Christ is manifestly the ēce Ordfruma ealra gesceafta 'eternal Creator (?) of all creatures' is not decisive, since ordfruma like fruma can mean 'first-ranking one' or 'prince' as well as 'creator,' but the reading 'Creator' here is well supported: in ll. 471–2 Christ himself tells the souls whom he is delivering from hell that he created them; in ll. 480–2 he says that he planted in paradise the tree that bore the forbidden fruit; in l. 488, still speaking to the delivered souls, he calls them his handgeweorc 'work of (his) hands'; in ll. 492–3 he says that it was he who had ordained the torment of hell as a retribution; and in l. 534 the poet calls Christ the Creator of angels (Scyppend engla), and the same in l. 562 (engla Scyppend), while in ll. 583–4 he calls him the Maker and Ruler of all creatures (ealra gescefta Wyrhta ond Waldend).

Admittedly, representation of Christ as Creator was by no means unheard of in patristic and mediaeval times. Clubb 1925 points out[49] that such scriptural passages as John 1: 3, Romans 11: 36, and Colossians 1: 16 were interpreted in this way, for example, by Ambrose (*Hexaemeron* 1.5.19, *PL* 14.131), and adds that the same view was represented in Old English in such passages as *The Advent* (*Crist I*) ll. 239–40 (Þū eart sēo Snyttro þe þās sīdan gesceaft mid þī Waldende worhtes ealle 'Thou [Christ] art the Wisdom who with the Ruler didst make all this broad creation' – which, however, ascribes to Christ at most a co-operative role in creation) and *Riddle 6* 1–2a (Mec gesette sōð sigora Waldend Crīst tō compe 'The true Ruler of victories, Christ, created me [the sun] for battle'). To these passages we may add several others. In *The Last Judgment* (*Crist III*) 1414–15, Christ says, Þā mec ongon hrēowan þæt mīn hondgeweorc on fēonda geweald fēran sceolde 'Then it began to grieve me that the work of my hands [mankind] should fall into the power of devils.' Similarly, in the Laws of King Alfred,[50] the statement is made that on VI dagum Crīst geworhte heofonas ond eorðan, sǣs ond ealle gesceafta þe on him sint 'in six days Christ made the heavens and earth, the seas and all creatures that are in them.' A particularly striking instance is the thirteenth of the *Vespasian Hymns*.[51] In it the hymnist, possibly Ambrose according to Kuhn p 186, addressing Christ as Creator of all things (*rerum Creator omnium*, glossed as wīsena Sceppend alra), who formed the man Adam at the beginning of the world and gave him a face like his own image (*qui mundi in primordio | Adam plasmasti hominem, | cui tuae imaginis | vultum dedisti similem*, glossed as ðū middangeardes in fruman gehīowadas mon, ðǣm ðīnre onlīcnisse ondwliotan saldes gelīcne), praises him for having humbled himself to take on human form in order to redeem mankind, whom he had formed of old (*ut hominem redemeris, | quem ante jam plasmaveras*, glossed as ðæt mon ðū alēsdes, ðone ǣr sōðlice gehīowades). Clearly we must suppose that the poet's or poets' age was not one that was prone to heresy-hunting in this matter. And yet, however strong the tradition of Christ the Creator may have been, it was not in the mainstream of Christian belief springing from the first words of the Nicene Creed: *Credo in unum Deum Patrem omnipotentem, Factorem coeli et terrae, visibilium omnium et invisibilium*. Strict orthodoxy allowed such passages as John 1: 3 to be taken only as meaning that the Father's work of creation was in some way mediated through Christ.

(5) Satan's followers blame and execrate him in Part I (53–64), and again tersely but comprehensively in Part III (728). A sense of the fitness of things is evident here, in that Satan is not to be the beneficiary of the bond of loyalty which he was the first to break. Yet the fact remains that the Satan of *Genesis B* does not experience this humiliation, to say nothing of the terror-inspiring ruler of fiends in *Juliana*.

(6) The above considerations are of unequal force. In general they all point in one direction, arguing for unity of the work, but in large part their effect is negative, weakening objections to unity rather than making a positive case for unity. Thus point (1) can prove at most only that the scribes of Book Two of MS Junius 11 identified the work they were copying as a single poem. Point (2) cannot prove more than common authorship of the three parts of the work, and at a more modest estimate only that all three originated so close together in time and place that common authorship is not precluded. Point (3) indicates that if the three parts were of separate origin someone has apparently joined them together, but leaves open the question of whether he integrated them so well that he can fairly

be called a poet working with different sources, or just stuck them together superficially. Points (4) and (5), dealing with motifs that are shared by the various parts of the work, do not necessarily prove that all were by one author, but only that if they were by various authors then those authors were working within the same tradition in several respects. The argument for unity is not complete, therefore, without evidence for unity in theme and structure.

## UNITY IN THEME AND STRUCTURE

Huppé and Finnegan have recognized the need for evidence of such unity.[52] To meet it, Huppé proposes that the single theme is the incommensurate might of God. Finnegan modifies this to make it consistent with the Christocentric nature of the whole work, accepts the view that Christ's omnipotence is emphasized in the total defeat of the devils in Part I, and goes on to focus on the manifestation of Christ's charity in Part II, thus broadening the theme to the revelation of Christ's character and the implications of this revelation for the conduct of man's life. As far as it goes, Finnegan's formulation is unshakable, but perhaps it does not go far enough. A conspicuous feature of Part I is revelation of *Satan*'s character, which Finnegan treats separately,[53] but which he does not bring into a sufficiently clear relationship with the revelation of the character of Christ to justify the prominence given to it by the poet. Nor does he show sufficiently the intimate link between Christ's omnipotence and his charity.

If one stands off from the work and looks at it as from a distance, macroscopically, without prejudging whether its 'Parts I, II, and III' are really parts of one poem or are three separate works, 'Part I' is seen to focus on Satan, 'Part II' to focus on Christ, and 'Part III' to be a short narrative of a direct confrontation between the two. Next it is possible to go one step farther and recognize that in 'Part I' Satan is depicted as lamenting the infernal consequences of his attempt to overthrow Christ and seize the supreme rule of heaven, and that in 'Part II' Christ is depicted as descending into hell to liberate the souls of some of those who died before his life and death on earth. In addition one recognizes that 'Part II' narrates not only Christ's descent into hell (the Harrowing of hell) but also, in brief form, all of Christ's post-Resurrection life up to and including the Last Judgment. Some awareness of the central Christian doctrine of divine charity (*caritas*) and diabolical cupidity (*cupiditas*) developed by St Augustine[54] may suggest to one, at this point, that the former is shown in 'Part II' and the latter in 'Part I,' in their respective archetypes, Christ and

Satan. Furthermore, the fact that 'Part I' depicts Satan in hell, and that 'Part II,' besides the Harrowing, depicts the subsequent life of Christ so as to culminate in his enthronement at the right hand of God the Father as judge of all mankind at the Last Judgment, may suggest that the poet of 'Part I' was concerned to show that the consequence of Satan's *cupiditas* was his abasement and that the poet of 'Part II' was concerned to show that the consequence of Christ's *caritas* was his exaltation. Now another look at 'Part III,' where Christ and Satan come into direct conflict with each other, shows the conspicuous presence there of *cupiditas* (as the sin to which Christ is tempted), rejection of *cupiditas*, and abasement.

In other words, the nearer one draws to the text by this approach the more it looks like a single work, for the concepts '*cupiditas* brings abasement' and '*caritas* brings exaltation' are the two halves of a proposition given as a saying of Christ in the gospels of Luke and Matthew: 'Whosoever exalteth himself shall be abased; and he that humbleth himself shall be exalted' (Luke 14: 11 AV; compare Matthew 23: 12 and Luke 18: 14).[55] It is my contention that *Christ and Satan* is a single work and that this gospel text, though the poet does not quote or closely paraphrase it, is in effect its theme. I mean to show how this contention is supported by closer examination of key words and key passages in the different parts of the text, but before doing so I want to mention two other things that complicate the picture in interesting ways.

The first of these is the relation of the 'might' motif which dominates the opening lines of the poem to the 'abasement-exaltation' motif which pervades the whole. What I have to say about this is scattered here and there through my discussion of the text,[56] but may be summed up in advance as follows: Christ's might accomplishes the defeat of the devils' self-exalting *cupiditas* and punishes them in Part I; Christ's might renders efficacious every step which through his self-abasing *caritas* he takes for the benefit of mankind in Part II; Christ's might thwarts and punishes Satan's attempt to destroy Christ's *caritas* by tempting him to *cupiditas* in Part III.[57] The *caritas* is the essential principle, the might its instrument.

The second is the special position of Part II within the whole of *Christ and Satan*. That the position of Part II is indeed special emerges most clearly from a consideration of sources and analogues of the poem and its various parts.[58] This consideration encourages us to think of Part II as the real heart of the poem; and in specific connection with Part II, St Paul's elaboration of the second part of Luke 14: 11 in his Epistle to the Philippians (2: 5–11 AV) is particularly relevant: 'Let this mind be in you, which was also in Christ Jesus: who, being in the form of God, thought it not robbery to be equal with God: but made himself of no reputation, and took upon him the form of a servant, and was made in the likeness of men: and being found in fashion as a man, he humbled himself, and became obedient unto death, even the death of the cross. Wherefore God also hath highly exalted him, and given him a name which is above every name: that at the name of Jesus every knee should bow, of things in heaven, and things in earth, and things under the earth; and that every tongue should confess that Jesus Christ is Lord, to the glory of God the Father.'[59] The abasement-exaltation motif is reinforced by the poet's not limiting the steps in Christ's descent to the Incarnation and the Crucifixion (indeed he treats them rather briefly), but concentrating his attention on the last and lowest descent of all, the Harrowing of hell, not mentioned in St Paul's Epistles, but familiar from the apocryphal *Gospel of Nicodemus* and connected in some way with the statement in the Athanasian Creed that Christ descended into hell.[60]

Let us now proceed to the closer examination of key words and key passages.

As the two halves of the abasement-exaltation theme are lyrically and dramatically embodied in the figures of Satan and Christ, in the same order as in the gospel texts, the two pre-eminent adversaries are partly matched and partly contrasted in the poet's diction. They are matched by being given similar or identical appellations: Satan in Part I (81) says that formerly in heaven he was a holy angel (hālig ængel), and the poet in Part II (585) calls Christ a hālig Encgel as he sits at the right hand of the Father. In Part I (21) Satan and his followers before their revolt are called the highest-ranking ones of the angels (engla ordfruman), and in Part II (657) the martyrs call Christ engla Ordfruma, which in this application may mean either 'Prince of angels' or 'Creator of angels.' The word ordfruma (without engla) in its meaning 'creator' is also used both of Satan and (presumably) of Christ in Part II: in l. 374 the poet calls Satan the author of evil (yfeles ordfruma), and in l. 441 Eve glorifies Christ as manifestly the eternal Creator of all creatures (ēce Ordfruma ealra gesceafta).

These two passages together adumbrate the contrast which is expressed elsewhere between Christian compassion and charity and Satanic overweening and covetousness. This contrast is expressed in pairs or sets sometimes of identical or cognate words and sometimes of semantically linked but different words, these pairs or sets sometimes occurring in the same part of the poem and sometimes in different parts. Thus the ambiguity of the word þingian 'talk' or 'intercede for' is subtly used in Part II when in l. 446 after the plunging of the fiends into yet lower darkness at the

Harrowing of hell, the poet says 'there Satan now talks gloomily' (þǣr nū Sātānus swearte þingað), in apparent reminiscence of the speeches in Part I in which Satan lamented his inability to rise and regain possession of heaven, and in l. 508 Christ tells the souls delivered at the Harrowing of hell that when he was pierced by a spear on the cross 'I interceded for you' (ic ēow þingade). Similarly the fallen Satan of Part I, in his futile covetousness to regain physical possession of heaven, laments (169) that he cannot reach heaven with his hands (mid handum ... heofon gerǣcan), but when in Part II (436) Eve reaches out her hands to Christ (rǣhte þā mid handum tō Heofencyninge) it is for the purpose of pleading humbly for his mercy. The covetousness of reaching is joined with a like covetousness of looking in the Part I Satan, who also laments (170) that he is not allowed to look up (to heaven) with his eyes (mid ēagum ... ūp lōcian), and quite consistently in Part III, Satan, seeking to make Christ sin through lust for power, shows Christ the kingdoms of earth and begins his speech (683) with the imperative 'look' (lōca), bidding him to look covetously on them. The contrast with a humbler looking in Part II involves Eve again, and the verb is not lōcian but wlītan: after her deliverance from hell at the Harrowing Eve was not allowed (408) to 'look on heaven' (wlītan in wuldre) until after her prayer of confession and petition.

A particularly illuminating cluster of words has to do with possession, power, and dominion: ǣht 'possession, property,' āgan 'have, possess,' gewald 'power, dominion,' onwald 'rule.' – Satan's 'lust for power and greed for universal possessions (both of which are sins of *superbia* rather than *luxuria* or *avaritia*...)' as shown by the words ǣht, āgan, and gewald has been mentioned by Isaacs 1968,[61] but apparently by no one else. – Here we must first distinguish the power which Christ has simply by virtue of his divine nature from the power which created beings seek to gain by covetous striving. The verb āgan and the noun gewald are each used only once to refer to this unique power of Christ, both in l. 118 namely, where Satan acknowledges that Christ has dominion over everything (āh him alles gewald). In reference to righteous men or their souls, neither ǣht, gewald, nor onwald is ever used. Since āgan is a verb of the most basic vocabulary often meaning simply 'have,' it could hardly fail to occur sometimes in this poem with an expression meaning 'righteous men' or the like as its subject, but there are only four such occurrences in all, and these are hedged about with careful restrictions. In a homiletic passage, the poet says (314) that righteous men in heaven shall have the joy of joys (āgan drēama drēam), and in a similar passage (361) that the blessed shall have life (līf āgon) throughout eternity; in ll. 505–6 it is Christ who assures the souls delivered from hell of his intention that they should have dignities conferred by the Lord and the splendour of a host (āgan Drihtnes dōmas ond duguðe þrym), and in ll. 553–4 the poet homiletically echoes part of these words of Christ with 'we' as subject (þær wē āgan Drihtnes dōmas). It is noteworthy that a righteous person is never represented as claiming to have or striving to have; they do not use the word āgan themselves except for the poet in l. 553. Furthermore, the things to be had by righteous persons are to some degree intangibles: joy, life, dignities, splendour. On the other hand, āgan is one of Satan's favourite words: he is using it constantly, often coupled with æht or gewald or both, and often picturing a quite tangible object of possession.

Thus in ll. 86–7, speaking of the heavenly mansions as strongholds or cities, he says that he intended, through overthrowing Christ, to have in his possession all dominion over them (āgan mē burga gewald eall tō æhte). In a later lament, and again together with a reference to his attempt to drive Christ from his throne, Satan says (174–5) that his goal was to have dominion over that joy, glory, and bliss (āgan mē þæs drēames gewald, wuldres ond wynne). Still later (252–3), quoting the words he used in heaven to incite the other angels to revolt, he expresses the goal in the same terms: '[Let us] possess as a property all this light of glory' (āgan ūs þis wuldres lēoht eall tō æhte). Not only in his rebellion, but in his recollections of his life in heaven and his laments for its loss, Satan shows that he regards his estate in heaven as a property. In ll. 95–6 he tells his fellows 'nor may we have heaven' (nē wē ūpheofon āgan mōten); in l. 107 he laments 'just now I had dominion over all glory' (nū āhte gewald ealles wuldres); in ll. 116–18 he says that he and his followers cannot expect that the King of glory will ever 'grant [them] a homeland, a land of habitation as [their] property, eternal rule, as he formerly did' (eard alēfan, æðel tō æhte, swā hē ær dyde, ēcne onwald); a few lines later (122–3), he is destined to 'have no joy with the angels above' (nænigne drēam āgan uppe mid ænglum); and in ll. 278–9 (in an echo of ll. 116–18) he is questioning whether the Eternal will ever 'grant [him and his followers] a home, a land of habitation as [their] property, as he formerly did' (hām alēfan, ēðel tō æhte, swā hē ær dyde). When Satan's followers execrate him in hell, they recognize this overweening and grasping nature of his, and throw it in his teeth in much the same terms, telling him in ll. 55–6 'it seemed to you alone that you had dominion over everything, heaven and earth' (ðūhte þē ānum þæt ðū āhtest alles gewald, heofnes ond eorþan), and in ll. 59–60 'you supposed in your magnificence that you possessed the world, the rule of all things' (wēndes ðū ðurh wuldor ðæt þū woruld āhtest, alra onwald).

In striking consistency with the character of Satan as revealed in these passages in Part I, the brief account of Satan's temptation of Adam and Eve in Part II, at the beginning of Eve's speech, shows Satan offering the very same temptation of covetousness to Adam and Eve, with āgan and gewald as key words. The horrible one persuaded us, says Eve (413–14), 'that we would have blessedness, a holy home, heaven under our dominion' (þæt wit blǣd āhton, hāligne hām, heofon tō gewalde). There is no mention here of the knowledge of good and evil as in the scriptural account, nor any hint of the mysterious false illumination that figures prominently in *Genesis B*. In Part III also, gewald is the inducement Satan holds out to Christ in the last and most significant Temptation (tō gewealde 686). This accords essentially with the account in Matthew, but the underlying irony is sharpened here by the fact that Satan, who in Part III is tempting Christ with the kind of gewald that is gained by covetous striving, has already acknowledged in Part I (118) that Christ has all-embracing gewald of an entirely different order, solely through his divine nature.

The place occupied in Satan's feelings by æht, gewald, and onwald is occupied in righteous men's feelings by such things as help, hope, and joy (help, hyht, and wynn). Even syntactically parallel to Satan's favourite prepositional phrase tō æhte (87, 117, 253, 279) are the expressions tō helpe in ll. 435 and 439, referring to Christ's coming 'as a help' to mankind in the Harrowing of hell and the Incarnation respectively; tō hihte in l. 641, where the poet implies that righteous men have Christ 'as their hope' unlike the wicked who forget him; and tō wynne in l. 198, where the poet in a homiletic passage urges his hearers to take the Lord of hosts 'as their joy.' In similar contexts but not as object of tō, help occurs in ll. 291 and 581, and wynn in ll. 507, 555, 592, and 648.

If the structure of *Christ and Satan* is indeed based on contrast between self-exaltation, which abases, and self-humbling, which exalts, the pairs and sets of words examined hitherto have illustrated that contrast for the most part somewhat indirectly. It becomes explicit, however, in another pair of passages, one from Part I (190–3) and the other from Part II (399–402a), starting with the same words, 'He went then to hell' (Hwearf þā tō helle). The passages will bear close scrutiny, to see in how much detail the contrast is carried out:

A              B             C

Hwearf þā tō helle  þā hē gehēned wæs, / Godes andsaca;  dydon his

D              E             F

gingran swā, / gīfre ond grǣdige,  þā hig God bedrāf / in þæt hāte hof þām is hel nama (190–3).

A         B         C         B

Hwearf þā tō helle   hæleða bearnum / Meotod   þurh mihte;   wolde manna

D         E         F

rīm, / fela þūsenda,   forð gelædan / ūp tō ēðle (399–402a).

In A, Satan and Christ alike go down to hell. In C, Satan is characterized as 'God's adversary' (Godes andsaca 191), and Christ as 'the Lord' (Meotod 400). Since the characterisation of Satan fills a half-line and the characterization of Christ does not, the poet has and uses the opportunity to present in B, as a counterpart to the declaration of Satan's abasement ('when he was abased,' þā hē gehēned wæs 190b), not one but two attributes of Christ: his compassion and his power. His Descent into hell is made 'for the children of men' (hæleða bearnum 399b) and is an exercise of his divine power (þurh mihte 400a). Thus Satan is represented as going to hell involuntarily in the abasement consequent on his attempt to exalt himself to the rank of deity, but Christ is represented as going to hell, by his own compassionate decision rendered effectual through his power, in the last and lowest of the steps that lead to his supreme exaltation. Then D, E, and F (in ll. 400–2a part of B and the whole of D, E, and F) show the involvement of Satan's followers and of mankind in the abasement and exaltation of the two great adversaries. In D, Satan's followers, grasping and greedy as himself, follow his example both in their voluntary attempt to exalt themselves and in their involuntary abasement. Their fate is expressed by a verb of action of which they are the subject (dydon ... swā 191), just as Satan's is (Hwearf 190), although in both instances only the punishment imposed on the rebels is stated, and the voluntary action that led to the punishment is merely implied. The counterpart in D to Satan's followers is the many thousands of human souls delivered from hell at the Harrowing, and they are made the object of a verb of action (wolde ... gelædan 400–1), since indeed their role is entirely passive, and the action is Christ's alone. Then E expresses the action of Christ (God 192, meaning Christ in the light of other passages that represent Christ as the punisher of the rebel angels) in driving the rebels down and leading the human souls up (though syntactically E is more closely linked with D in 400–1 than in 191–2), and F states the contrasting destinations of the rebel angels and the human souls.[62] This is a truly remarkable set of parallels, tightly structured and departing from complete rigidity at just those places where the departure itself makes a significant thematic point.

Such interrelations of vocabulary items and of syntacticometrical structures, extending on occasion as far as detailed parallelism between passages in different parts of the work, seem to me to complete the proof of the unity of *Christ and Satan*. Unity and genesis are of course two different questions, and the genesis of the poem will be discussed below, but if for example we were to find reason to believe that an Old English poem that could fairly be called the nucleus of Part II was already in existence at the time when the person who composed *Christ and Satan* in its present form set to work, then I believe we would also have to conclude that he must have adapted that hypothetical Old English poem so determinately to the sense of his own work that we would only be justified in calling it the *source* of Part II of *Christ and Satan*.

## EXPRESSION OF THE THEME IN THE WORK

Not as a further argument for unity, but for its own sake, it seems desirable at this point to make a consecutive survey of the poem, with the purpose of showing how, if the poem does indeed have the theme of self-exaltation, which abases, and self-humbling, which exalts, this theme (together with the corollary theme of the power of God the Son which was illustrated above in the Philippians text) is displayed through the structure of the poem in the order in which it reaches a reader or hearer:

God has power that is not like men's power. In this connection we need to take Huppé's word 'incommensurate' very seriously, and keep in mind texts like Isaiah 55: 8–9 (AV): 'For my thoughts are not your thoughts, neither are your ways my ways, saith the Lord. For as the heavens are higher than the earth, so are my ways higher than your ways, and my thoughts than your thoughts.' He does not acquire his power as men do by competition or warfare; he is not Supreme Being by ambition or striving: he simply is what he is, as he told Moses in the desert of Midian ('I am that I am,' Exodus 3: 14 AV). Indeed his nature is such that he can only manifest himself through what is lower than he is. Thus it is in Creation that his power *sui generis* is manifested to man: ll. 1–6.

The chain of references Meotod 2, hē 3, seolfa hē 4, his 6, Meotod 8, hē selfa 9, and Godes āgen Bearn 10, retrospectively, is impossible to break. Linearly, the identification of the Creator as God the Son in l. 10 catches us and probably the poet's audience as well somewhat by surprise. According to the orthodox view, God the Father is the Creator, operating through the Son to be sure, according to John 1:3, Colossians 1: 16, and the words of the Nicene Creed 'per quem omnia facta sunt.' The poet makes it sound different, makes the Son's role in Creation (and almost everything else) more autonomous and active: not taking a polemic tone and pretty certainly not exposing himself to a charge of heresy, he focuses on the Son almost exclusively. It is a matter of emphasis. Without implying that the Father is a *roi fainéant*, the poet allows him to remain well in the background: the Son is his topic.

Or rather, the Son is part of his topic. The other part, also introduced circuitously, is Lucifer-Satan, leader of rebel angels. He is not introduced as an individual until l. 34. First the rebel angels are introduced as a group (ll. 20–33), and significantly almost the first thing said about them is that they were engla ordfruman (l. 21), the highest-ranking angels. As such they were at the top of the entire hierarchy of created things. No being was higher than they were except God, and they could not possibly supplant him, since he was a being of an entirely different kind. They were created, he self-existent. The two kinds are incommensurable. Yet nevertheless they did seek to supplant God (ll. 22–24a), and as a result plunged immediately into the burning pit of hell (ll. 24b–33). The poet does not try to cope on the philosophical plane with the enduringly mysterious problem of the origin of evil, but he dramatizes vividly the nature of evil: seeking to aggrandize one's limited created self at the expense of the Supreme Being who is without limit and self-existent. It is St Augustine's *cupiditas* (*De doctrina christiana* 3.10.16, *PL* 34.72); the rebel angels are 'greedy and grasping' (grēdige ond gīfre 32). In the nature of the case the sinner falls by his attempt to rise. The poet does not here depict a vengeful or offended God inflicting punishment. On the contrary, 'God alone knows how he had exiled that guilty host' (God āna wāt hū hē þæt scyldige werud forscrifen hæfde 32b–33). The sin and the damnation are inseparable from each other in 22–24a and 24b–32a.

Thus in the opening lines already we have a contrast clearly drawn between God the Son, who manifests his unique power and exaltation by a descending movement, Creation, and Lucifer-Satan, who inadvertently plunges himself to the lowest depths of perdition by an absurd attempt to raise himself and destroy the Supreme Being that is unalterably above him. Christ, by descending and creating, is exalted; Lucifer-Satan, by seeking to rise and destroy, is brought low. Lucifer-Satan's action is clearly enough identified as *cupiditas*. Christ's act of Creation is so far not clearly identified as *caritas*, but already we may begin to surmise why the poet associates God the Son so emphatically with Creation. Creation is a descending movement, and the Son is that Person of the Trinity whose distinctive character is to descend. Finnegan's suggestion[63] of a link between the presentation of Christ as Creator and the doctrine that Satan fell because he refused to honour his Creator is very apposite here. By seeking to rise above his Creator, Satan negates the descending principle of Creation and thus becomes a destroyer.

In his first speech (36b–50), Satan, introduced to the poet's audience as 'the old one' (se alda 34), laments the loss of the glory (wulres blǣd 42) and the joys (wyn 43, drēamas 44) that he and his followers (wē 37, 41, 44, ic 48, mē 49) knew in heaven before their rebellion, and contrasts with them the woe and damnation (wēan ond wergu 42) which is now their lot in hell. He recognizes that he has lost heaven because of pride (for oferhygdum 50), but the self-reproach is evidently sterile. He condemns pride because of its consequences for him, not because it is wrong in itself. At heart he presumably still feels it (as later episodes in the poem will verify), and thus has good reason to say in an anticipatory rather than retrospective way, 'Because of pride I do not expect ever to have a better home' (ond mē bættran hām for oferhygdum æfre ne wēne 49b–50). For even if Origen's heresy of the devil's capability of being saved were a true doctrine, this Satan would nevertheless continue to be damned because he does not repent.

Satan's fellows, in reply (53–64), revile him for tempting them to evil by his lying claim to be God (53–57a). They gloat over his damnation (57b–58, 64b), and ascribe to themselves no share of blame. The poet nevertheless knows that they are sinful (synfulle 52, firenfulle 65), and specifically that they too have fallen by reason of pride and presumption (for oferhygdum 69, for ... anmēdlan 74). Even though Satan is unequivocally damned and unequivocally worthy of damnation, still there are degrees of damnability as well as of saintliness ('one star differeth from another star in glory,' I Corinthians 15: 41 AV), and the poet leaves little room for doubt that Satan's followers are even more despicable than he.

The remainder of Part I consists of further laments of Satan, with homiletic passages interspersed by the poet. In the laments the same principal motifs recur which have already been stated, and the homiletic passages reinforce these motifs and give them a moral application. The homiletic passages, with their forþon's and uton's and their Gemunan symle on mōde Meotodes strengðo (286), at times make the poet's Christianity sound almost like a self-seeking religion of *do ut des*. The sort of paraphrase that suggests itself is 'Let us be humble *in order that* we may be exalted' or even 'Since God is all-powerful we had better be humble if we know what is good for us.' This is not the poet's idea of religion, however, any more than it is St Paul's when he says plainly in I Corinthians 13: 3 that almsgiving and even martyrdom are worthless to anyone who proposes to gain by them.

The poet guards against misinterpretation on this crucial point by making it one of the most distinctive characteristics of Satan that he regards heaven as a property (see p 17 above), which Christ and righteous men do not. Besides his implication that help, hyht, and wynn are central to the charitable life of Christ and righteous men in the way that covetous desire for æht is central to the life of Satan and his followers, the poet uses metaphors of light and fragrance with the same function. Thus he says that a man living on earth 'has need that his face shine' (behōfað ... þæt him wlite scīne 209–10, compare l. 222) when he goes to the next world. The blessed souls shine brightly (295–6); the words of Matthew 13: 43, 'then shall the righteous shine forth as the sun in the kingdom of their Father,' are closely paraphrased in ll. 307–9a (as Clubb points out). The blessed souls who come from earth to heaven bring with them as their offering blossoms of fragrance, that is, in all likelihood, their good deeds, which embody the words of God (356–8). The figure of health versus sickness is used with similar effect to counteract the possible view that religion is a matter of *do ut des*: Satan expresses his own sadness of heart with a word that literally means 'sick' (sīc 275); Christ, on the other hand, brings us to heaven through his 'healing' (læcedōm 588), dispensing to men (581) not only help but also hǣlo, which of course has the double meaning of 'salvation' and 'health.' The healthy, sweet-smelling, luminous spirit which the poet commends to his hearers and readers is far from being an opportunistic calculation of the main chance in cosmic terms.

At the start of the section where the poet treats of the Harrowing of hell (366ff.), he recapitulates the theme of abasement through self-exaltation on the part of Satan and his fellows (371–79b), in terms very reminiscent of ll. 22–32a. It is not so much that exact words or formulas are repeated, but rather that in both passages the connection between the offence and the punishment is in no way arbitrary: the one follows naturally and inevitably, even inseparably, from the other. Then in the middle of a line (379) the poet makes an intentionally abrupt transition from the Fall of the angels to the Harrowing of hell: that is, from Satan's attempt to reach the highest point of exaltation, which brings him low, to Christ's lowest descent, which can only exalt and glorify him.

The specific details of the transition are significant, too: the last thing said about the revolt and Fall of the angels is that never again through eternity can they look in the face of the Eternal (377b–79a), so that when the Eternal actually approaches their dwelling in hell, it is fear (egsa 379b) that comes upon them. They apprehend him as din (dyne 380), storm (386), and a light (lēoht 388) which with all its beauty is a part of what terrifies them (egsan 384, 'frightened' afyrhte 384, egsa again 392 joined with dyne 393).

The *caritas* in the descending nature of God the Son is made evident in the Harrowing of hell, whereas it was only implicit in the Creation (see p 21 above). Moreover, Christ's speech (470b-512) to the souls he has just delivered from hell includes a retrospective account (488–512) of his Incarnation and Passion. These were of course the earlier stages of his descent, motivated by *caritas*, which culminated in the Harrowing. The exaltation and glorification which inevitably spring from his self-abasement are expressed in two ways. Spiritually he rises directly and immediately to heaven from the Harrowing of hell (456–8, 513–15), bringing with him the souls he has delivered. Physically (and spiritually) he bursts forth alive from his sepulchre, after the Harrowing of hell is completed, to begin a post-Resurrection life on earth (516–24).

In this section of his poem, the poet is able to follow the sequence of the clauses of the Athanasian Creed, 'descended into hell,' 'rose again the third day from the dead,' 'ascended into heaven,' and 'sitteth on the right hand of the Father God Almighty,'[64] adding details from the gospels and from Acts, because the sequence is chronological, and being such, recounts one by one the stages of the exaltation and glorification consequent on Christ's descent. The immediate rise to heaven is in the Harrowing of hell tradition, which is not supported by any of the four canonical gospels but flows from the apocryphal *Gospel of Nicodemus* and is supported by the Athanasian Creed; the Resurrection, post-Resurrection life on earth, and Ascension is in the canonical tradition of the gospels, the Acts, and the Athanasian and Nicene Creeds. The poet simply uses both side by side and feels no need to reconcile them.

The section that tells of Christ sitting on the right hand of the Father ends with l. 596. Moving along the current of the Creeds, we are not surprised to find that the poet next (597–641, with homiletic applications 642–62) tells of Christ's coming at the Last Judgment to judge the living and the dead. Yet this is no merely mechanical following of credal sequence. It is by virtue of his descent that Christ is with full rightness the judge of men, and he judges them according as they have lived by self-exaltation (*cupiditas*) or by self-abasement (*caritas*). It is characteristic of the wicked that, even while trembling before judgment, they expect to rise up into the glorious city (622–3); and in the homiletic reflections, martyrs are singled out (653) as the principal representatives of the righteous.

After the homiletic reflections on the Last Judgment, a passage of transition (663–6) opens Part III, which tells of the Temptation of Christ by

Satan in the wilderness. The placing of Part III out of chronological order
has disturbed many readers who on the whole are convinced of the poem's
unity. Yet if the theme is what it has here been argued to be, there is a
reason for putting the Temptation last. In terms of the exaltation-
abasement theme, Parts I and II without Part III would stand like two piers
of an arch with no span yet constructed to join them. The two modes of
existence, covetousness and charity, have been separately displayed
through their archetypes Satan and Christ, but the poet has not set the two
adversaries in direct confrontation with each other at any place where he
might naturally have done so, such as the overthrow of Satan and the other
rebel angels by Christ, or Christ's invasion of Satan's habitation at the
Harrowing of hell. If he had done so, the confrontation would have been
anticlimactically located in his work. In the synoptic gospels, however, he
found a canonically authenticated example of this very confrontation and
he used it, with no apparent consideration of chronology, for its climactic
value.

The choice of this episode, moreover, was good not only in terms of
climax and symmetry. The events of the Temptation do indeed fill out the
picture of abasement and exaltation shown in Parts I and II. Satan has found
at the beginning that he cannot rise to be God: now that God the Son has
humbled himself to human form in the Incarnation, perhaps he is so
vulnerable that Satan can bring him down to be a devil like himself. Satan
therefore seeks to lure Christ to sin through covetousness, the sin which
caused his own fall. The poet gives the three temptations in the same order
as Matthew 4: 1–11. First Satan tempts Christ to the most basic and
universal form of covetousness, that concerned with the needs of the body:
You are hungry, use your divine power to procure food by turning stones to
bread (670–2). The second temptation, in which Satan urges Christ to try
God's providence by casting himself down from the pinnacle of the temple,
is not well represented in the existing text of *Christ and Satan*, perhaps
owing to textual corruption at an earlier stage of transmission. Or perhaps
the poet, who took liberties enough in other respects, simply omitted the
second temptation because it did not suit his artistic purposes. Even if ll.
676–8 are the last words of Christ's answer to it,[65] they do not suffice to tell
us exactly in what terms the poet conceives the second temptation. In the
third, Satan tempts Christ to sin by covetousness in its most extreme form
(679–88): Be greedy, seek to rise to possession and power, receive at my
hand like a vassal from his liege lord (fōh hider tō mē 685b) the rule, not only
of all kingdoms of earth, as in the gospel, but of the Kingdom of heaven
(rodora rīces 687a). This last is the poet's addition, and a sufficiently strange

one. He evidently would not have found the confrontation fully representative of his meaning without it: as Satan fell in the beginning by grasping covetously for the highest possession, so he tempts Christ to fall to hell by grasping covetously for a rule and possession, and this too must be nothing less than the highest possession.[66]

This attempt by Satan to make Christ fall to hell by grasping covetously at the rule of earth and heaven fails. Through not chronologically (since the Harrowing of hell comes after the Crucifixion), yet dramatically, this is his final failure. The two natures meet face to face. Charity is mighty and prevails; covetousness is weak and succumbs.

In the third temptation, Satan's claim to have the Kingdom of heaven at his disposal is even more extreme in its absurd presumption than his first offence in seeking to supplant God. Again, the sentence Christ passes on him (689–709) is fully appropriate. For his covetous attempt to rise to the rank of deity, Satan had plunged into hell; for his even more presumptuous attempt to degrade Christ by tempting him to a like covetousness, he is to plumb hell's very bottom.

Satan does so (710–28). In doing so, he may in some degree be learning to know the full depth of the degradation to which his presumption has brought him, and thus we may be inclined to suppose, incautiously, that he is a developing character. Chronology, which should not after all be ignored, is against such a surmise; at the Harrowing of hell, 379b–98 and 443–55, he is indistinguishable from the rest of the cowering devils. After his plunge to the lowest depth, his fellows revile him. They are allowed the last word, and that word is a final curse. The whole passage from Christ's sentence to the devils' malediction (689–728), in harmony with the poet's homiletic desire to have a covetousness-deterring effect on his audience, is a very Tchaikovskyan finale, with plenty of cymbals and brass.

# 2

# Date and Dialect

In my view, then, the unity of *Christ and Satan* can be taken as proved. Even of those who have not accepted its unity, finding in the work no such thematic unity and structural coherence as that for which I have argued, almost no one has suggested an appreciably divergent time or place of origin of its parts.[1] At all events, the investigations of Graz 1894, Barnouw 1902, and especially Frings 1913[2] have so solidly established the metrical and linguistic homogeneity of the work that even if my thematic and structural arguments are less than compelling, we may legitimately seek to assign the existing work *Christ and Satan* as a whole to a particular time and a particular region.

Opinions concerning the date of the work have varied widely. At one extreme stands its early traditional attribution to Caedmon, along with the rest of MS Junius 11, which would place it in the seventh century; at the other, the willingness of ten Brink 1877[3] and Wülker 1896[4] to concede that it may have come into existence as late as the tenth century. The eighth and ninth centuries have obviously been most favoured.

Some arguments from literary substance or tone, besides tending to cancel each other out, have led to conclusions so wildly divergent as to demonstrate only their lack of an objective foundation. Ten Brink 1877 puts the work in the late ninth or early tenth century, partly because of the 'tenderness' and 'elegiac passion' of Satan's speeches;[5] but Sarrazin 1913 includes Part I of *Christ and Satan* in a list of poems which he ascribes to mid-eighth century Northumbria and considers comparable to *Beowulf* in 'tendermindedness' (*Gemütsweichheit*) and preoccupation with the emotional states of their characters;[6] and Brooke 1892 finds in the narrative an 'extreme simplicity, directness, and rude passion' which lead him to consider Book Two of MS Junius 11 'earlier than the rest of the book, except, perhaps, some portions of *Genesis*.'[7] Can they all be talking about the same work and in the same literary context? Can ten Brink's Satan be the Satan who desired and desires heaven as a property? Like ten Brink, Barnouw 1914 finds the 'sentimental Satan' of *Christ and Satan* inconceivable in an early work.[8] Ricci 1929a, on the other hand, classes *Christ and Satan* together with *Genesis* and *Exodus* as poems with a 'seventh-century mentality,' showing 'as yet no idea of the essentials of the new religion.'[9] Are we to suppose that Bede's or Aldhelm's grasp of the essentials of Christianity was similarly defective?

Other literarily based opinions about the date of the work, including some less vulnerable to objections, may be reviewed briefly. Groschopp 1883 ranks it among the oldest surviving works of Old English poetry, and thinks it may possibly be Caedmon's, on the ground of its simple and popular ('volkstümlich') mode of presentation.[10] (The linguistic forms which he cites as evidence of early composition, namely dual pronouns and the accusatives þec and ūsic, occur in late as well as early Old English.) Kühn 1883, though he considers *Christ and Satan* three separate poems and offers no closely reasoned argument concerning the date of the work, favours the eighth or ninth century, specifying that the style of Part I is by no means broad and does not show the complete decay of Old English poetry since the expansions of subject, object, and predicate by variation are still within the tradition of the best works, while Part II shows the stage of decay in which epic poetry is beginning to give way to didactic.[11] Morley 1888 thinks Part III is by Caedmon, without saying why.[12] Smith 1907 assigns the work probably to the end of the ninth century, linking Part II in theme and style with Cynewulf's *Crist*, by which she seems to mean *The Last Judgment* (*Crist III*), which is probably not by Cynewulf at all. However, she also says that *Christ and Satan*, three distinct poems in her view, shows a religious fervour and a comparatively rude form which might be considered to place it nearer to Caedmon than is *Genesis A*, *Exodus*, or *Daniel*.[13]

Grau 1908 dates Part II of *Christ and Satan* considerably later than Cynewulf, on the ground of a rather involved line of argumentation purporting to show that it presupposes the existence of a highly developed sermon literature in Old English; he also sees borrowing of detail from *The Phoenix* and *The Last Judgment* (*Crist III*), which he calls Cynewulf's, and argues that a literary treatment of the person of Satan would be quite impossible as early as Cynewulf.[14] Clubb 1925 says that the literary relations of *Christ and Satan* would indicate a date later than Cynewulf,[15] and Krapp 1931 agrees that the closest literary relations are with

Cynewulfian poetry.[16] Specifically, Clubb suggests the period 790–830, and Krapp repeats these dates, but is inclined to favour the earlier part of their range. Bracher 1937, dealing with the figure of understatement in Old English poetry, gives a frequency table on which *Christ and Satan* stands low, in the neighbourhood of such late Christian poems as *Crist*, the *Descent into Hell*, and *Judith*;[17] he makes no claim, however, that frequency of understatement can be used by itself as a criterion for the dating of individual poems, and indeed *Exodus*, which is generally considered early, stands adjacent to *Christ and Satan* in the table. Schirmer 1937 places *Christ and Satan* at the end of a tradition of religious lyric that begins with Caedmon's *Hymn*, and, without mentioning a specific date, he implies that it is late because the lyric quality is fading and giving way to a narrative and homiletic tone.[18]

Kennedy 1943 cites with approval Clubb's findings of a pervasive resemblance of *Christ and Satan*, especially Part II, to passages in the 'Cynewulfian' poems *Crist*, *The Phoenix*, and *Guthlac*, implying acceptance of Clubb's dating of the work as later than Cynewulf.[19] Malone 1948 agrees that the work shows the influence of the 'school ... of Cynewulf,' and cautiously assigns it to the ninth century.[20] Greenfield 1965, without mentioning Cynewulf, places it dubiously in the early ninth century.[21] Renwick and Orton 1966 say that it may have been written in the eighth century, and mention non-committally the view, familiar from Clubb and Krapp, that it is in 'the Cynewulfian tradition.'[22] Whitbread 1967 lists it along with *Andreas*, *Guthlac*, and *The Phoenix* as 'associated loosely with Cynewulf's age.'[23] Wrenn 1967 suggests that it may be considered 'a kind of bridge between the school of Caedmon and that of Cynewulf.'[24] Finnegan's suggestion that the Christocentricity of the poem may be a reaction against the Adoptionist heresy leads him to favour a date within the period 792–820,[25] but would be compatible with a somewhat later date, since the opponents of a heresy are sometimes not easily convinced that it is dead. On the whole, then, since Clubb 1925 or thereabouts there seems to have existed, among those who would place *Christ and Satan* chronologically on literary grounds, something like a consensus[26] that the work was composed probably not far from Cynewulf's time.[27]

We may now consider how this agrees with such attempts as have been made to date the work by linguistic criteria. Passing over the aberrant view of Hickes 1705 that the work is composed in a form of Old English strongly modified by the Danish invasions and accordingly belongs to the end of the tenth (Hickes says thousandth!) century,[28] and the view of Junius 1665, Thorpe 1832, and other early authorities, who would place it in the seventh century as Caedmon's work, we may say that the use of linguistic criteria in this connection begins with Groschopp 1883,[29] or more truly with Barnouw 1902. On the basis of relative frequency of the combinations article plus substantive, article plus weak adjective, article plus weak adjective plus substantive, and weak adjective plus substantive,[30] Barnouw dates *Christ and Satan* about 880, contemporaneous with Cynewulf's *Elene*, two or three decades later than *Juliana* and *The Ascension* (*Crist II*), both of which also bear Cynewulf's signature, two decades later than *The Last Judgment* (*Crist III*), and little earlier than *The Phoenix*, *Physiologus*, and *Guthlac B*.[31] Brandl 1908 similarly dates it not long after Cynewulf because of the relatively high frequency of the combination weak adjective plus substantive.[32] Richter 1910 uses a different set of linguistic criteria: loss of final -*u* after a long stressed syllable, loss of *h* in inflected forms of words like feorh or mearh, monosyllabic or dissyllabic quality of words with a final liquid or nasal such as wuldor or wæstm, and contracted versus uncontracted forms of words like frēa, fēa, or þēon. He also takes into account Brandl's evidence as well as the literary relationships proposed by Grau 1908 (see p 28 above). On the basis of these linguistic criteria and literary relations he concludes that *Christ and Satan* is probably not much later than Cynewulf, close in time to *Physiologus*, *The Phoenix*, and *Guthlac B*, and later than *The Last Judgment* (*Crist III*).[33] Thus his relative chronology is quite close to that of Barnouw 1902, though the absolute date which he assigns, the last half of the eighth century, is about a century earlier than Barnouw's.

Frings 1913 cites yet other linguistic features which according to him point to a comparatively early date not far from 750:[34] the unbroken *e* in tōwerpan l. 85; the invariable dative plural in -*um*; three occurrences (30, 41, 716) of past or preterit-present indicative plurals in -*un*; the consistent retention of the final -*u* of the *u*-stems sunu and duru, contrasted with prevailing -*o* for -*u* in words of other classes such as strengðo and hælo; the spelling sīdas for sīðas in l. 189; and possibly also the rather frequent occurrence of *æ* in unstressed final syllables, for example niðær and undær in l. 31 and noldæs in l. 728. Since he asserts that his conclusion about the date is consistent with that of Brandl 1908,[35] it is possible that he also has no quarrel with Brandl's dating of *Christ and Satan* not long after Cynewulf. (To be sure, the deviant spellings tōwerpan and sīdas are too isolated to be strong evidence for date, and the other features cited by Frings are by no means absent from later texts.)

Dating of Old English poetry by linguistic criteria has fallen out of fashion in recent decades, and objections have been made to it, partly on the ground that we cannot know which forms in a text come from the author and which from a copyist in the numerous cases where the meter is not decisive, partly on the ground that spatial as well as temporal differences of usage may be involved, and partly on the ground that in any case the Anglo-Saxon poets composed their work in an archaizing diction heavily dependent on traditional formulas, so that linguistic forms could survive in poetic use long after they had otherwise ceased to exist. These are not reasons, however, for completely discrediting and abandoning linguistic criteria, but only for using them cautiously, critically, and in conjunction with other evidence of a different kind. In this particular case it seems not likely to be an accident that the linguistic forms for the most part point towards the same conclusion to which several good authorities have been led by consideration of literary affiliations: that *Christ and Satan* belongs to a period slightly later than Cynewulf.

Conspicuous among the other conceivable dating criteria which might be applied, besides those we have already considered, are the metrical features of a poetic work. Graz 1894 brought some of these to bear on the question of unity of authorship of *Christ and Satan*, with results favourable to the hypothesis of a single author.[36] He deals with the comparative frequency of the various types and subtypes of half-line according to the system of Kaluza,[37] and the comparative frequency of the various alliterating sounds, in *Genesis*, *Exodus*, *Daniel*, *Christ and Satan*, and the first thousand lines of *Beowulf*. It seems possible to me that these features might have chronological significance if investigated more inclusively, and accordingly I have made a sampling of this kind. My tabulation of scansional data is limited to the comparative frequency of Type A half-lines with alliteration on the second lift only, among all first half-lines. This type is almost exactly equivalent to Sievers' Type $A_3$, or to Pope's types A63–A97 and A104–A107,[38] and will hereafter be called Type A Weak. The poems investigated were *Beowulf*, *Genesis A* ll. 1–234, *Genesis A* ll. 852–2936, *Genesis A* in toto, *Exodus* ll. 1–361 and 447–590, *Exodus* ll. 362–446 (a possibly interpolated section), *Exodus* in toto, *Daniel* ll. 1–278 and 362–764, *Daniel* ll. 279–361 (a possibly interpolated section), *Daniel* in toto, *Christ and Satan* Part I, *Christ and Satan* Part II, *Christ and Satan* Part III, *Christ and Satan* in toto, *Elene*, *Juliana*, *The Ascension (Crist II)*, *The Fates of the Apostles*, the Cynewulf canon (consisting of just those poems signed by Cynewulf, which are *Elene*, *Juliana*, *The Ascension*, and *The Fates of the Apostles*), *The Advent (Crist I)*, *The Last Judgment (Crist III)*, *The Phoenix*, *Guthlac A*, *Guthlac B*, *The Meters of Boethius*, *The Battle of Brunnanburh*, and *The Battle of Maldon*. Pope's figures were

Table 1

| Text | Percentage | Absolute |
| --- | --- | --- |
| Guthlac B | 3.82 | 21 out of 550 |
| Brunnanburh | 5.48 | 4 out of 73 |
| Genesis A 1–234 | 7.05 | 16 out of 227 |
| Phoenix | 7.76 | 52 out of 670 |
| Exodus 1–361, 447–590 | 7.80 | 38 out of 487 |
| Genesis A | 8.77 | 198 out of 2258 |
| Genesis A 852–2936 | 8.96 | 182 out of 2031 |
| Exodus | 9.11 | 52 out of 571 |
| Elene | 9.58 | 124 out of 1294 |
| Beowulf | 9.77 | 309 out of 3162 |
| Fates of the Apostles | 10.92 | 13 out of 119 |
| Cynewulf canon | 10.92 | 280 out of 2565 |
| Ascension (Crist II) | 11.76 | 50 out of 425 |
| Advent (Crist I) | 11.93 | 52 out of 436 |
| Juliana | 12.79 | 93 out of 727 |
| Last Judgment (Crist III) | 13.07 | 100 out of 765 |
| Daniel 279–361 | 16.25 | 13 out of 80 |
| Daniel | 16.59 | 115 out of 693 |
| Daniel 1–278, 362–764 | 16.64 | 102 out of 613 |
| Exodus 362–446 | 16.67 | 14 out of 84 |
| Meters of Boethius | 18.84 | 325 out of 1725 |
| Christ and Satan I | 18.99 | 68 out of 358 |
| Guthlac A | 19.00 | 148 out of 779 |
| Christ and Satan | 19.63 | 138 out of 703 |
| Christ and Satan II | 19.72 | 56 out of 284 |
| Maldon | 20.82 | 66 out of 317 |
| Christ and Satan III | 22.95 | 14 out of 61 |

accepted for *Beowulf*. For the remaining poems I made my own count, using the texts as printed in *The Anglo-Saxon Poetic Records* published by Columbia University Press, except that I used my own text of *Christ and Satan* (see microfiche), and took the text of *The Battle of Brunnanburh* from Anderson and Williams's *Old English Handbook*[39] and that of *The Battle of Maldon* from Sweet's *Anglo-Saxon Reader*.[40] (I have also tried to extend Graz's consideration of the comparative frequency of alliterating sounds to a larger body of Old English poetry, but since I have not been able to linearize the results in such a way as to make them possibly useful for relative chronology I do not give them here.) Hypermetric, missing, and conjectural first half-lines have been excluded from the count, as well as isolated half-lines. Table 1 shows, in percentage and absolute terms, the proportion of Type A Weak first half-lines to all first half-lines in the poems and parts of poems under consideration.

Several comments may fairly be made on the figures in Table 1. To begin with, it is noteworthy that items which are taken on other grounds to belong together have percentages which are not widely separated: this is true of the two parts of *Genesis A*, and of the four poems of the uncontroverted Cynewulf canon, and therefore, incidentally, these figures are favourable to the unity of *Christ and Satan* (as well as unity of *Daniel* and disunity of *Exodus*). Next, it is certain that order of ascending frequency of Type A Weak half-lines does not correspond simply to chronological order, for if it did, *Guthlac B*, *The Battle of Brunnanburh*, and probably *The Phoenix* as well would not appear so near the beginning of the list. This said, however, we can hardly fail to observe that the gap of more than three percentage points between *The Last Judgment (Crist III)* and *Daniel* appears to divide the poems considered into two groups which are in some way significant. On one side of the divide we find *Daniel*, *Christ and Satan*, *Guthlac A*, and the *Exodus* interpolation (if it *is* an interpolation), along with works which are known to be late, namely *The Meters of Boethius* and *The Battle of Maldon*; on the other, the Cynewulf canon and *Crist I* and *III* preceded by poems generally held to be early, namely *Genesis A*, the main part of *Exodus*, and *Beowulf* (overlapping slightly with the Cynewulf canon), with *Guthlac B*, *The Battle of Brunnanburh*, and *The Phoenix* enigmatically appearing very high in the list.

To account for this partly chronological and partly contradictory picture, I can suggest only a somewhat complicated hypothesis, as follows: In the earlier period of Old English poetry, up to and including the age of Cynewulf, sparing and judicious use was probably made of the Type A Weak half-line, roughly in the proportion of one to every ten lines as a device conspicuously imparting variety to the meter. (We can hardly suppose that it was ever regarded as a blemish, considering that the first datable half-line in English verse, Nū scylun hergan at the beginning of Caedmon's *Hymn*, is of this pattern; Bede does not say that the angel rapped Caedmon's knuckles and told him to start again.) Later, however, let us say from some time in the ninth century, there probably came to be at least two different traditions in the composition of Old English poetry, a conservative one which continued to keep the proportion of Type A Weak half-lines low, and a more permissive one whose practitioners resorted more freely to Type A Weak half-lines for relaxed ease and fluency of composition. Probably then the poets of *Guthlac B*, *The Battle of Brunnanburh*, and *The Phoenix* were working within the former of these traditions, one or two of them perhaps with excessive zeal; for such a late poem *The Battle of Brunnanburh* is also remarkably conventional in other respects such as the conspicuousness of litotes and of the beasts-of-prey motif. The poets of *Daniel*, *Christ and Satan*, *Guthlac A*, and *The Battle of Maldon*, in this view, were working within the other. Concerning the poet of *The Meters of Boethius* it might be more accurate to say that he was not working within any poetic tradition at all, but I would be reluctant to say the same of any of the others.

Something of a convergence, then, of data based on literary relationships, linguistic forms, and metrical practice would seem to indicate a date later than Cynewulf for the composition of *Christ and Satan*. On the basis of a careful review of the evidence, Kenneth Sisam is inclined to assign Cynewulf rather to the ninth than to the late eighth century.[41] Accepting his view, we may tentatively conclude that *Christ and Satan* was probably composed not far from the middle of the ninth century.

In seeking to ascertain the original dialect of *Christ and Satan*, one consideration must not be lost from sight. The text of *Christ and Satan* in the manuscript is the work of three scribes, Scribe A having written pages 213–15, Scribe B pages 216–28, and Scribe C page 229; and the work of all three was subjected to emendation by a Corrector. As has long been recognized, for example by Groschopp 1883 and Frings 1913, the text as we have it has been much normalized into late West Saxon, especially by Scribe B and the Corrector. The forms that have escaped this normalization are those to which we must look for evidence of an earlier stage or stages of transmission and for even a surmise concerning the original dialect. Kenneth Sisam, to be sure, in his study 'Dialect Origins of the Earlier Old English Verse,'[42] has argued, with much supporting evidence, that 'linguistic tests now available [do not] enable us to determine the dialect in which any longer piece of the earlier Old English poetry was composed.' However, he does not in this study take into account the fact that *Christ and Satan* is almost unique among Old English poems in containing right in the manuscript the changes made by a Corrector whose goal, normalization into late West Saxon, is identifiable, and who therefore inadvertently and indirectly gives us the opportunity to draw conclusions about the dialect features of the manuscript from which Book Two of Junius 11 was copied. These features are unmistakably Anglian.

The arguments of Sievers 1885a, who like Groschopp 1883 had argued in favour of Kentish, were effectively refuted by Frings 1913.[43] In fact, on the basis of a detailed study of the non-West Saxon features of the text[44] Frings concluded that the Junius 11 scribes had before them a text in a Mercian-Northumbrian border dialect resembling that of the Rushworth Gloss to the gospel of Matthew, and this view has remained unchallenged since his time. After the lapse of more than six decades in which much dialect study has been done, however, it seems appropriate to examine the evidence again, and I have done so, making use of Campbell's *Old English Grammar*.[45] In the report of that examination which now follows, I omit general Old English features like *ā* for Proto-Germanic *ai*, general non-West Saxon features like *ē* for West Germanic *ā* or for the *i*-mutation of *ēa*, and forms like *ȳ* for the *i*-mutation of *ēa* or the *y* of Scyppend (c ss 300–1) or fyrnum (c ss 317–18) that are readily explainable as West Saxon. My rule has been to list only features which are distinctively Anglian (though some overlapping with Kentish has proved impracticable to avoid) and those which may contribute to narrower localization of the text within the Anglian area.

The *i*-mutation of PG *a* or its equivalent before a nasal appears three times as *æ* in forms of ængel 'angel' in Scribe A's part of the text, against prevailing *e*. This *æ* is found in early Northumbrian and early Mercian texts; in later texts *e* is usual and *æ* is exceptional, though the Rushworth Gloss to Matthew[46] has *æ* alongside *e* in the ratio of 1[+] to 10 (c s 193 (d)). The Vespasian Psalter gloss,[47] a West Mercian text of the early ninth century, also has one occurrence of ængel (34, 6), according to Grimm's glossary to the Vespasian Psalter gloss,[48] against a much greater predominance of *e* than Ru.[1] shows. (The form mænego 'multitude,' however, which occurs three times in the sections of text written by Scribes B and C, alongside five forms with *e* in the work of Scribes A and B, may well be late West Saxon according to c s 380.)

PG *a* followed in consecutive syllables by *u* and *i* in that order appears twice in Scribe A as *ǣ* in forms of ǣce 'eternal(ly)' against predominant *ēce* found in A and B. This *ǣ* is found in vp, Ru.[1], and Northumbrian, and also in Kentish charters, where, however, *æ* is only a spelling for *e* (c s 237 (1) (c)).

The characteristically Anglian *a* (by retraction of *æ*) before *l* plus consonant, where ws and Kt. have *ea* by breaking (c s 143), is about equally frequent in *Christ and Satan* with *ea*.

For the normal breaking of *e* to *eo* before *r* plus consonant, *Christ and Satan* has alongside predominant *eo* a single occurrence of a spelling with *e* in tōwerpan 'distintegrate' (Scribe A). Such spellings are found in eMerc. and eNhb. texts, as well as in Kt. charters (c s 140). Clubb 1925[49] reports isolated occurrences of this *e* in Ru.[1] (awerp, werþe), to which may be added gehwerfæþ 'turn' in 7, 6.

The word for 'angry,' reconstructible for prehistoric OE. as *irrī-, might be expected to undergo breaking and *i*-mutation of the vowel of its first syllable. The breaking occurs, but the resultant *io* does not undergo *i*-mutation in non-ws, but on the contrary tends to merge with *eo*, so that all Angl. texts have iorre or eorre, and specifically both vp and Ru.¹ have eorre (c ss 148, 154 (3), 201, 294–5). What *Christ and Satan* has is eorre, twice in Scribe B alongside a single occurrence of ws yrre- also in B. To be sure, eorre might also be a Kt. form (c s 297).

Back mutation of *i*, that is its diphthongization to *io* (later usually *eo*) before a back vowel, is common to all dialects, but in certain dialects it does not occur before certain intervening consonants, and besides analogical extension of unmutated *i* is very frequent, so that on the whole both *i* and *eo* are widespread (c ss 212–17). One form in *Christ and Satan* which may have dialect significance is seoððan 'after(wards),' invariably (seven times) so spelled; Kt. and Ru.¹ have seoððan, vp seoðan, corresponding to ws siððan. The form seondon 'are,' occurring twice in *Christ and Satan* (in A and B with the *-on* added by the Corrector on the second occasion) alongside more normal sind, synd, syndon (each once and all in B), has been called Kt., and indeed siondon and seondan do occur in ninth-century charters of Kent and Surrey (c s 217), but there is no reason why it may not be Angl. as well: seondan occurs in a Worcester charter of 904 printed as no. 31 in Sweet's *Second Anglo-Saxon Reader*.⁵⁰

The unrounding of *o* to *a* in scealdon 'should' (once in A against eight occurrences of *(e)o* in A-B) is a predominantly Angl. feature, shared by vp, Ru.¹, and Nhb. (c s 156). The *a* of sweglbetalden 'surrounded with ether' (once in B) is probably to be accounted for in the same way, on the assumption that its second constituent corresponds to normal oe betolden, past part. of beteldan 'cover, surround.'

The *i*-mutation of *ā* (pg *ai*) appears as *ē* in *Christ and Satan* in clēne 'complete(ly)' (twice), forms of bedēlan 'deprive' (twice), gedēlde 'created' (once), forms of Hēlend 'Saviour' (twice), and gelēdde 'led' (once), all in A, against far more numerous examples of *ǣ* in the work of all three scribes. Several Angl. texts including both vp and Ru.¹ along with some Nhb. texts have *ē* in words of this class before dentals (c s 292); since the *Christ and Satan* examples are all before dentals too, we may reasonably ascribe them not to Kt., which has *ē* for the *i*-mutation of *ā* regardless of what consonant follows *ā* (c s 290), but to this Angl. development.

The diphthong *īo* is subject to *i*-mutation in ws only (c s 201 (3)). This presumably accounts for the occurrence in *Christ and Satan* of the unmutated nom. pl. form fēond 'fiends' (once in A and once in B, against no occurrences of any other nom. pl. form), with its characteristically Merc. *ēo* for earlier *īo* (c ss 294–5), where in ws the mutated form fīend or fȳnd would be expected.

The characteristically Angl. phenomenon of smoothing, that is monophthongization before a back consonant (even if *r* or *l* intervenes), is well represented in *Christ and Satan* (C ss 222–33). Examples of *e* by smoothing from *ea* are a form of esl (for exl) 'shoulder' (once in B), werg 'accursed' (seven times in A-B-C and never with any other stressed vowel than *e* but mostly with a parasitic *i* or *e* between the *r* and the *g*), and perhaps merced (once in B), if it stands for mercod (= mearcod) and means 'appointed, allotted.' Within Angl. the forms werg and merced agree equally well with VP and Ru.[1], but the form esl (for exl) agrees better with Ru.[1] than with VP, where forms like -sæx 'knife' and wæx 'wax' are almost invariable (C s 223). Examples of *e* by smoothing from *eo* are a form of werc 'work,' occurring once in A against four occurrences of forms of WS weorc in B, and just possibly merced if it means 'darkened, murky.' This *e* is general Anglian. An example of *ē* by smoothing from prehistoric Angl. *ēo* (which comes by breaking from prehistoric Angl. *ē*, equivalent to prehistoric WS *æ*, from WG *ā*) is nēh 'near,' occurring once in B and never in any other form (C ss 152, 222, 227). This *ē* is also general Anglian. Examples of *ē* by smoothing from *ēa* are ēc 'also' (once in B against one occurrence of ēac likewise in B), a single occurrence of a form of ēge 'eye' in C (against four occurrences of forms of ēage in B and C), and hēh(-) 'high' (eight times in A-B against only one occurrence of hēah-, which is in A); and an example of *ǣ* by smoothing from *ēa* is a single occurrence of þǣh 'though' in B (against two occurrences of þēah, also in B). In general *ǣ* is earlier and *ē* is later, but whereas both VP and Ru.[1] (with some Nhb. texts) have þǣh, VP has ēc and Ru.[1] (with some Nhb. texts) ǣc; it is possible that ēc and especially þǣh may have short vowels occasioned by lack of stress (C s 225). The smoothing of *ēo* is represented in *Christ and Satan*, contrary to expectation, not by *ē* but only by *ī*. The words in question are sīc 'sick at heart' (so spelled in its only occurrence, which is in B) and forms of līht (noun) 'light' (three occurrences in A-B against sixteen occurrences of forms of lēoht, also in A-B, counting occurrences of the adjective lēoht 'bright' and of lēoht- in a compound). The only thing comparable which I can find in Campbell is the occasional occurrence of *ī* rather than *ē* in the present system of verbs of Class II Strong in VP and Ru.[1], for instance līgende 'lying, speaking falsely' in both those texts (C s 227). Finally, an example of *ī* (general Angl.) by smoothing from *īo* is the sole occurrence of gelīhtan 'descend to,' which is in B (C ss 201 (4) and n 3, 222, 229). To be sure, this form might also be explained as WS, with *īo* becoming early WS *īe* by *i*-mutation and the *īe* later becoming *ī* or *ȳ*. If instead of meaning 'descend to' the word has a meaning like 'light the way' and belongs to the family of the noun lēoht 'light,' substantially the same possibilities exist for the the development of a form gelīhtan in Angl. or in ws.

Back mutation of *e* to *eo*, which occurs before any intervening single consonant in Kt., is more limited in ws and Angl.: in ws it occurs only before labials and liquids, in Angl. only before labials, liquids, and dentals, but not before the back consonants *c* and *g*, or, if it did take place before *c* and *g* as well, the *eo* shortly became *e* again, still in prehistoric Angl., by smoothing (c ss 205, 247). In vp, however, and to some extent also in Ru.¹, *eo* is extended by analogy to words where it is followed by *c* or *g*, for example spreocan 'speak' (c s 210 (2)). This same verb occurs only once in *Christ and Satan* in a form having the vowel grade of the present, and is there spelled (by Scribe A) spreocan, in agreement with the predominant spelling of vp and the occasional spelling of Ru.¹ Of course this form could also be explained as Kt., if there were independent evidence for Kentish origin or transmission of our text.

The 3d pers. sg. pres. indic. of strong verbs and of Class I Weak verbs almost never syncopates the vowel of the inflectional ending in *Christ and Satan*. Specifically, there are twenty-one occurrences of forms without syncope, and only one occurrence of a form with syncope, sit 'sits' in l. 217, where siteð would fit the meter equally well. Of the twenty-one without syncope none are contradicted by the meter and eleven are confirmed by it. The forms in question are cymeð 'comes,' dæleð 'bestows,' færeð 'comes,' fēreð 'goes,' hāteð 'commands,' haldeð 'holds,' ymbhaldeð 'encompasses,' ahefeð 'raises up,' lædað [sic] 'leads,' forlæteð 'forsakes,' lȳhteð 'gives light,' scīneð 'shines' (twice), gesēceð 'goes to,' sit 'sits,' siteð 'sits' (twice), tæceð 'shows,' þenceð 'intends' (three times), wriceð 'utters.' Syncope is general in ws (except for a mere sprinkling of 'forms of Angl. type') and generally lacking in Angl. (including vp, Ru.¹, and Nhb.), while early Kt. lacks syncope but tenth-century Kt. has syncope prevailingly (c ss 347, 731, 732, 733 and n 2, 734, 742, 751). Thus, setting aside the possibility of early Kentish origin or transmission, which lacks independent support, we may consider this overwhelming predominance of unsyncopated forms to be a conspicuous Angl. feature, while keeping an open mind to the possibility that it is a traditional feature of poetic diction not necessarily attached to a particular region.[51] Since it is well confirmed by meter, it is in any case a feature relevant to the origin of *Christ and Satan*, not merely its transmission.

Past participles of Class I Weak verbs, when they do not have adjective inflection, invariably end in *-ed* (once *-ad*) in *Christ and Satan*: there are twenty-five examples: †onæled 'burned' five times, †gebēged 'bent (transitive), gecȳðed 'made known,' [†]bedæled 'deprived' twice, [†]oðfæsted 'fastened on,' [†]gefēred 'fared,' [†]geflēmed 'put to flight,' [†]afylled 'filled,' [†]gefylled 'filled,' [†]hēahgetimbrad 'high-built,' [†]gehēned 'abased,' [†]gehēred 'heard' twice, alǣded 'led away,' [†]benēmed 'deprived,' genemned 'named' twice, with one occurrence confirmed by meter, geseted 'ordained,' [†]ontȳned 'revealed' twice. The twenty marked with a dagger plus one occurrence of genemned are confirmed by the meter, and none contradicted by the meter. Of course the form aseald 'banished' does not count, since it historically lacks a vowel before the -d (c s 753 (9) (a)). When such past participles add adjectival inflectional endings beginning with or consisting of a vowel, the e of -ed is invariably syncopated in *Christ and Satan*, with the sole exception of bescyrede 'deprived,' where no syncope is to be expected in any dialect on account of the short root syllable (c s 751 (3)); there are thirteen examples (bedælde 'deprived' three times, gefærde 'brought,' afyrhte 'terrified,' gelēdde 'led,' gesette 'established,' awyrgda 'accursed' and similar forms six times), none of them contradicted by the meter. This consistent relation between forms with and without a vocalic inflectional ending reflects Angl. conditions: specifically, the very same picture is seen in vp and Ru.[1] as in *Christ and Satan*; Nhb. too has -ed final, but frequent syncope in forms with vocalic inflection; ws, on the other hand, has syncope after root-final dentals even in forms without adjective inflection, and tenth-century Kt. shares this tendency (c ss 351 n 2, 643 (5) (d), 751 (3), 753 (9) (b) (7)). As for the aberrant form hēahgetimbrad, with its apparent switch to Class II Weak, it could be an instance of agreement with Ru.[1] and Nhb. (c s 752 near end) or with vp (c s 753 (2)).

The forms abǣlige '(he) offend' (subjunctive), herede 'guardian,' and various cases (in five occurrences) of wereg or werig 'accursed' (35, 126, 332, 628, 727) represent forms with a parasitic vowel after a stressed syllable and between r or l and a consonant such as are 'scattered through early texts' (Nhb., Merc., Kt.) and found also in late Nhb. (c ss 360–1). It seems best for reasons of meaning to take these five occurrences of wereg or werig, plus werga 710, as occurrences of an adjective meaning 'accursed' and etymologically connected with wergu 'damnation' (42), wærgðu 'damnation' (89), and awyrged 'accursed' (316, 415, 626, 674, 690, 698), not with wērig 'weary' (162, 343, 427, 448). Recognition of such an adjective was advocated by Hart in 1907[52] and accepted for two passages in *Beowulf* by Klaeber in his edition.[53] Once again we see the pattern that when our text shares a feature with Kt., it shares it also with Angl.

*Christ and Satan* has one occurrence of werud 'host,' uninflected, against five of gen. pl. we(o)roda; forms of w(e)oruld 'world,' on the other hand, invariably have *u* (nine times). These are examples of *u* unstressed but not in absolute final position (what Campbell calls 'protected *u*'); it is extensively preserved by VP, and remains frequent in Ru.[1] and late Nhb. (C ss338, 373).

As pres. participles of Class II Weak verbs with long root syllable *Christ and Satan* has only forms with no *i* (nor *g*), namely gnornende 'lamenting' and reordende 'speaking' (ms probably reodende until changed by Corrector to reordiende); frēfergendum is not a valid contrary example, since the verb here is originally frēfran, Class I Weak, whose regular pres. participle frēfrendum would scan much better in the passage in question. This again is an Angl. feature, unless perhaps it is to be taken as traditional poetic diction: *-ende* without *i* appears in some early Merc. glossaries and in verse generally as shown by the meter; VP occasionally has *-ende* after long syllables, Ru.[1] has *-ende* in all Class II Weak verbs; Nhb. has *-ende* nearly always after long syllables, and quite often also after short (C s757).

As 1st pers. sg. pres. indic. of the verb 'to be,' *Christ and Satan* has one occurrence of eam (in B) alongside four of normal OE eom (in A–B). This form is shared with Kt., VP, and Ru.[1] (C s768). (Once again what our text shares with Kt. it also shares with Angl.!)

The form feolo 'many, much' appears once in B, against two occurrences of fela and two of feola, all in B. This feolo, for earlier feolu, is an Angl. form (C s666). For that matter feola might also stand for feolu, since spellings like geara 'ready' occur in our text.

As Clubb 1925 points out,[54] 'the occurrence of six cases of nymðe in a poem of [this length] is favorable to Anglian, and against Kentish provenience.'[55]

The only mention I have found in Campbell of the form hær 'here,' which occurs once in A alongside seven occurrences of normal OE *hēr* in A–B, is that it occurs as an inverted spelling in ninth-century Kt. (C s128 n 2). This isolated form, however, is entirely too slim a basis for an argument in favour of Kentish origin or transmission of our text. Almost any other explanation of it would be preferable.

Raising of general OE *æ*(<PG *a*) to *e* is represented in *Christ and Satan* by quite numerous *e* spellings, in the work of all three scribes, of words such as forms of cester 'city,' feste 'firmly,' gefestnade 'established firmly,' gefreg(e)n '(I) heard, learned,' hefde, hefdon 'had,' hebbe '(I) have,' heleð 'men' (?), forms of ness 'stratum of the earth' (?), refnan (ms hrefnan) 'inflict,' scedes 'of shade, darkness,' forms of gesceft 'creature, created thing,' scref 'pit,' þes 'of the, of that,' segdest '(you, sg.) said,' onwecnað

'(they) awaken,' wes 'was,' wrece 'punishment' (once as an oblique-case form and once apparently by extension from oblique cases as a nom. sg. form), and *wrec-* 'exile,' some thirty-six occurrences in all, against far more frequent occurrences of spellings with *æ* (or with *ea* from *æ* by influence of an initial palatal consonant). Apart from the possibility that these *e* spellings might be ascribed to Kentish origin or transmission of our text (C ss288–92), which lacks independent support, they must be regarded as a Merc. feature, specifically one which our text shares with VP and not with Ru.[1] This *e* is 'fairly common' in some eMerc. glosses, 'very frequent' in l Merc. texts (*Royal Glosses* and *The Life of St Chad*), and 'practically universal' in VP, but it is 'practically absent' in Ru.[1], and 'ME sources show that it was limited to a small part of the vast Midland area' (C ss164, 168). S.M. Kuhn has argued from indirect evidence that a sound change of *æ* > *e* occurred also in the dialect of Ru.[1], but his evidence is highly dubious (C s259 and n 1). The closest affinities of *Christ and Satan* in this respect are with VP.

In most OE the equivalent of PG *a* when a back vowel follows in the next syllable is *a*, but in what appears to have been a quite limited area a fronting of this *a* to *æ* occurred; this *æ* then undergoes back mutation to *ea*, except before an intervening consonant which prevents back mutation or reverses it by smoothing, though sometimes in early texts *æ* is retained even before consonants which do not usually have a mutation-hindering effect (C ss164, 168, 206, 207). This feature is invariable in VP and frequent in eMerc. glossaries as well as WS transcripts of poetic texts (such as *Beowulf*). Three *æ* forms in *Christ and Satan* may belong here, namely nom. pl. bæðe 'baths' (WS baðu) (once in B), acc. pl. æpla 'apples' (once in B), and pl. pres. indic. mægon 'may' (once in A). However, the consonant group *-pl-* may have hindered the retraction of *æ* > *a* before a back vowel, and WS actually has æplas beside apla (C s158); and Campbell (C s767) lists mægon beside magon as by implication a WS form, presumably by extension of the vowel of sg. mæg into the plural. Less equivocal are three *ea* forms in *Christ and Satan*, gen. sg. eaples 'apple' (once in B), and forms of the Class II Weak verb leaðian 'invite, summon' (twice in B). The fact that no back vowel occurs in the gen. sg. *eaples* does not invalidate its evidence: the *ea* must have been extended to the gen. sg. from a form like the eappul- attested in VP. Here, then, as in the preceding point, our text has a feature most conspicuously represented in VP and not shared by Ru.[1]; we should not altogether forget that it may be a feature of poetic diction, but still, neither æppel nor laðian is a particularly poetic word.

The peculiar form *herm* 'malignant' (once in B), with *e* for normal OE *ea* by breaking of *æ* before *r* plus consonant, is nowhere treated by Campbell so far as I can see. However, a search of Grimm reveals the following occasional spellings in vp: bern 'children' (twice), dat. pl. bernum (once), erð '(thou) art' (twice), gen. pl. ferrá 'bulls' (once).

The 2d and 3d pers. sg. pres. indic. of the verb 'to have' are never hæf(e)st, hæf(e)ð in *Christ and Satan*, but always dissyllabic forms with *a* in the stressed syllable: the occurrences are hafus (once in A), hafest (twice in B), hafað (twice in B). This agrees with the invariable hafast, hafað of vp, but these forms are also found in ws prose (c s762).

In the unsyncopated Angl. 3d pers. sg. pres. indic. forms of strong verbs (see p 38 above), vp usually has no *i*-mutation, but does have *i* in verbs where the infinitive has *e*; Ru.[1] and Nhb. have no *i*-mutation and have *e* in verbs where the infinitive has *e* (c s733). Thus wriceð 'utters' in *Christ and Satan* (once in A) agrees with vp against Ru.[1], and contrary examples are lacking. The form færeð 'comes' in *Christ and Satan* (once in B) is of dubious significance: vp has -fereð, but Ru.[1] and Nhb. sometimes replace *a* by analogical *æ* (from forms like the pres. subj. and pres. part.) even in such forms as the infin. færan, so that a 3d sg. færeð should not surprise us in these dialects (c s744); and even ws occasionally has forms with *i*-mutation and no syncope like hætest (c s734).

In all other features significant for dialect, so far as I can tell, *Christ and Satan* agrees with Ru.[1] against vp.

Prehistoric OE *æ* before *r* plus consonant appears four times as *a* (by retraction), against some seventy-two occurrences of *ea* (by breaking) and one occurrence of an anomalous *e* (see pp 41–2 above): forms of swart 'black' (once in A and twice in B), and forwarð 'was damned' (once in A). The occurrence of *a* in this position is practically limited to Nhb., with 'a few similar forms' found in Ru.[1] and a few in eMerc. glossaries (c s144 and n 1). It is noteworthy that they are especially common in a labial environment: the *Christ and Satan* examples share this feature.

For the *i*-mutation of *æ*, *Christ and Satan* has *æ* in a single occurrence of a form of bættra 'better' (in A), against overwhelmingly predominant occurrences of normal OE *e*. There are many instances of this *æ* in Ru.[1] and Nhb. (c s327).

The *i*-mutation of Angl. *a* before *l* plus consonant appears twice as *e* in forms of (-)welm 'surge' (in A), once as *æ* in wælm (also in A). In the Angl. texts *æ* is practically universal, but ME evidence shows that this *æ* became *e* before the end of the OE period except in the West Midlands, and the only OE text to show undoubted traces of the beginning of this change is Ru.[1] (c s193(*a*)).

The *i*-mutation of Angl. *a* or *ea* before *r* plus consonant appears twice as *æ*, in wærgðu 'damnation' (in A) and gen. sg. wk. awærgdan 'accursed (one)' (in B), against seven occurrences of general non-ws *e* (in A–B) and seven of ws *y* (in B), besides a single occurrence in A of a form of hwearfan 'go, move about' which must be due to confusion between a Class I Weak verb hwerfan or hwyrfan and a Class II Weak verb hwearfian. This *æ* occurs in Nhb., and also in Ru.[1] (C s193(*a*)) and in eMerc. glossaries. Angl. smoothing is not involved, since *i*-mutation took place earlier than smoothing (C ss247, 255).

Normal OE *e* (<PG *e*) appears as *æ* in -ðægn 'retainer,' gen. sg. rægnas [sic] 'of rain,' gen. sg. swægles 'of heaven,' all in A, against predominant *e* in A–B. Ru.[1] shows 'a well-marked change *we-* > *wæ-*' and some indications of a similar change *-egn* > *-ægn* (C s328). The fact that our text shows *æ* in just these environments and no others indicates that we have here a real dialect feature, not a symptom of scribal incompetence.

The *i*-mutation of *ō* appears four times as *ǣ*, in dat. sg. onmǣdlan 'pride' (once in B), forms of æðel 'homeland' (twice in A), and a form of gefǣran 'bring' (once in A), against a predominance of *ē* (or its shortening *e*, once) in A–B. Examples of this *ǣ* are found in ws and Ru.[1] (C s198).

Loss of final *-n* occurs in acc. sg. wēa 'woe' (once in B), dat. sg. masc. wk. werga 'accursed (one)' (once in C with *-n* added by the Corrector), and uta 'let us' (twice in B), against otherwise invariable retention. This loss is a mainly Nhb. feature, shared to an extent by Ru.[1], which has frequent loss of *-n* in weak inflection, presumably both of nouns and of adjectives, and in some other categories as well (C s472). The ms forms heofen déman and ordfruman in ll. 656 and 657, where the context requires nom. sg. masc. forms of these weak nouns, may be reverse spellings reflecting the same sound change. For the sporadic occurrence of such forms in Ru.[1] see Clubb 1925, p 130, and the reference given there.

The following unstressed vowels are to be understood as exceptional occurrences, standing out against a general predominance of more normal spellings:

PG unstressed *-a-* (normal OE *-e-*) appears occasionally in gen. singulars as *-æ-* or *-a-*, thus nīðæs (ms in ðæs) 'enmity' (once in B), rægnas 'rain' (once in A), and as *-æ-* in uninflected words, thus niðær 'down,' undær 'under' (each once in A). This *-æ-*, which is the earliest recorded OE spelling in this position, is used with considerable historical accuracy in eNhb. and the eMerc. glossaries, but is rare in charters after about 770; later it comes to be used again, less discriminatingly, as a spelling variant of *-e-* in Ru.[1] and lNhb. (C ss333, 369 and n 3). Ru.[1] and lNhb., as well as eleventh-century texts, can also have *-a-* for this *-æ-* or *-e-* (C s379 and n 3). On the whole, this like other less than predictable unstressed vowels in *Christ and Satan* is probably to be ascribed to the late period of the manuscript (early eleventh century) and not to the considerably earlier period of the original poem.

Like PG unstressed *-a-*, PG unstressed *-ai-* has OE *-æ-* as its earliest recorded OE spelling equivalent (C ss331(7), 355(2)), and the subsequent developments of it were as stated in the preceding paragraph (C ss369 and n 3, 379 and n 3). As representatives of this sound in subj. plurals, mostly 1st pers. hortatory, *Christ and Satan* has one *æ* in cwēmæn 'please' (in B, changed by erasure to cwēman) and eleven occurrences of *a*, in beoran 'bear,' cēosan 'choose,' dēman 'extol,' gearwian 'prepare,' ongeotan 'understand,' hēran 'obey,' lūcan (ms) 'lock,' gemunan 'be mindful of' (three times), neoman 'take' (all in B), besides two occurrences of uta 'let us' (in B, against three occurrences of uton also in B). These instances of *-æ-* and *-a-* are probably to be explained in basically the same way as those in the preceding paragraph. However, the high frequency of *-an* here makes it look like something other than a sporadic phenomenon, especially considering that in the one place where *-æn* was written it has been corrected not to *-en* but to *-an*. Perhaps the pres. pl. subjunctive was formally identified with the infinitive. One occurrence of dat. sg. mihta 'might' in B (corrected to mihte), where the ending was likewise PG *-ai*, is to be explained as late confusion of unstressed vowels in accordance with C s379 and n 3.

PG unstressed *-i-* appears unchanged, where not lost, in earliest OE; later it becomes normal OE *-e-*, for instance in the ending *-eð* of the 3d pers. sg. pres. indic., where not syncopated (C ss731(*a*), 735(*b*)). For this, *Christ and Satan* has a single instance of *-að*, in lædað 'leads' (in B). This *-að* is found alongside *-eð* and *-æð* in Ru.[1] and Nhb. (C ss735(*b*), 752); it might also be, more generally, an eleventh-century feature (C s379 and n 3).

PG unstressed *-ijaz*, the nom. sg. masc. ending of *ja*-stem nouns and adjectives, is represented by *-i* in earliest OE, later ordinarily by *-e* (C ss 645, 576, 355 (3)). For this ending *Christ and Satan* once has *-æ*, in ðeostræ 'dark' (in A). In Ru.[1] and lNhb., unstressed *æ* can appear for *e < i* (C s 369 n 3). It is also possible that ðeostræ is to be taken as nom. sg. masc. weak rather than strong. In this case the PG ending was unstressed *-ô* (C ss656, 616), and normal OE *-a* (C s 355 (1)); this *-a* is stable until a late period (C s 375); Campbell does not specifically say in s 379 and n 3 that *-æ* could appear for it in Ru.[1], lNhb., and eleventh-century texts, but it does not seem impossible.

PG unstressed *-a-* before a nasal is represented by OE *-a-* from the beginning and this *-a-* is stable down to a late period (C ss 333, 375), for example in infinitives. The one occurrence in *Christ and Satan* of an infinitive in *-en*, namely oferhycgen 'renounce' in B, agrees with spellings found in Ru.[1], lNhb., and eleventh-century texts (C ss 379 and m 3, 735 (*i*)).

The prehistoric OE ending of the gen. pl. of weak nouns was unstressed *-anôm*, which appears early in OE as *-ana*, though the normal OE form is *-ena*, shared by VP and WS (C ss 616–17, 385). In *Christ and Satan* the form *-ana* once occurs, in sceaðana 'of (the) devils' (in A). This form is frequent in Ru.[1] and lNhb., where Campbell takes it as a survival (C s 617); however, the medial *-a-* might also be a mere replacement of *-e-* by confusion of unstressed vowels in a late text (C s 379 and n 3). Yet it is to be noted that the form gave trouble to the Corrector, which suggests that it may have come down into our text from an earlier stage of transmission.

PG unstressed *-a-* followed by a nasal which in turn is followed by a vowel (and therefore does not belong to the same syllable as the *a*) is represented in earliest OE by *-æ-* and in normal OE by *-e-*; this is the source of the endings of most strong past participles, which in normal OE end in *-en*, with *-e-* extended by analogy into the form where the *-n* is final from the forms where a vowel-initial adjectival ending followed the *-n* (C ss 731 (*h*), 334, 369). (This formulation is accepted from Campbell for lack of a better, but if it is correct, it is hard to see how the wk. gen. pl. ending *-anôm* of the preceding paragraph could have become *-ana* in earliest OE.) *Christ and Satan* has one strong past part. in *-on*, namely gewunnon 'fought' (in C). This is reminiscent of Ru.[1] and lNhb., which have occasional *-on* or *-an* due to 'failing distinction of unaccented vowels' (C s 735 (*k*) and n 1).

PG unstressed *-anþi*, the ending of the (3d pers.) pl. pres. indic., becomes OE *-að* (C ss 731, 332, 355 (4), 331 (3)), which is subject to relatively little variation. *Christ and Satan* has one pl. pres. indic. in *-eð*, namely stæleð 'accuse of' (in B), agreeing in this respect with Ru.[1] and Nhb., which occasionally have *-eð* (C ss 735 (*c*), 752), but also more generally with eleventh-century texts, in which such confusion of unstressed vowels is possible (C s 379 and n 3).

PG unstressed *-ō*, as in the nom. sg. of *ō*-stem nouns, became OE *-u*, which remained rather stable until a late period except for varying with *-o* (C ss 586–7, 589 (6), 353, 373). *Christ and Satan* once has *-e* as the nom. sg. of an *ō*-stem noun, namely in fæhðe 'enmity' (in B). This *-e* in place of *-u* or *-o* occurs also in Ru.[1] and lNhb., and more generally in eleventh-century texts (C s 379 and n 3).

The PG ending of the (3d pers.) pl. past and preterit-present indic. was unstressed *-unþ*, which became earliest OE *-un*, normal OE mostly *-on* (C SS 731 (*c*), 736 (*d*), 750, 735 (*e*), 373). *Christ and Satan* has numerous occurrences of normal OE *-on*, six occurrences of *-an* which could easily be lWS. (C S 377), and three occurrences of *-un* (sceolun 'shall' twice in A and gesāwun 'saw' once in C) which may well be survivals from an earlier stage of transmission but in any case could hardly be used for localization. On the other hand, it has eight occurrences of *-en*: æten 'ate' (in B), mōten 'may' (once in A and three times in B), mōsten 'might' (in B), sceolden 'were destined to' (in A), and þanceden 'thanked' (in B). Such *-en* forms are possible in Ru.[1] and lNhb., and also more generally in eleventh-century texts (C SS 735 (*e*), 379 and n 3).

Most of these phenomena of the vowels of unstressed syllables probably have little significance for localization, since in most instances they need not point to anything but a practically universal confusion of unstressed vowels by the early eleventh century when our manuscript was written. The wk. gen. pl. in *-ana* may be an exception, and possibly also the very frequent 1st pers. pl. hortatory subjunctives in *-an*.

The pres. part. of the Class II Weak verb beofi(g)an 'tremble' appears in *Christ and Satan* as beofigende (once in B). We would expect *-iende* in WS, Kt., or VP, but *-igende* in Ru.[1] or Nhb. (C S 757). The situation is quite similar with pl. pres. indic. eardigað '(they) dwell' (once in A): WS and Kt. have *-i-* before *-a-*, VP *-i-* before all vowels, Ru.[1] *-ig-* prevailingly, Nhb. mainly *-ig-* though sometimes *-i-* before *-a-* (C S 757).

A single instance occurs in *Christ and Satan* of a pl. pres. indic. of a Class II Weak verb without the historically justified *-i(g)-*: leaðað '(they) summon' (in B). Comparable forms occur in Ru.[1] and Nhb. (C S 757 p. 334). This form also gave the Corrector trouble (he thought it was an error for lǣdað 'lead,' Class I Weak), so that it may come from an earlier stage of transmission. The form lange in l. 504, if correctly interpreted as a sg. pres. subj. of langian 'long,' is another example of the same feature (C S 757).

The only form of the sg. pres. subj. of the verb 'to be' which occurs in *Christ and Satan* is sēo (five times in B). WS has sīe (sī, sȳ), VP sīe, and lNhb. sīe (alongside sē); but a ninth-century Surrey charter has sēo (alongside sīo) and Ru.[1] has sēo (alongside sīe, sȳ, sē) (C S 768 (*d*)).

All in all, when we try to see what is beneath the lWS garb which in MS Junius 11 has been not too successfully imposed on *Christ and Satan*, we can hardly fail to recognize a Mercian text. Features which our text shares with Northumbrian or Kentish it invariably shares with Mercian as well, except for the one erratic spelling hær. Within Mercian it sometimes agrees with both VP and Ru.[1], sometimes with VP against Ru.[1], sometimes with Ru.[1] against VP. At this point a caution is in order. The reason why references to VP and Ru.[1] have been so frequent in the above summary of dialect features is that these are the only Mercian texts that can be definitely localized. The Vespasian Psalter gloss is an early ninth-century Lichfield text,[56] and the Rushworth gloss to the gospel of Matthew is a tenth-century text from Harewood on the river Wharfe in the West Riding of Yorkshire, a few miles north-northeast of Leeds.[57] There is much less detailed evidence about the dialect of other parts of Mercia. In particular, how far a locality could be from Harewood and still share dialect features with Ru.[1], or how far a locality could be from Lichfield and share dialect features with VP, are impossible matters to determine.

On the basis of the dialect evidence assembled here, three possible conclusions about the provenance of *Christ and Satan* recommend themselves. First, there may have been for all practical purposes only a single Mercian stage of transmission, and that in a dialect close to that of Ru.[1]; in this case the features resembling VP would be explained as belonging to traditional poetic diction. Second, there may have been for all practical purposes only a single Mercian stage of transmission, and that in the dialect of an unidentified locality, probably somewhere between Harewood and Lichfield, which shared some of the dialect features of both Ru.[1] and VP. Third, there may have been two quite distinct Mercian stages of transmission, one accounting for the dialect features resembling Ru.[1] and the other for those resembling VP; in this case the relative age of the two stages would remain to be settled.

The first possibility, though it would account satisfactorily for eaples and leaðian, can hardly be considered the best, as there seems to be no particular reason to attribute the other VP-like peculiarities of our text to poetic diction; this is particularly true of the quite frequent *e* for general OE *æ*. The second possibility has an attractiveness based on a realistic recognition of our ignorance of Mercian local dialects, but is probably also to be rejected: two of the Ru.[1]-like features of our text, namely the occasional loss of final -*n* and the occasional occurrence of *a* before *r* plus consonant after a labial, have a distinctly Northumbrian flavour, and may not have extended farther into the Mercian area than the border strip to which Ru.[1] belongs. This leaves the third possibility, which is open to neither of these objections: it seems most probable that *Christ and Satan*, prior to MS Junius 11, underwent two distinguishable stages of transmission, which we may call North Mercian and West Mercian.

Which of the two is the older, and therefore the more likely to have been the dialect in which the poem was composed? It might be thought that the stage of which the fewer traces appear is the older, since Stage A (whichever that is) has been overlaid both by Stage B and by the lws of MS Junius 11, whereas Stage B has been overlaid only by lws; but a decision is hard to reach even on this basis. The list of North Mercian features is the longer, even if we exclude most of the evidence from unstressed vowels, but most of them are represented by very few examples, and none by anything like the thirty-six occurrences of *e* for general OE *æ* on the West Mercian side. Nevertheless, apart from this one feature the West Mercian stage seems more obscured than the North Mercian. Accordingly I would say very tentatively that West Mercian may have been the earlier stage of transmission and therefore at least imaginably the poet's dialect, and North Mercian an intermediate stage of transmission.

Two morsels of non-linguistic data, though not to be considered real evidence, furnish some ground for a surmise about where and when *C & S* may have been composed.

(1) The most closely related source or analogue of *C & S* Part II that has been discovered is *Blickling Homily* 7.[58] The correspondences of detail are mostly not close, but the correspondences in large-scale features may fairly be called compelling. *Blickling Homily* 7, in turn, has as one of its sources a Latin homily, Pseudo-Augustine 160 in *PL* 39.2059-61, which it follows so closely as to be almost a literal translation from par. 1 l. 13 to par. 5 l. 10 of Pseudo-Augustine 160 as it appears in *PL*.[59] At this point *Blickling Homily* 7 departs from the *PL* text of Pseudo-Augustine 160, and for some time follows very closely a passage of Latin text found in the *Book of Cerne*, specifically in that part of it which was the prayer book of a ninth-century Bishop Aethelwold, probably the one who was Bishop of Lichfield 818–30.[60] Thus one branch of the stream of tradition which flowed down into *C & S* may possibly have passed through Lichfield in the early ninth century.

(2) The thirteenth of the hymns in the *Vespasian Psalter* alludes in its sixty-eight lines to no less than ten of the motifs occurring in *C & S*, including some which by no means obviously belong together, for example Christ as Creator and the immunity of believers to harm inflicted by the devil.[61] The *Vespasian Psalter* gloss is said by its most recent editor Sherman Kuhn to be a Lichfield text of the early ninth century.[62] Of course it was not necessarily through the *Vespasian Psalter* that the *C & S* poet had direct or indirect access to the Latin hymn, if indeed he had such

access. Still, it is suggestive that early ninth-century Lichfield here bobs up again.

On pp 34 and 48 above, independently of these two conceivable Lichfield connections, I had tentatively suggested that *C & S* was probably composed not far from 850 and in a West Mercian rather than a North Mercian area. The Lichfield associations, if associations they are, at least do nothing to weaken these tentative conclusions; and no nonlinguistic data have come to light that even tenuously suggest any other period or locality.

# 3

# Sources, Influences, Traditions

No single source has been discovered, and probably none will ever be, for *Christ and Satan* as a whole. An immediate or almost immediate source, handled with rather great freedom, is identifiable for Part II; but for the most part we must content ourselves with identifying the traditions within which our poet worked and some of the important influences taking effect on him by way of ultimate, indirect, and partial sources.

The most recent examination of the sources, influences, and traditions – a thorough one – has been made by Finnegan 1977: pp 37–55, repeating with some compression and some amplification his findings recorded in Finnegan 1969: pp 69–150 and Finnegan 1974a. In treating Part I here it will hardly be necessary to do more than abstract, with at most an occasional question or objection, Finnegan's published work, where ample references will be found.

The principal Part I motifs which Finnegan locates within their respective traditions are the Fall of the angels, Christ as target and punisher of the angelic rebellion, the location and description of hell, and the character of Satan. Concerning the Fall of the angels, Finnegan 1977[1] shows that the *Christ and Satan* poet does not follow the tradition that the angels fell through lust, which, as a development of the account in Genesis 6: 1–4 of the 'sons of God' begetting children on the 'daughters of men,' originated in Jewish Apocryphal writings such as the *Book of Jubilees* and was continued in early Christian patristic writings from Justin Martyr to Ambrose (late fourth century). Instead, he follows the tradition that the angels fell through pride, which became established around the end of the sixth century with the writings of Gregory the Great, though not originated by him.

The *Christ and Satan* poet's representation of the angels' rebellion as directed against Christ and punished by him, Finnegan finds,[2] is contrary to almost all patristic writings, which depict the rebellion as directed against God the Father. However, he finds a basis for it in verse 6 of the Epistle of Jude and in Bede's commentary on that Epistle, in which it is Christ who punishes what Bede calls the 'rebel angels' (*praevaricatores angelos*). Finnegan also refers to a late seventh-century Ascension Day homily falsely attributed to the late fourth-century Greek writer Epiphanius of Salamis,[3] in which Satan speaks of the 'Son of Mary' as his opponent and says 'From the heavens he threw me down to earth like a little whirling stone.'

Concerning the location of hell, the main rival traditions documented by Finnegan[4] are, on the one hand, that the fallen angels are 'in some aerial confinement, with the pains of hell, though prepared, reserved until after the Last Judgment,'[5] a tradition represented in the Jewish Apocrypha and in Christian writers as late as Ambrose, and, on the other hand, the tradition of a subterranean hell, represented by Augustine, Gregory the Great, and Bede. It is of course to the latter that our poet adheres.

Concerning the description of hell, Finnegan 1977[6] shows that the most conspicuous elements in the poet's account of the physical pains of hell, fire, ice, and serpents, are well represented in writings in the Christian tradition that were composed in England, such as Bede's *Ecclesiastical History of the English People* and two of his commentaries on Epistles in the New Testament, or very well known there, such as the *Visio Sancti Pauli*, a Latin translation of a third-century Greek text. It is especially in the latter that a wealth of such descriptive details occurs. One such correspondence is the statement in the *Visio* that the devils who torment sinners in hell have sparks flying from the hairs of their heads and out of their mouths, just as Satan in *C & S* 78 emits sparks when he speaks. As Finnegan points out, the parallels cited by Clubb 1925[7] from canonical and apocryphal scripture never refer to hell or Satan. However, since two of them refer to prophets, Hill 1972 is probably right in suggesting that the sparks Satan emits parody the prophets' speech, which burns 'with the fire of charity rather than that of torment.' The poet probably knew the *Visio* passage as well as one or more of the scriptural passages, and may have used the motif of the sparks as a grisly parody of prophets' fiery speech and also of the inner radiance of angels and good men which he mentions in ll. 210 and 222–3.

In his section on the character of Satan, Finnegan 1977[8] takes issue with those critics, like ten Brink 1877 and Brooke 1892, who find the Satan of *Christ and Satan* a weak character by contrast with the defiant one of

*Genesis B*, and therefore an inferior artistic creation. Accepting in part, and developing, a line of thought deriving from Huppé 1959 and Greenfield 1965, he reasons quite rightly that our poet's Satan must necessarily be wretched rather than haughtily defiant in order not to shift 'the audience's interest away from the omnipotence of the Son,' an essential feature of what Finnegan defines as the poem's theme, 'the revelation of the character of Christ and man's moral obligation in relation to this revelation.' For reasons already indicated,[9] it seems necessary to add that the *Christ and Satan* poet displays the character of Satan fully and in an unattractive light for the sake of the contrast between Satan, who incarnates powerless would-be self-exaltation, and Christ, who is divine omnipotence expressed through self-abasement from the Incarnation, or even the Creation, to the Harrowing of hell.

Structurally, Part I of *Christ and Satan* is a series of plaints of Satan, interspersed with invectives against Satan by the devils and homiletic passages addressed by the poet to his audience. Plaints of Satan (Lucifer) occur in a number of Christian writings earlier than our poem, as shown by Abbetmeyer 1903 and Clubb 1925, and therefore may be seen as a tradition which the poet used in a structurally central way, no matter how skilfully or unskilfully, in shaping Part I. Since Finnegan 1977 treats them very briefly and rather dismissively,[10] it seems desirable to treat them more fully here. What may be the earliest one is a speech by Lucifer in ll. 89–116 of the poem 'De originali peccato' by Avitus of Vienne (d. ab. 519).[11] Another occurs in the Ascension Day homily ascribed to Epiphanius of Salamis[12] which has been mentioned earlier.[13] Interest in Lucifer's state of mind after the Fall appears in England in the Latin works of Aldhelm, Bishop of Sherborne (d. 709). In his *De Octo Principalibus Vitiis*, ll. 296–302,[14] though not in Lucifer's words but in the poet's, Lucifer's angelic glory before his Fall is set in sharp contrast with his damned state; and in the riddle *Lucifer*,[15] spoken throughout by Lucifer in the first person, mostly in his identity as the morning star (Isaiah 14:12), ll. 6–8 express his identity as the fallen angel and contrast his former happiness under God's law with the vengeance that has struck him down. This tradition continues into Old English most conspicuously in *Christ and Satan*, but also in other passages of Old English poetry, notably in *Genesis B* 356–441 (by way of Old Saxon), where Satan is the speaker, and in *Guthlac A* 577–684, where a troop of demons speak to Guthlac, trying to drive him to the sin of despair, and are answered by him. The *Genesis B* and *Guthlac* passages are regarded as analogues rather than sources of *Christ and Satan*; it has been suggested by Clubb 1925, however, that *Christ and Satan* and the *Guthlac* passage may have a common lost source.[16] The section of *Genesis A* dealing with the Fall of the angels (15–91) contains no speeches, but shows an interest in their state of mind which puts it broadly within the same tradition.

This tradition has its relevance to the *C & S* poet's depiction of the character of Satan, for the tone of the lamentations in the different works where they appear varies between plaintive and defiant, according to the context and the authors' intentions, dramatic or homiletic or both. Thus the tone is defiant in Avitus and in *Genesis B* because Satan is speaking immediately after his Fall and is already forming the idea of retaliating against God through the temptation of Adam and Eve, whereas in the Pseudo-Epiphanius boastfulness and defiance are lacking in the Ascension Day context, since Christ has already freed the souls of men from bondage to the devil. The Satan of our poem is so far from being defiant that he has been called 'sentimental,'[17] and described as sounding 'like a preacher,'[18] but as was shown above, this view is a misapprehension. His regret for the loss of his former state is shot through with cupidity and power hunger growing out of pride, and these are the very qualities of character that have led him to forfeit heaven and bar him from regaining it. With a partial and sterile insight (Ne mæg ic þæt gehicgan, hū ic in ðǣm becwōm, in þis neowle genip 179–80 'I cannot understand how I came into this deep darkness') he recognizes that his exile is his inevitable and interminable fate as a rebel, without in the least repenting his rebellion, and recognizes too that even his schemes of retaliation by leading men to damnation cannot succeed as he desires, since he lacks power over believers' souls (145–9, 266–9) owing to Christ's loving kindness, which obviously he does *not* recognize.

In this respect he does to be sure sound more like the Ascension Day Satan of the Pseudo-Epiphanius than like the just fallen Satan of Avitus and *Genesis B*; but obviously this despairing attitude on Satan's part is more appropriate in a poem which also contains an account of the freeing of men's souls through Christ's Harrowing of hell (*Christ and Satan* viewed as a single poem) than in one that does not (Part I of *Christ and Satan* viewed as a separate work not connected with Parts II or III). At any rate the point to be kept in mind here is that, as is soundly and carefully argued by Finnegan 1969 with some differences of approach and emphasis,[19] the poet has every right to represent Satan's character and state of mind in the manner best suited to his context and his theme. The character ought to be judged in terms of the context and the author's intention, not compared in vacuo with a character from another work.

Turning from the lamentations of Part I to the angelology which Part I shares with Part II, we find that Gregory the Great's 34th Homily on the

Gospels[20] is a significant though indirect source for this, especially for the identification of Lucifer as a member of a particular order of angels, or perhaps as himself constituting an order of angels.

The first and most conspicuous segment of Part II of *Christ and Satan*, after a short introductory or transitional passage (366–79a), is an account of the Harrowing of hell, given in ll. 379b–512. The ultimate source of this, as of many other accounts of the Harrowing of hell in English and other languages, is the *Descent into Hell* which represents itself as being the narrative of two sons of the high priest Simeon, by name Karinus and Leucius, and which was appended, probably in the fifth century, as a second part to the apocryphal book variously known as the *Gospel of Nicodemus* (= *Evangelium Nicodemi*) or the *Acts of Pilate*,[21] though the central idea of Christ's descending into hell and freeing the souls of the righteous from bondage is at least as old as the second century. The connection between the *Christ and Satan* Harrowing of hell and the *Descent into Hell* in the *Gospel of Nicodemus* has been recognized since Hickes 1705,[22] but it is in fact quite indirect and tenuous, since *Christ and Satan* omits many of the motifs which make up the narrative of the *Descent into Hell* and on the other hand, even in its much abbreviated form, contains much that is not found in the older text. Eve's plea in ll. 409–24, 436–41 is a striking example of such an addition.

A much more closely related source or analogue was suggested by ten Brink 1877,[23] namely the Easter sermon which is the seventh of the *Blickling Homilies*, a tenth-century English collection.[24] Unlike the *Descent into Hell* in the *Gospel of Nicodemus*, *Blickling Homily* 7 does not treat the Harrowing of hell as a self-contained whole, but instead agrees with *Christ and Satan* Part II in making it the first of a sequence of narrated events of Christ's post-Crucifixion life in chronological order ending with the Last Judgment. Correspondences of word and detail are mostly not close, so that scholars in general have expressed the relationship cautiously.

There is a closer but not exact correspondence between the two works in the selection of the events narrated between the Harrowing of hell and the Last Judgment, as follows: Christ rises from his sepulchre; he appears to his disciples; he shows his wounds to overcome doubt of his Resurrection (in *Christ and Satan* only, he stays on earth forty days); he ascends into heaven (in *Christ and Satan* only, he sends the Holy Spirit to strengthen his disciples at Pentecost); he takes his seat at the right hand of God the Father. All this is very succinct in *Blickling Homily* 7, taking up just over fourteen lines by the most generous count in Morris's edition (pp

89–91) against eighty-four verse lines in *Christ and Satan* (513–96). Even so the poet lacks two references to the distinction between Christ's human and divine natures which the homilist finds it necessary to make, at the Resurrection and in regard to his enthronement at the right hand of the Father, and on the other hand the poet has the following significant items, among others, which the homilist lacks: in the appearance of Christ to his disciples, the place is Galilee and the spokesman for the disciples is Simon Peter; at the showing of the wounds Didymus (that is, Thomas) is mentioned by name; and as he sits at the right hand of the Father, Christ bestows help and healing every day on men on earth. Thus even if the homily stands only in a somewhat indirect relation to the poem, these differences give us the impression of a poet who handles his sources with considerable freedom, and who in this section may be modifying them to yield a more graphic picture of Christ in relation to individual human beings on this earth, giving effect to the same divine charity that was shown in the Harrowing of hell. Nevertheless, it can be seen that the poet in Part II is working within a tradition that views the post-Crucifixion life of Christ from the Harrowing of hell to the Last Judgment as an interconnected whole. If the concept of this sequence as a unity goes back to the Creed, as suggested by ten Brink 1877,[25] then the Blickling homilist has already expanded it with material from the New Testament by adding the appearance to the disciples and the showing of the wounds,[26] and the *Christ and Satan* poet has expanded it further in the same way by adding the forty days on earth and the gift of the Holy Spirit at Pentecost.

With no attempt at an exhaustive treatment, a few of the most obvious likenesses and differences between the *Blickling Homily* 7 and *Christ and Satan* versions of the Harrowing of hell may be noted. In both the devils make a speech of lamentation on the approach of Christ, but there is little resemblance between the two except that both express Christ's power and the devils' fear; in particular, the devils' speech in the homily sounds in large part like their side of an altercation with Satan, whereas the devils in the poem show a different attitude, always saying 'we' and never 'thou.' (To be sure, there is a lacuna in the *Christ and Satan* text shortly before this speech and we cannot absolutely exclude the possibility that it contained something more like what the homily has.)

The homily alone, but not the poem, then has two speeches of the delivered souls to Christ. At this point in the homily Adam and Eve have not yet been set free; Adam utters a prayer to Christ for mercy, is released, and utters a prayer of thanksgiving, after which the process with some variation is repeated for Eve. In the poem it is Eve alone who is not yet allowed to look into the glory of heaven; she utters a prayer to Christ for mercy and is then released. In that part of Eve's speech where she entreats mercy in the name of her descendant Mary, the two texts have the greatest similarity, amounting at one point to virtual identity of wording. Eve says in the homily 'þū wāst þæt þū of mīnre dehter, Drihten, onwōce,'[27] and in the poem 'Hwæt, þū fram mīre dohtor, Drihten, onwōce' (438). (The fact that this utterance can be scanned as a line of verse in the homily as well as in the poem does not necessarily prove the poem prior to the homily.)

After Eve's release, in the homily, Abraham leads the delivered souls in a short doxology which closes the account of the Harrowing. In the poem the delivered souls, called the family of Abraham, lift Christ up with their hands as all proceed together to their heavenly dwelling, and the account of the Harrowing closes with a speech of some forty-two lines (470–512) by Christ to the delivered souls, linking the Fall of man to his own work of Redemption.

In the entire account of the Harrowing, insofar as the homily may be taken to represent the poet's source, he has handled his source with great freedom. This time, apart from the closing speech by Christ, the poem generally diverges from the homily in the direction of compression, with fewer than ninety lines of verse (379b–468), ignoring the apparent lacuna after line 383, against just over a hundred lines of prose in the homily.[28] In the poet's scheme of things, if the view of the overall structure of *Christ and Satan* which has been expressed here is correct, Christ's Descent into hell is the farthest reach of his self-abasement through redeeming love of mankind, and is given no more than its due prominence as the necessary condition of his supreme exaltation, which is expressed in his Resurrection, his Ascension, his enthronement at the Father's right hand, and his coming to judge mankind at the Last Judgment.

It is precisely in their accounts of the Last Judgment that the poem and the homily diverge farthest from each other. After a passage of transition and general description of the Judgment,[29] the homily recounts the six traditional signs before Judgment, one every day for six days,[30] and the Judgment itself, which comes on the seventh day;[31] and the homily then closes with an exhortation to humility and mercy and charity whereby we may earn eternal blessedness, finding our Judge merciful.[32] The poem (597–662) has almost nothing of this. Specifically, it has nothing about the six signs before Judgment; its account of the Judgment itself hardly resembles that in the homily at all, except for commonplaces like the archangelic trumpets and the mention of the Judge's right hand or right side; and its exhortation is couched in entirely different terms from that in the homily.

Because of this great divergence, Grau 1908[33] maintained that the *Christ and Satan* poet's source was not *Blickling Homily* 7 as we now have it, but an earlier version of it with a different concluding section on the Last Judgment, that concluding section being represented by the corresponding part of a prose homily that begins on page 382 of MS Hatton 116 in the Bodleian Library at Oxford.[34] Grau's parallel-column comparison[35] of *Christ and Satan* 597–662 and Hatton 116 shows that both homily and poem have the Judge's speech of welcome to the blessed (616–18) and his speech of condemnation to the damned (626–7), the departure of the damned into the torments of hell (629–41), a passage of exhortation (642–6), and a description of the joys of heaven, with mention of the martyrs and with a short song either of the martyrs or of all the blessed (647–62), not all these parts being in the same order in both texts.

At no point, however, is there close correspondence of detail. Even the speeches of the Judge to the blessed and the damned are about as different in the two texts as they could be while still conveying the same pair of messages, quite apart from the fact that the homily gives them in Latin, staying close to the text of Scripture and translating only the first in full, and the poet in English. After the two judgments are pronounced, the damned in the homily tamely 'go with great lamentation to the torments of hell' (swīþe hēofigende [sic Hofmann; Grau reads beofigende 'trembling'] hellewītu sēcaþ), whereas in the poem it is the demons who 'summon' the damned to hell (leaðað 630) and 'shove' them into the abyss (scūfað 631), there to torment them through eternity by 'accusing' them of their sins (stæleð 638). The passage of exhortation and the description of the joys of heaven are also by no means similarly phrased in the two works.

Roughly speaking, the poet seems to diverge about as much from Hatton 116 in his account of the Last Judgment as he does from *Blickling Homily* 7 in his account of Christ's post-Crucifixion life from the Harrowing of hell through the Ascension. This is consistent with Grau's hypothesis that the poet's source was a now lost earlier homily, *Blickling Homily* 7 with a Hatton 116 conclusion, since we could then say that he was following it with the same rather high degree of freedom from beginning to end. But on the other hand, this hypothesis of Grau's is not a necessary one. The poet may here have been drawing from two different homiletic traditions (one represented by *Blickling Homily* 7 and one by Hatton 116), quite possibly by auditory memory rather than consultation of a written source or sources, and combining and modifying them to suit himself.

*Blickling Homily* 7, in turn, or rather as much of it as recounts the post-Crucifixion life of Christ from the Harrowing of hell through the

Ascension and the enthronement at the right hand of the Father, has as one of its sources a Latin sermon for Easter which formerly was falsely attributed to Augustine and which is numbered 160 in *PL* 39.2059–61. This is not surmise but certainty, and was first observed by Förster 1906.[36] The dependence is great, amounting through considerable stretches to literal translation, at least from the twenty-fifth line of *Blickling Homily* 7 in Morris's edition (p 83)[37] through Morris 87/24–5.[38]

At this point, however, *Blickling Homily* 7 has a passage [39] which does not occur in Pseudo-Augustine 160 as printed in *PL*, and which may be summarized as follows:[40] Adam and Eve have not yet been set free; Adam prays to Christ for mercy and is released, after which he says a prayer of thanksgiving; Eve, still in bonds and weeping, prays to Christ for mercy, invoking her descendant the Virgin Mary, and is released, after which she says a prayer of thanksgiving; and the patriarch Abraham, with the other delivered souls, utters a doxology, bringing the account of the Harrowing to a close. Förster 1906[41] has found the source of this also, in the *Book of Cerne* (Cambridge University Library MS Ll.1.10), specifically in that part of it which was the Latin prayer book of a ninth-century Bishop Aethelwold, probably the one who was Bishop of Lichfield 818–830.[42] On leaves 98*b* to 99*b* of the manuscript,[43] in fact, prayers of Adam and Eve at the Harrowing which are obviously the source of those in *Blickling Homily* 7 are appended consecutively to a passage in large part identical with that portion of Pseudo-Augustine 160 from which the immediately preceding part of *Blickling Homily* 7 is taken. It will be well to state the correspondence in some detail.

On *f* 98*b*,[44] the *Book of Cerne* after an introductory rubric has a passage beginning *Aduenisti redemptor mundi*[45] and ending *pone signum uictoriae in inferno*,[46] which corresponds exactly to Pseudo-Augustine 160, par. 4 ll. 7–25,[47] with omission of a part bracketed by Migne as occurring in few manuscripts; and *Blickling Homily* 7 follows this text closely, also with omission of what Migne brackets, from Þū cōme tō ūs, middangeardes Alȳsend[48] to sete nū þīn wuldres tācn in helle.[49] The *Book of Cerne* then has about ten lines of text (*f* 98*b*, l. 12 to *f* 99*a*, l. 4) not represented in Pseudo-Augustine 160 nor in *Blickling Homily* 7; but its rubric in lines 4–5 agrees except for slight modification and rearrangement of words with Pseudo-Augustine 160, par. 5, ll. 2–3 (*postquam audita est postulatio atque altercatio innumerabilium captivorum*). In the next few lines of text,[50] the *Book of Cerne* omits the statement in Pseudo-Augustine 160 that the delivered souls now turn their torments against their torturers, but otherwise stays rather close to Pseudo-Augustine 160 through the words *humili supplicatione cum ineffabili gaudio clamantes*.[51] From the beginning of Pseudo-Augustine 160 par. 5 to this point, *Blickling Homily* 7 on the whole follows Pseudo-Augustine 160 more closely than it does the *Book of Cerne*. There follows a short prayer of the delivered souls to Christ, in which the *Book of Cerne*[52] diverges in words and substance from Pseudo-Augustine 160.[53] In this prayer *Blickling Homily* 7 sticks rather close to the text of Pseudo-Augustine 160, where the prayer ends[54] with the words *Jucundentur in ascensu tuo fideles tui, aspicientes cicatrices corporis tui*.

It is immediately after this prayer that the *Book of Cerne* departs completely from Pseudo-Augustine 160, with a rubric *Adam autem et eua adhuc non sunt desoluti de uinculis*.[55] In agreement, *Blickling Homily* 7 introduces its next segment of text with the words Adam þāgӯt & Eua nǣron onlӯsde, ah on bendum hīe wǣron hæfde.[56] In the prayers and release of Adam which follow, the *Book of Cerne*, from *Tunc Adam lugubri ac miserabili uoce clamabat ad dominum dicens*[57] to *qui satiat in bonis desiderium meum*,[58] is closely followed by *Blickling Homily* 7, from Adam þā wēpendre stefne & earmlicre cēgde tō Drihtne, & cwæþ[59] to mīne geornnesse mid gōde þū gefyldest.[60] To the *Book of Cerne*'s rubric *Adhuc eua persistit in fletu dicens*[61] then answer *Blickling Homily* 7's words Eua þāgӯt on bendum & owōpe þurhwunode; hēo cwæþ.[62] The remaining lines of *f* 99*b* of the *Book of Cerne*[63] are taken up by the first few sentences of Eve's (first) prayer to Christ, beginning *IUstus es domine et rectum iudicium tuum* and ending *et ne declines in ira ab ancilla (tua)*. Here too *Blickling Homily* 7 follows the *Book of Cerne* closely, from Sōþfæst eart þū, Drihten, & rihte syndon þīne dōmas[64] to nē þū ne gecyr on erre from þīnre þēowene.[65] Immediately after *f* 99*b* of the *Book of Cerne* a quire has been lost. It is a justifiable supposition that the beginning of the missing quire contained the rest of Eve's prayer for mercy, her release, and her prayer of thanksgiving, in a form not very remote from that found in *Blickling Homily* 7.[66] With hardly less confidence it may also be supposed that this was followed in the *Book of Cerne* by the doxology of Abraham and the other souls which follows the Eve section in *Blickling Homily* 7.[67] However, since this part of the *Book of Cerne* is missing, we cannot be certain of the precise degree of indebtedness of *Blickling Homily* 7 to the *Book of Cerne* in that part of Eve's prayer for mercy where she invokes the Virgin Mary,[68] which is the place where *Christ and Satan*[69] is closest in wording to *Blickling Homily* 7.[70]

After the Abraham doxology the close dependence of *Blickling Homily* 7 on Pseudo-Augustine 160 resumes. The Latin homilist's account of

Christ's post-Harrowing life begins with the words *Facta præda in inferno*, *vivus exiit de sepulcro*,[71] for which *Blickling Homily* 7 has Mid þon þe Drihten þā þā herehȳhþ þe hē on helle genumen hæfde, raþe hē lifgende ūt ēode of his byrgenne.[72] The correspondence continues to be close through the words *quia Christus Dominus et de sua divinitate nihil minuit, et hominem quem fecerat liberavit*[73] and forþon þe hē his godcundnesse nān wiht ne gewanode, þā hē þone menniscan līchoman onfēng, & ūs of dēofles anwalde alēsde.[74] From this point on the two homilies go their separate ways: Pseudo-Augustine 160 has nothing more except a single concluding sentence, whereas *Blickling Homily* 7 after a transitional passage launches into its long account of the Last Judgment and especially of the signs before the Judgment, as we have seen earlier.

From this chain of detailed correspondences, the relevant general conclusion to be drawn for our purposes is that the poet of *Christ and Satan* Part II was working within a homiletic tradition that viewed the post-Crucifixion life of Christ as an interconnected unity: in a Latin representative, the sequence extended as far as the Ascension and the enthronement at the right hand of the Father, and in an Old English representative, as far as the Last Judgment. To supplement what was said earlier (p 55 above), it was not the author of *Blickling Homily* 7 who first introduced into that sequence two items found in the New Testament but not in the Creed, namely the appearance to the disciples and the showing of the wounds; Pseudo-Augustine 160[75] gave him the precedent for including these.

In our tracing of the sources of *Christ and Satan* Part II, it remains to be pointed out that paragraphs 3 and 4 of Pseudo-Augustine 160[76] are very close in wording to what in effect is the ultimate source for this whole tradition, that is, the *Descent into Hell* appended as a second part to the *Gospel of Nicodemus*,[77] in particular to sections of Chapters 6 to 8 of that text in the version known as Latin A.[78] The comparable sections comprise, in the *Descent into Hell*, a speech expressive of fear made by 'Hell and death and their wicked ministers'[79] to Christ, a rebuking speech of Hell to Satan, and a prayer of the captive souls to Christ; in Pseudo-Augustine 160 the first two of these are merged into a single speech of the infernal demons to Satan, expressing both fear and rebuke. After the passage of this material through so many hands, however, practically no specific detail of it has survived into *Christ and Satan*.

Especially for Parts I and II of *Christ and Satan*, a number of poems of the supposed Cynewulfian school including some with Cynewulf's signature and some without, have been proposed by Clubb 1925 as vital influences on tone and phrasing, though not as sources in the narrow sense. The verbal parallels on which Clubb partly bases this proposition begin to become frequent after l. 194, a little past the middle of Part I, and continue so through Part II, Part III being too short and containing too little hortatory material to yield more than trivial parallels.[80] For the section of Part I extending from l. 194 to the end, Clubb lists[31] six parallels with poems that have Cynewulf's signature and thirteen with Cynewulfian poems lacking the signature, distributed as follows: three with *The Ascension (Crist II)*, one with *Juliana*, two with *Elene*; and two with *The Advent (Crist I)*, three with *The Last Judgment (Crist III)*, six with *The Phoenix*, one with *The Dream of the Rood*, and one with *Andreas*. For Part II, Clubb lists[82] at least six parallels with *Crist II*, which has Cynewulf's signature, and the following twenty-six parallels with Cynewulfian poems that have not: two with *Crist I*, at least seven with *Crist III*, two within the twenty-nine lines in the Exeter Book variously assigned to the end of *Crist III* or the beginning of *Guthlac A*, five with *Guthlac A*, one with *Guthlac B*, four with *The Phoenix*, at least two with *The Dream of the Rood*, and at least three with *Andreas*.

To be sure, recent scholars in the field of Old English have tended to be quite sceptical of the suggestion that verbal parallels between Old English poems may indicate influence, especially since Magoun 1953 and others following him have given rather copious demonstrations of the oral-formulaic character of Old English poetry. Nevertheless, there are reasons why Clubb's view and his data should not be dismissed out of hand. First, he seems to have intentionally abstained from listing inconsequential passe-partout formulas like wordum sægde or and (infinitive) hēt. Of course the decision where to draw the line is a difficult one, but at any rate his most striking examples comprise such correspondences as that between

> Ðā mē gehrēaw    þæt mīn handgeweorc
> carcernes    clom ðrōwade
> *(Christ and Satan* 488–9)

and

> Ðā mec ongon hrēowan    þæt mīn hondgeweorc
> on fēonda geweald    fēran sceolde
> *(Crist III* 1414–15)

or that between

> Ūs is wuldres lēoht
> torht ontȳned,  þām ðe teala þenceð
> (*Christ and Satan* 555–6)

and

> Ēow is wuldres lēoht
> torht ontȳned,   gif gē teala hycgað
> (*Andreas* 1611–12)

or between

> behōfað  ...
> ...  þæt him wlite scīne
> þonne hē ōðer līf   eft gesēceð
> (*Christ and Satan* 209–11)

and

> Is ūs þearf micel
> þæt wē gæstes wlite   ...
> ...   georne biþencen
> (*Crist II* 847–9).

The last example, incidentally, shows how the same idea can be conveyed without the use of any common formula.

Second, as Clubb points out,[83] verbal correspondences of *Christ and Satan* with the other poems in MS Junius 11 ('so-called Caedmonian poems') are so few and slight as to be negligible. This cannot be more than partially explained by differences of subject matter, and may well suggest to us that within the overall oral-formulaic tradition there must have been narrower streams of tradition – poetic schools, if you will – and that the *Christ and Satan* poet may have belonged to the same one of these as the authors of poems somewhat vaguely called Cynewulfian.

Third, this idea receives support from Clubb's sensitive observation[84] that 'the similarities in diction ... do not adequately measure the general resemblance ... with the Cynewulfian poems. Wherever, in the latter, there occur extended exhortations, or passages describing the bliss of heaven or the torments of hell (often in connection with the Judgment Day), one is sure to recognize an affinity in conception and tone between those passages and those in *Christ and Satan* which treat the same themes.'

A notable example of this larger-scale affinity[85] is the resemblance between Christ's speech to the delivered souls in *Christ and Satan* 470–512 and Christ's speech to the sinner on Judgment Day in *The Last Judgment* (*Crist III*) 1379–1468 plus an echo in 1492b–1493 of 1414–15.[86] The differing contexts, Harrowing vs Last Judgment, occasion some obvious differences between the two passages. Thus in *The Last Judgment* 1408b–1411 Christ gives a short account of the great hardships suffered by Adam and Eve from the Fall until their death, relevant to the poet here because Adam and Eve represent all mankind and because their earthly sufferings prefigure the eternal damnation pronounced on unrepentant sinners at the Last Judgment, but not relevant in *Christ and Satan* where Christ is in the act of delivering Adam and Eve from hell. Also the poet of *The Last Judgment* lets Christ speak of his Incarnation with Nativity imagery (1421b–1427), showing his helplessness as an infant in swaddling clothes lying in a manger as part of the hardship he endured for thankless humankind, whereas the *Christ and Satan* poet lets his Christ, who does not have the same motivation for reproach, tell of his Incarnation as sparely as possible (494–495a) and without any details of the Nativity, purely as the first active expression of his compassion for mankind, the first stage of the voluntary self-abasement which has now culminated in the Harrowing. For like reasons, Christ's sufferings on earth up to and including the Crucifixion are narrated much more circumstantially by the Christ of *The Last Judgment* (1428–53) than by the Christ of *Christ and Satan* (494–9, 508b–512); the Christ of *The Last Judgment* tells, but the Christ of *Christ and Satan* does not, how he was buffeted, spat on by evildoers, made to drink vinegar and gall, scourged, reviled, and made to wear a crown of thorns. Again, the Harrowing is not the place for such sharply pointed reminders.

But apart from these differences required by the difference of theme of the two poems, the two passages correspond closely in narrative sequence and thought sequence: Christ created Adam and Eve and placed them in paradise in the Garden of Eden; they heeded the devil, forfeited paradise thereby, and went to hell; grieved at the infernal sufferings of his creatures, Christ came to earth and was born of an earthly mother for the benefit of mankind; he suffered much on earth in order to save mankind; while still a young man he endured plots and persecutions that culminated in his being crucified, having his side pierced with a spear, and dying on the cross; all this he did so that he might deliver human beings from the power of the devil and bring them to heavenly bliss. Besides, there are occasional close resemblances of wording, as at *Christ and Satan* 471 and 488–9 (*The Last Judgment* 1379–1380a and 1414–15), with little or no formulaic identity of half-lines. At the very least the poets were evidently drawing on the same tradition, homiletic or poetic or both.

It seems, then, a likely conclusion that the *Christ and Satan* poet was working within the sphere of influence of a poetic school that we can fairly associate with the person and example of Cynewulf, and that this is particularly evident in Parts I and II.[87]

For his account of the Temptation of Christ in Part III the poet would seem, in the words of Clubb 1925, 'to have depended upon his well-stocked, but not especially accurate, memory of Gospel story';[88] and the concluding part of the poem, after the Temptation itself, is evidently his invention.

The Temptation of Christ was naturally a favourite topic for comment by the church Fathers, and by homilists and others following them. For a careful investigation of this body of commentary in its possible relevance to *Christ and Satan*, we are indebted to Finnegan, who has traced it[89] through Jerome, Augustine, John Chrysostom, Gregory the Great, *Blickling Homily* 3, and Aelfric (valuable as showing the vitality of the patristic tradition on this matter in England though presumably later than the *Christ and Satan* poet). The principal points made by these commentators are the following: Christ by his example showed us how to conduct ourselves when tempted (all commentators); this example is the more effective inasmuch as it was in his human nature that Christ was tempted (Augustine, Gregory, *Blickling Homily* 3, Aelfric); this example is the more effective for baptized Christians inasmuch as Christ was tempted after his baptism (John Chrysostom, Gregory); Christ, tempted in his human nature, gave us an example by overcoming temptation, not by divine power, but by the means available to human nature, humility and patience (Augustine, Gregory, *Blickling Homily* 3, Aelfric); and as Christ's being tempted at all shows his human nature, so the fact that angels ministered to him after the Temptation shows his divine nature (Gregory, Aelfric).

None of this is at all made explicit in *Christ and Satan* Part III, which has no passages of homiletic exhortation whatever. Recognizing this absence of homiletic exhortation, Finnegan examines chiefly the manner in which the poet here departs from or modifies the tradition embodied in Scripture and commentary.[90] The poet's modifications occur mainly in connection with the final temptation. To the account in Matthew 4: 1–11 the poet has here added the statement that Satan lays hands on Christ and lifts him up on his shoulder, and when Satan offers Christ the lordship over earth and its inhabitants it is on condition that Christ accept this lordship from Satan as a vassal would accept a fief from his lord. In Finnegan's reading the physical assault on Christ and especially the ascription of mean ambition to Christ constitute a 'monstrous hybris,'[91] in view of what the poem has already shown of the all-encompassing might of Christ, and this makes the violent response of Christ, so unlike the patience dramatized in Matthew and lauded by Gregory, 'perfectly intelligible, perhaps even psychologically and aesthetically necessary.' In the concluding paragraph of this section, Finnegan says that the Temptation (presumably as recounted in Part III of the poem) expresses Christ's dual nature as God-Man, and that Part III as a whole 'provides ... a concrete illustration of how man is to react to the devil,'[92] an example which would be recognized without any need for homiletic exhortation. That the conduct illustrated by the poet is less meek and patient than that praised by the commentators, he says, 'is at once a measure of the poet's independence in relation to sources, a guide to his sense of aesthetics, and, perhaps, an indication of his personal theological beliefs as to how man should confront temptation.'[93]

Not every part of these conclusions, however, is acceptable. Certainly the account of the Temptation in Part III does express both Christ's human and his divine nature, as Finnegan says, for the first temptation (670–2) is intended by Satan to work through bodily hunger, and Christ's answer to the last temptation is made in his identity as Lord of all created things (695), King of mankind (696), God (703). But for this very reason the poet cannot possibly be presenting Christ here as an example of how human beings should overcome temptation. Rather we must suppose that the poet is here deliberately turning his back on the commentators' tradition of Christ as an example, choosing rather to modify his source in a way that reinforces his theme of the incommensurate might of Christ.[94] In this way he is able to end his poem by a juxtaposition of the supreme exaltation of Christ with the extreme abasement of Satan.

Moreover, what is probably the most drastic modification of his scriptural source made by the poet in Part III has somehow escaped notice hitherto.[95] It is that the Satan of the poem proposes that Christ receive at his hands, as does a vassal from his lord, dominion not only over earth and its inhabitants (folc ond foldan 685), but also over the realm of heaven (rodora rices 687). This would be a 'monstrous hybris' indeed, except that the word 'hybris,' having its original reference to Greek tragedy, scarcely seems the right one to apply to a proposition of such combined audacity and absurdity. In this passage rodora rīces alliterates with riht, as Satan calls on Christ to show himself the rightful (riht) King of angels and men by receiving dominion over the realm of heaven from Satan. At the only other place where rodera rīces occurs (347) it also alliterates with riht; there the poet tells us that the rebel angels by their revolt in heaven wanted to deprive Christ of the realm of heaven, but he held it by right (on riht). The echo forces upon us the question: Who should know this better than Satan? Yet here in Part III Satan is trying to induce Christ to damn himself by receiving from Satan what Christ has always had, what Satan has never had, and what Satan is already damned for trying to snatch away wrongfully from Christ. This is apart from the additional absurdity of imagining that Christ could show himself the rightful King of angels and men by accepting their rule in such a subordinate manner from Satan, even supposing Satan had it to give. One wonders how Satan could be so blind, could so combine knowing and not knowing. Was he thrown into confusion by Christ's combined human and divine nature? If Christ was to such a degree man on the cross as to cry 'My God, why hast thou forsaken me?,' perhaps he was to such a degree man in the Temptation that a possibility existed of his yielding to it. Or is the true explanation a different one? The poet does not tell us unless by implication. Perhaps the most satisfying explanation is this: Just as in the revolt in heaven Satan's pride and pride-generated ambition blinded him to the impossibility of exalting himself in Christ's stead by being unlike Christ, so in the Temptation his pride and pride-generated malice blind him to the manifold impossibility of inducing Christ to damn himself by a like wrongful self-exaltation.

However that may be, the introduction of the realm of heaven into the last temptation is a vital factor in motivating the poem's powerful ending; for the punishment imposed by Christ on Satan, to plunge to the very bottom of hell and measure its full depth, is in every way appropriate to Satan's offence. It is directed alike at his self-exaltation, his malice, and his unknowing.

Perhaps our discussion of the sources of *Christ and Satan* would not be complete without some mention of a hymn of 68 short lines (64 in *PL*) attributed to St Ambrose which may be found in *PL* 17. 1205–6 and which is also the thirteenth of the hymns in the *Vespasian Psalter*. In its brief compass this hymn alludes in turn to the following topics that are all treated in *Christ and Satan*, sometimes quite briefly, sometimes of course at greater length: Christ as Creator; the Fall of man; the Incarnation of Christ; the resurrection of the dead; baptism; the Crucifixion of Christ; the immunity of believers to harm inflicted by the devil; the Harrowing of hell;

Christ as Physician; and Christ as Judge at the Last Judgment. All of the correspondences except the first and seventh, admittedly, are with Part II of *Christ and Satan*; and no mention is made of the revolt and Fall of the angels nor of the Temptation of Christ. On the whole, it seems impossible to state definitely just what relation the hymn has to our poem, but the combination of so many shared topics when one of the texts is so short, and especially the combination of Christ as Creator with the Harrowing of hell and the Last Judgment, suggest something more than coincidence.

# 4

# An Hypothesis about the Genesis of the Work

Our study of sources, influences, and traditions leads to a view of the origin of the poem which resembles that of Clubb 1925[1] in general outlines. The main point of agreement is on the proposition that the poem as a whole evolved out of Part II. This follows almost as a necessary consequence from the fact that Part II is within a homiletic tradition associated with Easter Sunday and narrating Christ's post-Crucifixion life from the Harrowing of hell to the enthronement at the right hand of the Father or to the Last Judgment, whereas neither Part I nor Part III gets the elements of its structure from any particular homiletic or literary tradition.

To say that the poem as a whole evolved out of Part II does not necessarily mean that Part II ever existed by itself except as a more or less elaborated idea in the mind of the poet. He may have composed it first or he may not, we cannot be sure. In the clause Hwearf þā tō helle 'he went then to hell,' said in l. 190 of Satan and in l. 399 of Christ, the adverb þā fits perfectly in its simple and most usual temporal sense of 'then' in l. 399, but sounds slightly forced in l. 190, since Satan is already in hell. As far as it goes, this may be a slight indication that Part II was composed first, but it is not strong evidence. Either way, in composing it he seems to have departed from tradition in two notable ways, so far as we can judge from a comparison with *Blickling Homily* 7. First, he sharpened the focus on the person and character of Christ in the Harrowing of hell by greatly shortening the speech of the devils at Christ's approach (retaining in it their fear of Christ's might and eliminating from it the element of rebuke to Satan which would be distracting here), by allotting speeches to none of the human characters except Eve, who in her plea for mercy represents herself as ancestress of the Virgin Mary and therefore an indirect agent of Christ's Incarnation, and by giving Christ a long speech at the end of the Harrowing in which he explains the nature and purpose of his work of Redemption. Second, he expanded the account of events from the Resurrection to the enthronement at the Father's right hand, so that in the end almost exactly the same amount of space is given to the Harrowing of hell (about 147 lines) and to the events from the Resurrection through the Last Judgment (about 150 lines). The effect of these changes is to present a Christ whose might (mihte, 400) is shown in his compassion as he abases himself to the lowest depths for sinful man, and also more overtly (miht, 604) in the exaltation which is the proper and natural consequence of this divinely charitable self-abasement, and to give equal prominence to abasement and exaltation.

Seeing Part II, composed or in his mind, as a work on the theme 'Christ humbled himself and was exalted,' whether or not he was thinking of it consciously in the words of Philippians 2: 5–11,[2] the poet with his homiletic turn of mind could hardly fail to think of its converse 'Lucifer exalted himself and was abased.' Again, he may or may not have thought of this consciously in the words of Luke 18: 14. With the contrast in mind, we may suppose, the poet set to work to present Satan in his abasement, bewailing but not repenting the pride and covetousness which led him to exalt himself and therefore be overthrown. Once again the poet seems to have had some concern for proportionate length: Part I and Part II as we have them, ignoring lacunae, are respectively 365 and 297 lines long. In composing Part I, however, the poet lacked literary models for anything more than a single lamentation of Lucifer-Satan. Accordingly he resorted, not too successfully, to what ten Brink 1877[3] called 'variation applied to larger proportions.'[4] The reviling of Satan by his followers which had been or was to be eliminated from Part II was put to a use here which accorded better with the poet's overall design of concentrating on Satan in Part I and on Christ in Part II; but at least for most modern tastes, Part I suffers from repetitiousness. It is not justifiable, however, to find fault with it for not giving us a strong or manly Satan. This Satan is not the poet's hero, intentionally or otherwise. Nor is he penitent.

Having focused in turn on each of his two archetypal characters, Satan for self-exaltation and Christ for self-abasement, the poet must next have seen how he could bring his work to a dramatic and moving close by a direct confrontation of the two. Christ's Temptation in the wilderness gave an excellent opportunity for this. The poet did not greatly concern himself with chronology, and neither should we. What he did do was to make a slight but drastic change in the last temptation, letting Satan offer Christ dominion over heaven as well as earth. This heightens the archetypal quality especially of the character of Satan, since he exalts himself in words by implying that he possesses something that has always been Christ's by right. At the same time, by displaying the emptiness of Satan's implied claims and the weakness of his character, it throws into strong relief the incommensurate might of Christ and exposes Satan to the farthest extreme of abasement. In the sentence Christ imposes and Satan's acceptance of it, moreover, the focus of the poet's attention returns for one last moment to the weakness and malice that prevail throughout Satan's dominion, as the motif of the devils' reviling of Satan, excluded from its traditional place in the Harrowing of hell, is allotted climactic prominence in the final words of the poem.

5

# *Christ and Satan* in the Tradition of Old English Poetry

The pervasive importance of Christian belief and tradition in Old English poetry, penetratingly shown for *Beowulf* by scholars as early as Friedrich Klaeber in his first edition of *Beowulf*[1] and J.R.R. Tolkien in his essay 'Beowulf: The Monsters and the critics.'[2] has come within the past two decades or so to be recognized for almost the entire body of Old English poetry, including those works that have customarily been called heroic or elegiac as well as those that have always been known to be Christian. This ampler recognition has been brought about by scholars who have applied to Old English poems the principle of allegorical or typological interpretation presented by St Augustine of Hippo in his *De doctrina Christiana* and by other church fathers, whereby all writings, sacred or secular, contain within their surface meaning, like a kernel within its shell, a deeper meaning that expresses some aspect of God's universe as conceived in spiritual terms with moral implications: the eternal God, the Fall of the angels, the Creation, the Fall of man, the redemptive work of Christ including but not limited to the Incarnation, Crucifixion, Resurrection, and Ascension, the later vicissitudes of the church in the world, the Last Judgment, and eternal punishment or blessedness – the list is representative but not exhaustive. This typological interpretation, applied to Old English poetry by a good number of recent scholars, among whom B.F. Huppé and D.W. Robertson are prominent, has yielded an abundant harvest of insights sure to be of enduring value.

The diction and imagery of even the strictly Christian poetry in Old English, however, is conspicuously and in large part heroic. The embarrassed sense of lack of connection which many of us for honesty's sake must admit to feeling when we read this poetry undoubtedly comes mainly from this source: to us in our century the poems are not the successful marriages of form and content that they were to their Anglo-Saxon audience. To focus our attention on either the heroic or the Christian at the expense of the other is to perpetuate this lack of connection. What we need to do is to attempt to reconstruct in our imagination the fusion of two verbal cultures which occurred, as Alvin A. Lee says in his book *The Guest-Hall of Eden*, when 'the aristocratic, heroic diction and techniques of the Germanic tradition ... were ... put to use in a new poetry inspired by scriptural history with its morally and spiritually intelligible scheme for interpreting human life.'[3] It is to Lee, in the work just mentioned, that we are indebted for a pioneering and eloquent survey of almost the whole of Old English poetry with this very aim of enhancing our capacity to feel in the poetry the imaginative unity which was there for its makers.

The four poems of MS Junius 11, together with *Judith*, *The Advent* (*Crist I*), *The Dream of the Rood*, *The Descent into Hell* (in the Exeter Book), *The Ascension* (*Crist II*), *The Fates of the Apostles*, *The Last Judgment* (*Crist III*), *The Judgment Day I* (in the Exeter Book), and *The Judgment Day II* (in Manuscript 201, Corpus Christi College, Cambridge), constitute the most direct expression in Old English poetry of the pattern of God's universe according to its narrative statement in scripture and church tradition. In terms of comparative closeness in imagery and surface content to this central and overt expression of the Christian theme, though not in terms of date of composition, nearly all the remainder of Old English poetry is arrangeable, though only very approximately, in three concentric circles. The first of these, adjacent to the core, consists of the saints' legends *Andreas*, *Juliana*, *Elene*, *Guthlac A*, and *Guthlac B*, besides *The Phoenix*. The second, outside the first, includes such reflective poems as *The Menologium*, *The Seasons for Fasting*, *The Order of the World*, *The Wanderer*, *The Seafarer*, *Resignation*, *The Riming Poem*, *The Ruin*, and *The Grave*. The third and outermost includes most notably *Beowulf*, which of all Old English poems offers us by far the most narrative and imagery reflecting the heroic age.

In this fourfold corpus of poetry, the force of the heroic tradition in diction and imagery is greater, for the most part, as we move outward from the centre. The *Beowulf* poet, for example, consistently avoids reference to Christ, and even the most cursory second look at Chambers' *Beowulf*[4] reminds us forcibly that knowledge of the heroic background is indispensable for understanding the poem; whereas conversely the *Christ and Satan* poet includes in his passages of exhortation many features that are homiletic rather than heroic. Yet the fact remains that in every part of this poetry the heroic and the Christian traditions are present together as an imaginative unity.

The component motifs of the scriptural and traditional narrative presented most directly in Old English by the central group of poems begin with 'The Celestial Kingdom' existing from all eternity, and go on through the Fall of the angels, the Creation, and the various stages of the fall and redemption of man, to the Last Judgment.[5] The narrative line that runs through the whole, though the poets often show that they feel free to treat their material out of chronological order because of the typological links that bind earlier and later events together in timeless eternal relevance, is the breaking of the transcendent joy and unity of the heavenly host by the rebellion of Lucifer and his followers, and the ensuing struggle between the heavenly and hellish powers for the souls of men, culminating at the Last Judgment in the final triumph of good over evil. Seen thus, the subject matter of this entire group of poems is the archetypal struggle between Christ and Satan,[6] and the single poem that expresses it most directly and inclusively is *Christ and Satan* itself.[7] Accordingly it is the Junius manuscript that occupies a central position in this central group, and within the poems of the Junius manuscript *Christ and Satan*, though not of the highest poetic quality, is thematically central, touching on principal events of the archetypal struggle, from Christ as Creator of the universe and of angels, on through the rebellion of Lucifer and his followers *against Christ*, to the victory of Christ over Satan when tempted in the wilderness, the Harrowing of hell, and Christ judging mankind at the Last Judgment.

One of the chief determining shapes of the imaginative unity of the heroic and Christian traditions in Old English poetry is the set of images and ideas associated with the *comitatus*, the basic unit of Germanic society both on the Continent and in early Anglo-Saxon England. The word *comitatus* is Latin and was first applied to the Germanic peoples by Tacitus in his *Germania* about 100 AD. It designates the group consisting of a lord (often dryhten or ealdor in OE) and his thanes (OE þegnas or dryhtguman, singular þegn or dryhtguma). This group was held together and rendered formidable in combat by a sacred bond of loyalty between lord and thane. This bond was reinforced by mutual material benefits (the lord's generosity, the thane's duty to defend his lord unto death) but at the same time yielded such rich emotional rewards that lordlessness and separation from one's fellow thanes were the most dreaded part of the condition of exile. In the Old English poetry the concept of the *comitatus* is changed and extended under the influence of the Christian tradition, as the imagery associated with it comes to be applied to 'particular Christian communities, the whole Church on earth, the community of the blessed in heaven, or all of these in mystical harmony,'[8] and to have other specifically Christian applications as well. This expansion renders inappropriate the strictly heroic word *comitatus*, so that Lee adopts in its stead the Old English word *dryht*, which is used in both heroic and Christian contexts, and it will be well to follow his example.

'The Celestial Kingdom,' the first of the component motifs of the scriptural and traditional Christian narrative central to the poems of MS Junius 11, is what Lee calls the dryht of heaven. Its foe from the beginning to the end of time is the dryht of hell, called into existence by the rebellion of Lucifer and his followers, who at their expulsion from heaven are transformed into Satan and his devils. On earth there is 'the paradisal or golden gift-hall ... symbolized in Eden,' and by contrast 'the ruined dryhtsele (dryht-hall or dwelling) found when death and destruction hold sway in middle-earth.'[9] In poems showing conflict between human societies, moreover, one society, such as the Israelites in *Exodus* and in *Daniel*, is the earthly equivalent of the dryht of heaven, and the other, such as the Egyptians or the Babylonians, the earthly equivalent of the dryht of hell.

*Christ and Satan* fits into this framework, strongly attesting and reinforcing it in many ways, but at the same time showing some distinctive features in its treatment of the heroic-Christian imagery. The dryht of heaven, sublimely imaged in *Genesis* 1–14, is indistinctly shadowed forth in *Christ and Satan* 19 after the account of the Creation and before that of the Fall of the angels, and thereafter pictured more fully either through the eyes of Satan and his followers as the condition of blessedness they have lost, or by the poet in passages of exhortation as the condition of blessedness in store for good men, or by Christ as the condition of blessedness to which he is leading the souls delivered from hell.[10]

The dryht of hell, as debased a parody of heroic as of Christian qualities, is omnipresent in foreground or background from its first mention in line 20 through all the rest of Part I (20–365); it is still conspicuous in fright and defeat at the beginning of the account of the Harrowing of hell (366–405) and as subjected to greater punishment after the deliverance of the souls (443–55) and later as meting out punishment to the damned souls after the Last Judgment (628–41); its final appearance in the poem is in Part III, the Temptation of Christ, when as 'hell-dwellers' (694) and 'captives' (715) the 'multitude of devils' witness Satan's humiliation and pronounce their curse on him (725–8). The 'paradisal ... gift-hall ... symbolized in Eden'[11] is referred to indirectly by Eve at the Harrowing of hell (*Christ and Satan* 412–20) and represented with fuller imagery by Christ (470–84). No ruined dryht-hall amid death and destruction on earth[12] is pictured in *Christ and Satan*, since the immediately mentioned consequence of Adam and Eve's eating the forbidden fruit is their punishment in hell (417–20, 484–6), rather than the intervening years of their exile on earth.

Depiction of a wicked dryht on earth at first seems to be entirely lacking, but is nevertheless present in light but telling touches. Human souls that are damned or subject to damnation are mostly shown as individuals rather than members of a social unit; they are 'naked men' in l. 135, 'those souls that [Christ] is not willing to have as his own' in ll. 145–7, 'men' (designated, to be sure, by the warriorly word mecg which occurs in *Beowulf* in heroic contexts as the second element of compounds) who wail and gnash their teeth in l. 334, the 'unclean' or 'evil' ones in ll. 608–9, the 'evildoers' or 'accursed ones' consigned to eternal punishment at the Last Judgment in ll. 619, 626, 619–41. On the other hand they are a 'heathen troop' in l. 268, where the noun used is scealu, reminiscent of Beowulf's handscalu, 1317; and the nearby context suggests that as 'warriorly men' (hæleða 270) they may have been damned for their part in the 'strife,' ie, breach of the ties of kinship (unsibbe 271), stirred up by the devils among the 'nations of men throughout middle-earth' (272), where the nations (mægðum) are considered as groups of kinsfolk, like the mægþum subjugated by Scyld in *Beowulf* 5. Even allowing for the paleness of heroic reference in hæleð, evident in its other five occurrences in *Christ and Satan*,[13] this is after all quite a bit of heroic resonance to pack into five lines. The persecutors of Christ on earth too are sketched sharply, however briefly, in terms appropriate to a wicked earthly dryht: they are 'warriorly men' (secgas 497, beornas 509). Both these words are often laudatory heroic epithets in *Beowulf* and elsewhere but are capable of being applied to men of a wicked dryht like that of Sodom in *Genesis* 2560 or the builders of the tower of Babel in *Genesis* 1680. Again, they are 'rulers of a kingdom' plotting and accomplishing Christ's bodily death (rīces boran 499); compare Beowulf's request that Hrothgar should be the 'guardian,' mundbora, of his thanes if he should die, 1480, but also the dragon as mundbora of the treasure, 2779.[14]

In the poet's hortatory passages his audience's identity as an earthly dryht of good men, that is, as the body of the church on earth, is often left to be inferred in the most indirect way possible, from his first person plural subjunctives: 'let us take...' (198), 'let us remember..., choose..., bear..., remember...' (202–6), 'let us remember..., prepare...' (286–7), 'let us proclaim..., extol..., unlock..., understand...' (298–301), 'let us rightly purpose...' (593), 'let us ... resolve...' (642). Sometimes they are only appealed to as individual believers: 'each of men' in l. 194, and similarly in ll. 209–11, 283–5, 304–6, 363–5. Yet even in these two forms of reference heroic diction and imagery have a certain prominence, seemingly being used rather perfunctorily at times, at other times with real impact, and often characteristically intertwined with imagery from the Christian tradition, which on the whole predominates in these passages. Thus 'each of men' is hæleða æghwylc (194). Believers are urged to take as their joy the 'Lord of hosts' (weoroda Drihten 198), the 'Ruler of angels' (engla Waldend 199); the first of these epithets is both heroic and Christian in *both* its parts, and in the second the Christian loanword engel is joined to a native word waldend that originally meant an earthly ruler but was soon almost entirely appropriated to Christian use, being used in *Beowulf*, for example, only in reference to God. In 202–6 believers are exhorted to remember 'the holy Lord' (þone hālgan Drihten), to choose for themselves a 'dwelling place in glory') (eard in wuldre) with the 'King of all kings' (ealra cyninga Cyninge), and to bear in their breast 'kind thoughts' (blīðe geþōhtas), 'love as of kindred' (sibbe), and 'wisdom' (snytero), and to remember 'truth' (sōð) and 'right' (riht), five qualities savouring of the Christian tradition. Indeed four of them are the two pairs of complementary qualities that figure in Psalm 85: 10: 'Misericordia et veritas obviaverunt sibi: justitia et pax osculatae sunt.' (AV: 'Mercy and truth are met together; righteousness and peace have kissed each other.') Specifically, blīðe geþōhtas is equivalent to *misericordia*, sibbe to *pax*, sōð to *veritas*, and riht to *justitia*; and the fifth, wisdom (snytero), is represented in the Old English metrical translation of the same psalm verse (*The Paris Psalter* 84: 9) by glēawe cræftas. Yet at the same time sibb is a word showing an especially intimate fusion of heroic and Christian values, just as cyning, eard, drihten, even wuldor, perhaps even hālig, all native words, must have had meanings expressive of the material or non-material values of a dryht before they were appropriated, each in its own greater or lesser degree, to Christian use. In 209–11 'he that dwells here in worldly joys' (wunað weorulde wynnum) is admonished that his 'countenance should shine' (wlite scīne) when he goes to another life in heaven; the first collocation reminds us that the righteous king Hrothgar's company of thanes were on wynne when they welcomed Beowulf (2014), but the second echoes Matthew 13: 43 *tunc justi fulgebunt sicut sol*, 'then shall the righteous shine forth as the sun,' rather than any heroic motif.[15]

In 283–5 'he whose heart is strong' (se ðe his heorte dēah) is admonished in unimpeachably Christian terms to 'drive away presumptuous thoughts, hateful sins' (afirre frēcne geþōhtas, lāðe leahtras), but his characterization as strong-hearted reminds us that in one of the most often quoted celebrations of the heroic life it is said that fate often preserves an undoomed warrior when 'his courage is strong' (his ellen dēah, *Beowulf* 573). In 286–8 the believers are exhorted to remember God's 'strength' (strengðo), which he manifested also in the Creation (2), as Beowulf three times remembers or trusts in his own strengo 'strength' (once it is called the 'strength that God gave him') at a critical juncture in the accomplishment of his three heroic deeds (*Beowulf* 1270, 1533, 2540); but the 'green street' (grēne strǣte) which they are to prepare, leading up to the angels, belongs to a pervading strand of paradisal Christian imagery represented (not exclusively) by the all-green earth given to Adam and Eve at their Creation (*Genesis* 197), the all-green earth after the Flood (*Genesis* 1517), the all-green land promised to Abraham (*Genesis* 1751), and the green bottom of the Red Sea as the tribe of Judah crossed (*Exodus* 312). The imagery applied to the believers in 298–301 seems at first glance almost totally Christian, with its exhortations to 'proclaim' or 'preach' (cȳþan), to 'extol' (dēman), and to 'unlock' (onlūcan) the Ruler's 'treasure chest' (locen) so as to 'understand spiritually' (ongeotan gāstlice), that is, to use typological interpretation. However, the causative-denominative verb cȳþan has an original sense of 'make known, announce, disclose' which is not limited to a specialized reference to Christian preaching and can be used in decidedly heroic and pagan contexts, as when in *Elene* 161 Constantine before his conversion asks his sages to 'disclose' (cȳðan) to him by their 'magical incantations' (galdrum) what god it is who has sent him the vision of the cross; the denominative verb dēman, too, in its meaning 'extol,' corresponds to the radically heroic meaning 'glory, fame (especially after death)' of its root word dōm, and in this sense it is said of the twelve warriors who rode around Beowulf's memorial barrow that they 'extolled his courageous works' (ellenweorc ... dēmdon, *Beowulf* 3173–4); and even the verb onlūcan echoes the heroic formula 'unlocked his word-hoard' (wordhord onlēac), whose occurrences include *Beowulf* 259 and the first line of that unmatched repository of heroic tradition, *Widsith*. The passage 304–6 likewise contains Christian imagery with pagan and heroic connotations sometimes discernible: it admonishes the hearers to 'renounce wickedness' (mān oferhycgen), 'be pleasing to God' (Meotode cwēman, where the word Meotod is argued by Grein, *Sprachschatz der angelsächsischen Dichter*, to have had an original pagan meaning of 'fate'), and 'extinguish sin' (synne adwǣscan); the man who does so is said to be 'blessed' (ēadig), which could mean 'favoured by fortune' in a heroic context as well on the evidence of compounds in *Beowulf* such as sigeēadig or sigorēadig 'victorious,' 1311, 1557, 2352, and tīrēadig 'glorious,' 2189.

Somewhat analogously, what is promised in 363–5 to the good Christian who intends to 'obey the Saviour' (Hælende hēran) is 'glory' or 'splendour' (blæd), not exactly the same as the blæd of Scyld's son Beowulf which burst forth far and wide in *Beowulf* 18 but unmistakably resonating with it. No heroic resonance at all seems to be present in 593–5, where the exhortations to believers are to 'obey the Saviour' and to 'be pleasing to Christ'; but in 642–4, at the beginning of the last passage of exhortation, heroic and Christian strands are again inextricably mingled, in that the believers are admonished not only to 'obey the Saviour,' but also through 'the grace of God' (Godes gife) to be mindful of 'spiritual splendour' (gāstes blēd), for gifu means both 'grace' and 'gift,' and is the same word as is repeatedly used for the gifts by which a lord shows his generosity to his thanes, reinforcing materially and sacramentally the bond of loyalty that unites the dryht, for example in *Beowulf* 1173, 1958, and in gāstes blēd the originally heroic word blæd or blēd is joined with the native but by now fully Christianized word gāst 'spirit,' as waldend was joined with engla in 199.

When the church on earth is shown in its relation to Christ in heaven, dryht imagery and traditional Christian imagery are again mingled in varying proportions: 207–8, 290–1, 550–1, 579–82. When believers are said to bow before the throne and pray to the Ruler for mercy, the key words hēhseld 'throne,' Anwalda 'Ruler,' and ār 'grace, mercy' (207–8) all attest how complete the fusion can be. Though anwalda does not seem to occur in Old English poetry except in reference to God, as where it is coupled with ār in *Beowulf* 1272, it must of course originally have meant an earthly ruler. Hēhseld, used in *Christ and Satan* only of a heavenly throne whether in a divine or Luciferian context, is in origin a throne or 'high seat' or earthly rule, as in *Beowulf* 1087 the hēahsetl 'high seat' (a metathetic variant of hē(a)hseld) which together with its hall Finn grants to the Danish remnant in the uneasy truce after the battle of Finnsburg is the emblem of Hengest's lordship over the thanes of the slain Hnaef. And ār, meaning divine grace or mercy in *Beowulf* 1272 as in *Christ and Satan* 208, is used in *Beowulf* 1099 of the lordly generosity with which Finn swears to treat the Danish remnant under Hengest, and more specifically of the lordly generosity that is a bond of loyalty within a dryht in *Beowulf* 1182 and 1187, where Queen Wealhtheow urges King Hrothgar's nephew Hrothulf to treat Hrothgar's young sons 'with kindness' (ārum) after Hrothgar's death, in memory of the 'benefits' (ārna) that Hrothgar and she bestowed on Hrothulf when he was young. Lines 290–1 have little if any heroic flavouring, and ll. 550–1 scarcely more, though the lord there is to be thanked 'by deeds and works' (dædum ond weorcum). However, in 579–82 Christ as the 'Lord of hosts'

(Drihten weoroda, compare 198 and p 76 above), sitting at the right hand of the Father, 'dispenses' gifts every day (dæleð) to the 'children of men on earth' (hæleþa bearnum geond middangeard, compare 270 and p 75 above), altogether in the manner of an earthly lord showing generosity to his dryht, just as Hrothgar 'dispensed' (dælde) treasures in Heorot, *Beowulf* 80, 1686. There is even an instance in *Beowulf* 20–4 of a prince's reinforcing the loyalty of his thanes with gifts while still under the tutelage of his father. But Christ's gifts are 'help and salvation' or 'help and healing' (help ond hælo), in which the direct Christian meaning is very much to the fore.

The souls of men in heaven are part of the 'Heavenly Dryht' in the 'Celestial Kingdom,' and share in its 'Transcendent *Dream* (Joy)'[16] along with their fellow thanes the angels, and in this respect are not to be viewed as an earthly dryht. The blessed and the damned at the Last Judgment (608–41), similarly, are depicted as joining the dryht of heaven and the dryht of hell, and for that reason they also do not need here to be separately taken into account. Yet there is one further earthly dryht of good men in the poem, namely the apostles (520–45, 570–1, 573–8), though their relation to the theme of the poem is somewhat peripheral and the poet seems to introduce them mainly as witnesses to the Crucifixion, Resurrection, and Ascension, which were decisive stages in the abasement and exaltation of Christ, and as recipients of his 'gift' of the Holy Spirit at Pentecost (gife 571, compare 644 and p 78 above). They are only once called by the Christian loanword apostolas (570), which in the immediate context of Pentecost may even have conveyed some of its etymological meaning of persons sent forth to preach. Four times they are called gingran (521, 525, 530, 571). This word, being a substantivized comparative of the adjective geong, giung 'young,' has a meaning more like 'disciple.' It is hard to be sure whether it was used in pre-Christian times to designate a relationship existing within the dryht; conjecturally it might have designated an apprentice warrior serving as a tried warrior's attendant. Whether this is so or not, it is notably absent from *Beowulf*, and seems to occur only in the religious poetry, besides frequent occurrences as jungaro in the Old Saxon religious epic of the *Heliand*. Lucifer-Satan too has 'disciples' (gingran 191), the dryht of hell parodying the apostolic dryht here as it parodies the dryht of heaven elsewhere.

Heroic resonance is sparse but striking in the lines devoted to the apostles by the *Christ and Satan* poet: they have 'spiritual splendour,' either identical with or inspired by their Lord (gāstes blēd 526, compare 644 and p 78 above); their spokesman Simon Peter hails the risen Christ as 'adorned with glory' (dōme gewurðad 536), as was Beowulf, lord of thanes, man of brave deeds, coming into the hall to greet Hrothgar after slaying Grendel's mother, *Beowulf* 1645; the 'blood' (544) that Christ had shed from the wound in his side is swāt, etymologically and in prose meaning 'sweat,' but frequent in heroic poetry such as *Beowulf* in the transferred sense 'blood,' which it probably acquired as a truncated kenning, perhaps standing for heaþoswāt 'sweat of battle, ie, blood,' which also occurs three times in *Beowulf*.

All these references glorify Christ as Drihten (529) rather than the disciples as thanes, and indeed the disciples have not exactly performed with distinction as a dryht. The poet probably does not want to make them appear as too clearly having analogous virtues to those of a dryht, like the 'scanty troop' of faithful 'heroes' in *The Dream of the Rood* (mǣte weorode 69, beornas 66) who entomb and bewail their King; when the disciples in our poem are 'strengthened' (geswīðde 571) at Pentecost, it is by Christ's 'gift' of the Holy Spirit. At the same time the poet censures them only lightly, mentioning Thomas's doubt but not Peter's denial, and letting their human insufficiencies pale into insignificance beside his fervid denunciation (573–8) of the hell-black deed of Judas, who 'sold the Son of the Ruler for silver treasure' (bebohte Bearn Wealdendes on seolfres sinc 576–7).

Yet even while glorifying Christ with resounding heroic imagery in his post-Resurrection life among the disciples, the poet gives equal or greater prominence to imagery with strong resonance in the Christian tradition. Christ sends 'all-bright angels' (englas eallbeorhte 521) to summon the disciples. The 'spiritual splendour' (gāstes blēd 526) of the disciples is a fusion (p 78 above) of the heroic and Christian. Christ is not only 'Lord' (Drihten 536) and 'King' (Þēodne 533), but also the 'holy Son of God' (hāligne Godes Sunu 527), 'the Eternal' (se Ēca 531), 'Creator of angels' (Scyppend engla 534), 'the Dear one' to Thomas and the other disciples (se Dēora 542), the 'Saviour' (Hǣlend 543, compare 575 where the heroic Drihten is coupled with Hǣlend), or simply 'God' (523), and the collocation 'God in Galilee' (God in Galilēam 530, compare 523) seems to allude to the mysteriousness of the Incarnation, as 'God on the gallows' (God on galgan 549) embodies the shocking strangeness of the Crucifixion. Finally, the heroic '(battle) blood' that flowed from Christ's side (swāt 544) is transmuted in the next line into 'baths of baptism' (fulwihtes bæðe 545), just as the poet had let us know a few lines earlier through Peter that if Christ was 'adorned with glory' like a victorious hero (see pp 79–80 above) it was because the heathen had put him in hateful bondage (536–40), his abasement leading to his exaltation.

Yet all earthly dryhts, whether fully realized or less than fully realized, whether good, wicked, or humanly imperfect, are altogether subordinate to the thematic focus of the entire poem: the dryhts of heaven and hell (p 74 above), and especially their lords Christ and Satan, archetypes of self-abasing charity and self-exalting cupidity. It is in connection with these that the *Christ and Satan* poet's particular use of blended Christian and heroic imagery is now to be examined.

To begin with, there is a body of vocabulary that directly expresses lordship or thaneship. The word cyning 'king' in nine of its ten occurrences is applied only to Christ (or possibly sometimes to God the Father) and never to Satan. (In the tenth occurrence, as the genitive plural cyninga in mid ealra cyninga Cyninge 'with the King of all kings,' 204, it has presumably its usual human application.) It is sometimes associated with other words expressive of power, dominion, or prowess, such as eard 'dwelling place, homeland' (203), cester 'city, stronghold' (257, 655), rīce 'kingdom' (260), seld 'throne' (661), some of them hardly more characteristic of heroic than of traditionally Christian imagery, but sometimes with words which distinctly bring the Christian sense into the foreground, such as āna Cyning 'King alone' (260), Cynincg alwihta 'King of all creatures' (615, 669), Cyning engla ond monna 'King of angels and men' (687–8), Cyning moncynnes 'King of mankind' (697). Fusion of heroic and Christian traditions can be sensed here, but also some lessening of the impact of cyning as an heroic word. This is carried somewhat farther in the compounds Heofoncyning 'King of heaven' (three occurrences) and Wuldorcyning 'King of glory' (five occurrences), both of which are applied only to Christ (or the Father). The word anwalda 'ruler,' used only twice and only of Christ or the Father, has been discussed above (p 78) with reference to its occurrence in 208, where its association with hēhseld 'throne' and ār 'grace, mercy' makes it almost a textbook example of fusion of the heroic and the Christian. Its other occurrence, in 640, is a less striking example of the same, since there it is in variation with Frēodrihten 'noble Lord' (required for the alliteration in 639 though the manuscript has only drihten).

The word drihten itself is of course *the* word for 'lord of a dryht,' and is recorded in this sense at least from *Beowulf* to *The Battle of Brunnanburh*. Since it is also one of the most commonly used words for God (Father or

Son) in all Old English poetry, it played a principal role in keeping alive the simultaneity of heroic and Christian resonance that is so pervasive in that poetry. In our poem it is used, in some forty-five occurrences, only of Christ (or the Father). Dryhtnes līht 'the light of the Lord' 68, þone hālgan Drihten ēcne alra gescefta 'the holy Lord eternal of all creatures' 202–3 (compare 512), Drihten Hǣlend 'the Lord Saviour' (three times), ēce Drihten 'eternal Lord' (nine times), engla Drihten 'Lord of angels' 396, 519, and Drihten God 'Lord God' 451, 515 (compare 314) are examples of collocations that enhance the Christian resonance; Drihtenes þrym 'the power or splendour of the Lord' 164, adrīfan Drihten of selde 'drive the Lord from his throne' 187 (compare 256), weoroda Drihten 'Lord of hosts' 198 (compare 580 and p 76 above), Drihtnes mihtum 'by the power of the Lord' 231 (compare 604), and Drihtnes dōmas 'the judgments (or glories) of the Lord' 506, 554 are examples of collocations that have both heroic and Christian resonance in *both* key words. With Drihtenes þrym one may compare þēodcyninga þrym 'the glory of kings of the peoples' (*Beowulf* 2) alongside the more frequent uses of þrym in reference to God or heaven; and with Drihtnes dōmas, the well-known use of dōm in heroic contexts to mean 'fame after death' (for example *Beowulf* 885, and see p 77 above). The compound frēodrihten, whether it means 'noble lord' or 'dear lord,' apart from its use in *Christ and Satan* to refer to Christ (or possibly once to the Father), is in its other poetic occurrences[17] used only of an earthly master, even in *Guthlac B* 1021; it is addressed to Hrothgar by Wealhtheow in *Beowulf* 1169, and used of Beowulf in his relation to Wiglaf in *Beowulf* 2627. Therefore it would seem to be a compound with enhanced heroic resonance. As if to counterbalance this, it is joined with distinctively Christian motifs in all four of its occurrences in *Christ and Satan* (including two in which frēo- is inserted by emendation for the sake of alliteration): the help afforded to human souls by the Harrowing of hell in 434–5, the suffering of the Crucifixion in 546–7, the glory of the Ascension in 564–6, and the hope which the souls damned at the Last Judgment had forgotten to fix on their Lord in 639–41. As the first three references are to Christ, the fourth probably is too, since what is meant must be the hope of the Atonement, of which the Harrowing is an emblem.

The word fruma, etymologically related to OE forma 'first,' has three principal branches of meaning: 'beginning,' 'originator,' and 'ruler.' It occurs once in *Christ and Satan*, in the last of these meanings, referring to Christ as burhlēoda Fruma 'Ruler of the people of the (heavenly) city' (560), which resonates for example with Hrothgar as lēodfruma 'ruler of a people' in *Beowulf* 2130, Moses as lēodfruma of the Israelites in *Exodus*

354, and the Emperor Constantine as lēodfruma in *Elene* 191. At the same time it is embedded in distinctively Christian imagery, that of the Ascension.

The poetic word meotod, used twenty times in *Christ and Satan* and always of Christ (or the Father), except for Lucifer's lying claim that his son was the Meotod of mankind, must have had a different meaning in pre-Christian times, since it is a native word; but the indications are that that meaning was 'fate' or the like (see Grein's *Sprachschatz* and p 77 above), and in any case it is not found anywhere in reference to an earthly ruler. Evidently, then, only its context could determine heroic or Christian resonance, since the word Meotod itself means 'God' in Old English poetry without any underlying suggestion of the ruler of a dryht. It is quite otherwise with þēoden 'king,' which of course meant 'king' in pre-Christian times, and is used not only of Christ or the Father but also of earthly rulers in Old English poetry of all periods. In its seven occurrences in *Christ and Satan* it always refers to Christ (or the Father). Heroic resonance predominates in its first occurrence, where the rebellious Lucifer is vexed that the 'King' (Þēoden 246 – Christ or the Father?) is 'strong and unyielding' (strang ond stīðmōd 247), like the strong and resolute Christ in *The Dream of the Rood* 40, stripped for the combat of the Crucifixion by which he will conquer death and hell, or like Beowulf standing stīðmōd before the dragon but too strong to use a sword without breaking it (*Beowulf* 2566, 2684). In 597 Christ or the Father is an 'illustrious King' (Þēoden mæra), like Hrothgar, Heremod, Beowulf (*Beowulf* 129, 1715, 2788), and many another lord of an earthly dryht, but in the distinctly Christian context of the Last Judgment and with 'almighty God' (ælmihtig God 598) as a variational equivalent of 'illustrious King.' Elsewhere Christ is Lord of a heavenly dryht as 'King of angels' (Þēoden engla 387, 664). In the latter of these passages the contextual reference is to Christ's suffering death at the Crucifixion. In the former there is more heroic imagery of a kind appropriate to Christ's warfare against hell in the Harrowing: the 'King of angels' is also a 'Thane' or 'Warrior' (Þegen 387, perhaps as 'God's Thane') and comes 'with a host [of angels]' (mid þrēate) like the 'armed troop' that Beowulf brings to Denmark (īrenþrēat, *Beowulf* 330). In 660 the 'thanes' (þegnas) of Christ's heavenly dryht, who are angels (651) and souls of the blessed (651) including martyrs (653) and patriarchs (654), are praising him as 'King' (Þēoden) in a context rich with heroic imagery: 'Helmet (= Protector) of men (= warriors)' (hæleða Helm 656), with which we may compare examples like King Beowulf as Wedra helm 'helmet of the Geats' (*Beowulf* 2705), and also the rebellious Lucifer's reference to the Father or Christ as Helm þone micclan 'the great Helmet' (*Christ and Satan* 251) and Satan's lament over his exile from the Father or Christ as duguða Helm ('Helmet of hosts' 164); 'splendour' (þrym 660, compare 164 and p 82 above); and 'song at the throne' (sang æt selde 661), like the 'song and music' in Hrothgar's royal hall (sang ond swēg, *Beowulf* 1063).

The word waldend retains its original meaning of an earthly ruler in barely a handful of its very numerous occurrences in Old English poetry (compare p 76 above) and therefore its heroic resonance is less than that of such a word as drihten (compare pp 81–2 above). On the whole, this resonance is not strongly reinforced by context, either. Christ is 'Ruler of victories' (sigora Waldend 217, as is God in *Beowulf* 2875, *Genesis* 126, 1112, *Exodus* 16, *The Phoenix* 464, and elsewhere) in a passage (216–23) where heroic and Christian diction mingle to the eventual advantage of the latter: the poet's hearers are exhorted in Christian homiletic style to 'make [their] way to the place where he himself sits,' the 'Ruler of victories,' the 'Lord Saviour' (Drihten Hælend 218), in the beloved 'home' (hām 218), on a 'throne' (hēhsetl 219), surrounded by 'troops' (fēðan 220) or 'companies' (-þrēatas 221) who praise the 'Lord' (Drihten 221) by words and deeds, and whose 'countenances shine' (wlite scīneð 222) 'through eternity' (geond ealra worulda woruld 223) with the 'King of glory' (Wuldorcyning 223). In Drihten Hælend an heroic is combined with a Christian epithet (compare p 82 above); hām is a word of great emotional force in both traditions; the impact of the word hēhsetl in a Christian context owes much to its importance as an emblem of lordship over a dryht (compare p 78 above); fēðan are always troops of fighting men in the five occurrences in *Beowulf*, but in *Christ and Satan* 220 they are troops of angels and the blessed; the þrēatas are reminiscent in one way of the īrenþrēat 'iron company, armed and armored company' led by Beowulf to Denmark (*Beowulf* 330) except that these in *Christ and Satan* are hālige heofenþrēatas 'holy companies of heaven'; Drihten is a single-word fusion of the heroic and Christian traditions (compare pp 81–2 above); the shining countenances are drawn from Matthew 13: 43 (compare p 76 above); geond ealra worulda woruld is modeled on the Christian Latin phrase *in saecula saeculorum*; and Wuldorcyning is a compound in which the original heroic force of cyning has undergone some weakening (compare p 81 above).

Christ is 'Ruler of hosts' three times (weoroda Waldend 563, also 188, 252, unless the latter two refer to the Father). Like 'Lord of hosts' (weoroda Drihten 198, compare p 76 above), this epithet is both heroic and Christian in both its parts. The nature of the immediate contexts is quite varied. In 563 the Ascension is being narrated in scriptural terms, and the variational equivalent of weoroda Waldend is engla Scyppend 'Creator of angels' (562). In 252 and especially 188, where Satan is regretting the consequences of his rebellion against the 'Ruler of hosts,' the heroic imagery is more fully developed. In 252 Satan is recalling his exhortation to his followers to scorn 'the great Helmet (= Protector)' (Helm þone micclan 251, compare pp 83–4 above), the 'Ruler of hosts,' and to 'possess' (āgan 252) 'as a property' (tō æhte 253) 'this light of glory' (þis wuldres lēoht 252). The 'light of glory' seems to have none but Christian resonance, but æht and even to some extent āgan are used in a possibly unique way by the *Christ and Satan* poet to show Satan's damnable incomprehension of the nature of divine power, by diction that expresses in debased form the heroic motif of a lord's generosity with material rewards to the thanes of his dryht (see pp 16–18 above). In 188 the 'Ruler of hosts' (weoroda Waldend) is also the 'Lord' (Drihten 187, compare pp 81–2 above) whom Satan intended to drive 'from his throne' (of selde 187, compare what is said of hēhseld 'throne' on p 78 above), and the consequence is exile, an often recurring heroic motif here expressed by the favourite word wreclāstas 'steps of exile' (188).

This same word wræclāst(as) is used twice in *The Wanderer* (5, 32) and once in *The Seafarer* (57) in graphic evocations of the solitary wanderings of a banished man, not only deprived of the material joys of the mead-hall (*Wanderer* 27), the feasting (*Wanderer* 36), the music (*Seafarer* 44), the receiving of treasure (*Wanderer* 32, 34, *Seafarer* 44), but also deprived of the company of his fellow thanes (*Wanderer* 34, 53) and of his beloved generous lord (*Wanderer* 22, 25, 35, 37, 41, *Seafarer* 41). More strikingly, a close analogue to the particular way in which the word wreclāstas in *Christ and Satan* joins the motif of banishment to that of enmity to God is found in *Beowulf* 1352 in reference to Grendel, who treads the 'steps of exile' (wræclāstas) as a member of the manslaying tribe of Cain (*Beowulf* 100–14).

The use of Waldend in the genitive in expressions that identify Christ as 'Son of the Ruler' (Sunu Waldendes 395, Waldendes Sunu 119, Bearn W(e)aldendes 195, 576) can hardly be felt to produce much heroic resonance, since these expressions only paraphrase the scriptural 'Son of God.' The 'Ruler's treasure chest' (locen Waldendes 300) is in an unequivocally Christian context: the poet's hearers are exhorted to unlock it by spiritual understanding, that is, by allegorical interpretation. The rebel angels sought by war to make themselves 'rulers of glory' (wuldres waldend 24), as God is wuldres Waldend in *Beowulf* 183, *Daniel* 13, and elsewhere. Whatever relevance wuldor originally had, possibly as an attribute of majesty, to the conditions of heroic life in a dryht, it must certainly have moved a long way in the direction of 'heavenly glory' or 'heaven' when it could be coupled in the genitive with Waldend. In 125, where Satan recalls his presumptuous claim to be 'Ruler of creatures' (wihta Wealdend), that is, God, the accompanying wihta emphasizes the universality of God's rule. In the remaining four occurrences likewise the accompanying words constitute a distinct Christian framework: when Christ is called 'Maker and Ruler of all creatures' (ealra gescefta Wyrhta ond Waldend 583–4), the Creation and the universality of Christ's rule are emphasized; in 586 Christ the 'Ruler' (Waldend) is a holy Angel sitting in heaven 'with [his] prophets' (mid wītegum); in 607 Christ the 'Ruler' (Waldend) is to come to this earth at the Last Judgment 'with clouds' (mid wolcnum) like the cloud(s) of the Ascension (563 and Acts 1: 9); and whether the 'Ruler of angels' (engla Waldend) in 199 is Christ or the Father, the effect of the whole phrase is Christian rather than heroic (compare p 76 above).

Besides cyning, anwalda, drihten, fruma, meotod, þēoden, and waldend, there is one other word expressive of lordship, namely aldor 'lord,' which has an importance out of proportion to its few occurrences in our poem, because it is used both of Christ or God as Lord of Creation and also of Satan in his relation to the other rebel angels, and because in both applications it is paired off with þegn 'retainer, thane,' the one word most expressive of thaneship (see p 81 above), and therefore shows very clearly the particular way in which the *Christ and Satan* poet uses dryht imagery to represent the relation between God or Christ and his creatures and between Satan and his fellows. The reference to God the Father as 'Lord of the heavens' (heofna Ealdor 566), welcoming Christ the 'noble Lord' (Frēo-drihten 565) to his heavenly 'home' (hām 566) at the Ascension, is of only minor significance in this respect. In 650–62, however, the angels and blessed souls in heaven (651), including martyrs (653) and patriarchs (654), are vividly realized as a heavenly dryht of 'thanes' (þegnas 660), praising amid 'glory' (þrym 660, and compare p 82 above) and 'song' (sang 661, and compare p 84 above) 'at the throne' (æt selde 661) their Lord who is 'Lord of all' (ealra Aldor 662). The sweetness and harmony of the heavenly dryht is parodied by the discord and malice of the infernal. Satan is 'lord of fiends' (fēonda aldor 76), but it is these same fiends who have just been reviling him, saying how they detest him, and gloating in the midst of their own torment over the torment suffered by him (51–64). Even when he tells them what they are to do – seek out dwelling places (112–14) or stir up strife among the nations of men on earth (270–2) – there is no suggestion that they do so as a service to him.[18] In 323 again he is 'their lord' (heora aldor), advancing to rebellious combat at the head of his 'troop' (on fēþan 324, and compare p 84 above), and they are 'his thanes' (his þegnas 326), but lord and thanes alike must dwell in a horrible homeland (326–7) where they are bound fast in fire and flame (324–5), and besides it is impossible to hear of Satan as a lord and the other rebel angels as thanes without remembering the contempt and malevolence they showed him in the earlier passage. He is 'their lord' (ealdor heora) again in 373, but only as what Milton was to call the 'author of ... ill' (yfeles ordfruma 374), with the traditional emphasis on the rebels' sin of overweening pride (371–3) and its appropriate eternal punishment (375–9).

Thanes (þegnas) too are either of the heavenly dryht or parodically of the dryht of hell, as we have just seen in reference to lines 660 and 326. Even Christ is a 'Thane' (Ðegen 387), presumably God's Thane, at the Harrowing of hell: to call him a Thane and therefore a member of the dryht of heaven does not seem to our poet a lesser ascription of honour than to call him 'King of angels' (Ðēoden engla 387) alliteratively in the same line. Even Judas (or perhaps Satan, whose earthly representative he is) is in 425 a (traitorous) 'thane of the Saviour' (þegen Hǣlendes), letting us see at the same moment the heavenly dryht which he has deserted and the infernal dryht which he has entered.

These are all the occurrences of þegn as a simple word. The compound aldorðægn 'lord-thane, ie, chief among thanes' is used of Satan in 66 with scathing sarcasm. It is the very word which was used in *Beowulf* 1308 to identify Aeschere, Hrothgar's 'secret-knower and ... counsel-bearer' (rūnwita ond ... rǣdbora 1325), but as applied here to Satan immediately after the other devils' first stream of invective against him, it can only remind us that Satan no more has the qualities of a lord in hell than he had the qualities of a thane in heaven. The bond of loyalty broken in heaven is not restored in hell. In fact the tables are turned in the only other occurrence of a compound ending in þegn, when Satan as the tempter of Adam and Eve is more realistically called the 'servant of hell' (handþegen helle 484). Both these compound words achieve part of their effect through the implied contrast with the ascription of honor to Christ as God's Thane (387). Christ, humbling himself to death and hell and exalted in glory, is both Thane and Lord; Satan is neither.

A dryht has joy (drēam); there are nineteen occurrences in *Christ and Satan*, seventeen of them in Part I, twelve referring to what Satan and the devils have lost on parting from the heavenly dryht and four referring to what angels and good men have in the heavenly dryht. The place of its joy, or of its abundant and varied joys, is its hall (sele, three occurrences in *Christ and Satan*, besides a single occurrence of wīnsele 'wine hall' and two of windsele 'windy hall'), classically exemplified for Old English poetry by the dryhtsele Heorot in *Beowulf*. Satan says in 94 that there is in hell no 'wine hall of exultant ones' (wloncra wīnsele). Since neither wlonc nor wīnsele occurs elsewhere in *Christ and Satan*, this phrase needs to be circumspectly examined. To judge from the five occurrences of wlonc and three of its abstract noun wlenco in *Beowulf*, wlonc is a word with two faces. When in *Beowulf* 341 the poet calls Beowulf 'wlanc man of the Geats' (wlanc Wedera lēod) he must mean that he is vigorous and high-spirited, and therefore he may be assumed to have the same laudatory intent in calling Wulfgar a wlonc hæleð 'vigorous and high-spirited warrior' in 331; and in turn Wulfgar's intention to praise Beowulf is clear when he says that he supposes Beowulf to have come to Hrothgar's land not as an exile but 'because of vigour and high spirits' (for wlenco 338). In 2953, similarly, Ongentheow retreats to his stronghold when Hygelac approaches, because he has heard of 'the martial prowess of the vigorous and high-spirited man' (wlonces wīgcræft). Unferth's intention, however, is obviously not laudatory when he says that Beowulf and Breca undertook their swimming contest 'out of presumption' (for wlence 508) and 'because of a foolish boast' (for dolgilpe 509), nor is the poet's when he says that Hygelac in his Frisian expedition 'presumptuously asked for trouble' (for wlenco wēan āhsode 1206). Grendel's mother bearing away her human prey is to Hrothgar a 'monster exulting over carrion' (atol æse wlanc 1332), and the dragon after its death is spoken of as no longer 'exulting over its treasured possessions' (māðmæhta wlonc 2833). On balance it is altogether likely that the *Christ and Satan* poet meant wlonc here to carry an idea of foolhardiness and presumption closely akin to the 'overweening pride' (oferhygd 50, 69, 114) that is the fatal sin of Satan and his fellow rebels, and therefore meant wloncra wīnsele to stand out as incongruous with the other terms with which it is grammatically co-ordinate: 'the glory of a blessed one' (ēadiges tīr), 'joy of the world' (worulde drēam), and a 'host of angels' (ængla ðrēat). The incongruity would be one of the touches by which the poet portrays the self-deception on Satan's part which led to his rebellion.

Whether wloncra wīnsele is genuine or suspect as an heroic representation of heaven, it is certain that all other occurrences of sele alone or in combination in *Christ and Satan* refer parodically to the habitation of the dryht of hell. Two occurrences (320, 385) are in the compound windsele 'windy hall,' apparently created by word play from wīnsele and probably the poet's own coinage, since it is not attested elsewhere by the Bessinger-Smith *Concordance*[19] nor by Clark Hall's *Concise Anglo-Saxon Dictionary*, and both in 320 and 385 it was first written winsele, the *d* having to be added later by the scribe or the Corrector. It is prepared for by the expression 'this windy hall' (þes windiga sele 136). It is not certain what appropriateness the poet intended the reference to wind to have; perhaps we are to think of a hot blast of combustion sweeping endlessly through hell to torment its denizens. The remaining references are to hell as 'this vast hall' (þyssum sīdan sele 131) and 'the hall of the damned' (þone werigan sele 332).

It is not easy to see why the word sele is never used in any of the passages in *Christ and Satan* that describe the habitation of the heavenly dryht of angels and blessed souls nor even in any indirect reference to heaven unless Satan's wloncra winsele itself is one, but at any rate this conforms to the situation in Old English poetry as a whole. The Bessinger-Smith *Concordance*[20] gives twenty-five occurrences of sele alone not counting the three in *Christ and Satan*, twenty-four occurrences of sele as the first constituent of a compound, and forty-four occurrences of sele as the final constituent of a compound not counting the three in *Christ and Satan*, and only one of them refers to heaven: sele in *The Judgment Day I* 92. Perhaps this is because the hall image is absent from biblical depictions of the heavenly city; but at any rate the concept of the sele as the place of the joy and comradeship of thanes, as well as of mutual loyalty and love between thanes and their lord, in earthly dryhts of good men representing the dryht of heaven, was available to be parodied in reference to the dryht of hell, as is done in five (if not all six) of the *Christ and Satan* passages.

Conspicuous among the joys of a dryht in its hall was minstrelsy, 'song and music' (sang ond swēg, *Beowulf* 1063, and compare also 89–90). Though similar imagery is found also in biblical accounts of heaven, the heroic rather than the Christian tradition seems likely to have been the most operative source of Satan's bitter memories of former enjoyment of sang (234) and swēg (236) around the heavenly throne. The *Christ and Satan* reference to song in heaven in 661, and the statement sanctas singað 'the saints sing' 355, can hardly be felt to have any heroic resonance, as they possibly might if swēg were in their immediate context. In the remaining references to song in heaven in our poem, 45, 143, 145, swēg is equally lacking, but seems to be suggested by a kind of word-play in the formula song on swegle 'song in heaven' (45, 143), which thus indirectly suggests song and minstrelsy in a hall. This formula is not recorded outside of *Christ and Satan*, but sang or singan is accompanied by swegl in at least two other passages which represent the singing of a heavenly dryht: *Andreas* 869 (þǣr wæs singāl sang ond swegles gong) and *The Phoenix* 635 (singað on swegle sōðfæstra gedryht).[21] No parodic reference is made to song in depicting hell. Apart from 236, swēg is used of the 'music of the angels' (engla swēg 402) at the Harrowing of hell, where there is a parodic as well as a direct reference since the devils apprehend the angelic swēg as 'din' (dyne 403), and is used also of the 'music in the clouds' (wolcna swēg 563) at the Ascension. It is gruesomely parodied in hell by the 'viper's music' (nēdran swæg 102).

The generous dispensing of treasure by the lord to his thanes is an essential feature of the life of a dryht, expressed by a rich vocabulary in numerous heroic contexts in Old English poetry. Some words of this vocabulary became the proper words for central attributes of God the Father or of Christ, such as ār 'mercy' or gifu 'grace.' In the only occurrence of ār in *Christ and Satan*, the poet speaks of a time when we human beings 'intend to bow before the high throne and beg the Ruler for mercies' (tō hēhselde hnīgan þencað, ond þone Anwaldan āra biddan 207–8). In one of the two occurrences of gifu in *Christ and Satan*, the reference is to the 'gift' (gife 571) of the Holy Spirit at Pentecost, a 'gift' which is at the same time the 'grace' of God; in the other, the poet in a homiletic passage is urging his hearers to 'be mindful, through God's grace, of spiritual splendour' (þurh Godes gife gemunan gāstes blēd 644). Besides the occurrence of conspicuously heroic diction in the immediate context of ār and gifu in two of the three passages (hēhseld 207, Anwalda 208, blēd 644), the words ār and gifu themselves in heroic contexts elsewhere have material meanings which support and, as it were, incarnate the spiritual meanings which our poet is expressing: the tangible 'benefits' conferred by Hrothgar and Wealhtheow and expected to be reciprocated by Hrothulf (see p 78 above), and the 'gifts' dispensed by Hrothgar, Offa, and many another earthly ruler (see p 78 above) – outward and visible signs of an inward and spiritual grace.

Similarly, a lord's act of dispensing gifts to the thanes of his dryht, often expressed by the verb dǣlan and in *Beowulf* 71 by gedǣlan, is mirrored in *Christ and Satan* by a single use of each of these verbs. Christ at the right hand of his Father 'dispenses' (dǣleð 580) each day to men on earth not gold nor arm rings but 'help and salvation' (help ond hǣlo 581, and compare pp 78–9 above). More complexly, in ll. 19–21 (Drēamas hē gedēlde, duguðe ond geþēode, Ādām ǣrest, ond þæt æðele cyn, engla ordfruman, þæt þe eft forwarð), a difficult passage, the objects duguðe '?hosts,' geþēode 'peoples,' and especially Ādām 'Adam,' cyn 'kind of beings,' and ordfruman 'the most exalted ones' seem to require for gedēlde a sense of 'created' which is elsewhere attested weakly if at all, while the object drēamas 'joys' seems to require for gedēlde a combination of the sense 'created' and the more usual sense 'dispensed' or 'imparted.' ('Joys he imparted by the Creation of hosts and nations, of Adam foremost and of that excellent order of beings, the most exalted of the angels, who afterwards fell into damnation.') Probably part of the solution to the puzzle lies in the consideration that to create *is* to impart, that is, that anything is created in order to be bestowed upon someone and thereby give joy. Probably too the first three lines of the poem should be read in the same light: 'It became evident to dwellers on earth that the Lord had might and strength, when he established the regions of earth,' that is, at the Creation of the universe. This passage is not meant to confront us with a chronological problem, causing us to object that nothing could be evident to dwellers on earth at a time when they did not yet exist and to wonder how to solve the apparent contradiction, but it is meant to be understood timelessly: God's Creation of the universe is an eternal reality which at any time gives evidence to earth dwellers of his might and strength, just as it also at any time imparts 'joys' (drēamas 19) to his creatures themselves. Christ's *caritas* is thus manifested in the act of Creation, clearly identified here as his act rather than God the Father's (see also p 21 above); the Creator and Bestower of all things is made immediate in human terms to the Anglo-Saxon audience, by the gedēlde in l. 19, as a generous Lord.

A lord, especially a generous one, is often called in Old English poetry sinces brytta 'dispenser of treasure': examples are Hrothgar (*Beowulf* 607, 1170), Hygelac (*Beowulf* 1922, 2071), Pharaoh (*Genesis* 1857), Abimelech (*Genesis* 2728), Holofernes (*Judith* 30), Constantine (*Elene* 194), and an unnamed lord (*The Wanderer* 25). It is never used of God the Father nor of Christ in *Christ and Satan*, nor in any other Old English poem so far as can be ascertained from the Bessinger-Smith *Concordance*;[22] probably sinc had too stubbornly material a meaning to be spiritualized. However, sinc occurs once in *Christ and Satan* and brytta twice. In 577 we are told that Judas sold the Son of the Ruler 'for silver treasure' (on seolfres sinc); in 23, that the rebel angels thought they might be 'dispensers (= lords) of heaven' (swegles brytan); and in 124, that Satan had said that he himself was '[God,] the Lord of heaven' (swægles Brytta). It is as if the poet had broken the phrase sinces brytta into its parts and degraded each part by association with Judas or the devils, so that they could not convey a sense opposite to what he intended.

This is in harmony with the manner in which certain words expressing possession and domination, æht 'property,' āgan 'possess,' gewald 'dominion,' onwald 'rule,' are with few and carefully delimited exceptions appropriated to diabolic references and made to characterize the 'greedy' and 'grasping' devils (grǣdig, gīfre, 32, 192) as primal examples of *cupiditas*.[23]

A familiar group of three words denoting a dwelling place or landed property, hām 'home,' eard 'land, homeland, dwelling place,' and ēðel 'land of habitation, home,' are somewhat differently treated. Though they have such a large area of meaning in common that sometimes one and sometimes another of them is used in otherwise identical contexts,[24] each of them does have some specialization of meaning setting it off against the others. Among those strands of meaning which belong specifically to the heroic tradition, we can distinguish the following: (1) The place in which a lord's rule and generosity are exercised (hereafter 'lord's place'); (1a) The specific seat of a lord's rule and generosity, such as a hall, fortress, or city (hereafter 'lord's seat'); (1b) The whole domain or territory of a lord (hereafter 'lord's domain'); (2) Landed property bestowed by a lord on a thane (hereafter 'lord's gift'). These meanings have different prominence relative to each other in the three words, besides any other specializations of meaning in any of the three.

In the occurrences of hām it is the meaning 'lord's seat' which is most strongly attested. When King Beowulf's hām (*Beowulf* 2325)[25] is burned by the dragon, it is called the 'gift-seat of the Geats' (gifstōl Gēata 2327), and we are told that lavish rewards were conferred on Ongentheow's slayers by Hygelac 'when he came [back] to his Residenz' (þā hē tō hām becōm, *Beowulf* 2992). In *Beowulf* 713–20, Heorot as Hrothgar's 'home' (hām) is surrounded by an especially imposing array of such appellations: 'the high hall' (sele þām hēan), 'wine-hall' and 'hall' (wīnreced, recede), 'goldhall' (goldsele), and 'hall' (heal-). The reading of *Juliana* 683–8 is enriched if the phrase in þām þȳstran hām is understood as a parodic application of this same sense of hām: Heliseus and his thanes together have gone to hell, and 'in that gloomy home' [so unlike the lordly one he possessed on earth] his 'thanes' (þegnas), the 'band of comrades' (genēatscolu), need not [any longer] expect 'allotted fiefs' (feohgestealda witedra) 'from their chieftain' (tō þām frumgāre), need not expect that in the 'wine-hall' (wīnsele) 'on the beer-bench' (ofer bēorsetle)[26] they will receive 'arm rings' (bēagas) or 'embossed gold' (æpplede gold). In *Genesis* 33 what Satan hopes to gain for himself by rebellion against God is 'a home and a high seat of rule' (hām and hēahsetl); what he gets by way of retribution from an angry God is, parodically, a 'home of exile' (wræclicne hām 37) in a hell filled with wailing.[27] (This infernal home reflects ironically the heroic sense of hām as a 'lord's gift'[28] at the same time as it makes a mockery of Satan's overweening attempt to set himself up in God's stead in a home which is a high seat of rule, a 'lord's seat.')

This sense of 'lord's seat' is appropriated to heaven as 'the Lord's seat of rule' in three passages in *Christ and Satan*. In a homiletic passage, ll. 216–20, the poet exhorts his hearers to go to where the Lord Saviour is enthroned on his 'high seat' (hēhsetl) 'in that beloved home' (in ðǣm dēoran hām). In ll. 255–7 Satan and his fellows say that they 'wanted to drive the lord from his beloved home, the King from his city' (woldon ... Drihten adrīfan of þām dēoran hām, Cyning of cestre). In ll. 564–6, at the Ascension of Christ, God the Father extends his hand and leads Christ 'to the holy home' (tō þām hālgan hām) which is thenceforward to be the seat of the Son's rule and generosity at the Father's right hand, as is made explicit in ll. 579–82. A grimly ironic parody of this sense occurs in ll. 412–14, when Eve says that Satan, tempting her and Adam to eat the forbidden fruit, persuaded them that they would gain thereby a 'holy home, [namely] heaven as their dominion' (hāligne hām, heofon tō gewalde).

The case that can be made for use of hām in the sense 'lord's gift' is not equally compelling, but such a meaning does occasionally show through, however faintly. In *Widsith* 93–6 the 'home' (hām) to which Widsith returns is identical with his father's ēþel, the 'land' (lond) given by their lord Eadgils. In *The Battle of Brunnanburh* 9–10, when the poet says that Aethelstan and Eadmund often defended in battle the 'land, treasure, and homes' (land..., hord and hāmas), the hāmas must be the manorial properties held of the king by his subjects. Similarly in the Finn Episode in *Beowulf*, when in l. 1127 the surviving Frisian warriors are said to go to 'the homes and the high fortress' (hāmas ond hēaburh) during the winter truce, the hēaburh (singular) must be Finn's Residenz (though the larger context will hardly allow us to take it to be the same Finnsburuh which the Danes defended against the Frisians' attack), and the hāmas (plural) must be the Frisian thanes' homes which they hold of Finn. In *Beowulf* 2998, when Hygelac gives his daughter to Eofor as an 'ornament of the home' (hāmweorðunge), it is a legitimate inference that the home she is to adorn is equally Hygelac's gift, especially since an ample grant of land by Hygelac to Eofor and Wulf has just been mentioned in ll. 2994–5.

Since this gift of land and a simultaneous gift of interlocked rings are in l. 2995 called 'rewards' (lēan) for the slaying of Ongentheow, mention of hām in specifically Christian context as a reward, or as something to be earned by service, works, or valour, may be understood to reflect this heroic connotation while adapting it to Christian homiletic purposes. Thus in *Guthlac A* 65–70 we hear of holy persons who fix their hopes on heaven, knowing that an eternal 'home' (ēðel, ms eleð) awaits all those who on earth 'serve' (þēowiað) the Lord and 'by their works' (bī gewyrhtum) 'petition for' (wilniað) 'that precious home' (þæs dēoran hām). In ll. 790–803 the same poet describes the righteous as those who carry out here 'in words and works' (wordum and weorcum) the imperishable precepts of the King of glory and in their lifetime on earth 'earn' (earniað) a 'home on high' (hāmes in hēahþu); further, he calls them chosen 'warriors' (cempan) dear to Christ and says that they 'overcome' (oferfeohtað) the enemy. In *The Fates of the Apostles* 115–20 Cynewulf exhorts us to pray that we may enjoy the 'home on high' (hāmes in hēhðo) where the King of angels renders to the pure a 'timeless reward' (lēan unhwīlen). The poet of *The Phoenix* says in ll. 482–4 that a 'blessed man/warrior' (ēadig eorl)[29] 'earns by zeal/valour' (earnað on elne) a 'home' (hāmes) in heaven with the high King, and in ll. 598–600 that the 'works' (weorc) of every person will shine brightly 'in that joyous home' (in þām blīþan [ms bliþam] hām) before the face of the eternal Lord. Parodically, the *Genesis* poet tells in ll. 36–8 that God created for Satan a 'home of exile' (wræclicne hām) 'as a reward/retribution for his work' (weorce to lēane) of rebellion.[30] In these six Christian passages it is thus possible to discern a connection with a heroic sense of hām as 'lord's gift,' but the connection is in varying degrees indirect, and it seems likely that even for the Anglo-Saxon audience a large share of their emotional power derived from the feeling, probably common to all cultures, that 'there's no place like home.'[31] The same is doubtless true of certain passages, like *Guthlac A* 220–2 and *Riddle 39* 8–9 (besides *Genesis* 36–8), in which lack or deprivation of a home is spoken of in terms of exile – even though exile as such is a favourite heroic motif. In numerous other passages where heaven or hell is spoken of as a home bestowed, but where no stronger colouration is imparted by specific mention of reward, service, or exile, the reflection of the 'lord's gift' sense is even fainter and the lion's share of their poignancy seems to come from the universal feeling of attachment to one's home. Some examples are these: *Genesis* 945–7, *Guthlac B* 833–5, and *Guthlac B* 868–71, all referring to Adam and Eve's home in Eden or the loss of it by the Fall, and therefore, typologically, to heaven or hell; *Andreas* 102–5; *Andreas* 225–9 and 1683–5, where hām might be taken to refer to heaven as Christ's or the Trinity's seat of rule and generosity or as the dwelling bestowed upon the souls of the righteous, or both; *Soul and Body I* 66–71, where it is the sinful body that ordains hell as a dwelling place for the soul;[32] *The Dream of the Rood* 147–8; *Elene* 919–21; *The Last Judgment* (*Crist III*) 896–8; *Guthlac A* 9–10, 96–8, 673–80; *The Phoenix* 591–4; *Juliana* 321–3 and 526–30, where hell may be understood as the seat of rule and punitive generosity of 'the king of hell-dwellers' (hellwarena cyning 322) or as the dwelling allotted by God to the devils; *The Seafarer* 117–20; *The Judgment Day I* 23–5; *The Paris Psalter* 106.35, where the 'home' (hām) which God 'established' (staðelude) 'for the hungry' (hungrium) is typologically heaven, and 122.1, where the 'heaven homes' (heofonhāmas) may be God's seat of rule or, because of the plural form, the dwellings bestowed on the souls of the blessed; *The Seasons for Fasting* 148–51; *The Metrical Preface of Wærferth's Translation of Gregory's Dialogues* 5; and *Instructions for Christians* 262. In one passage otherwise similar to these, *Guthlac A* 654–7, the heroic sense of hām as a dwelling place bestowed by a lord on a thane is somehow reinforced by the presence of eard and ēþel: Guthlac is telling how his heart is spurred on, and his way lighted, towards 'that better home' (þām betran hām), 'that most precious eternal homeland' (þām lēofestan ēcan earde), where his '[manorial] estate' (ēþellond) is beautiful and joyous in the Father's glory.[33]

In *Christ and Satan*, when hām refers to hell, there is always an implication that it is the home bestowed by God (that is, Christ) upon Satan and his fellow rebels. This meaning is even explicit in ll. 177–8, where Satan says not only that he has been 'led away from light into this hateful home' (alæded fram lēohte in þone lāðan hām) but also that he has been 'parted from that shining dryht' (asceāden fram þære scīran driht)[34] and receives some indirect reinforcement in l. 49, where Satan contrasts his state as one who cannot expect a 'better home' (bættran hām) than hell with the felicity of those who praise the Lord 'around the high seat' (ymb hēhseld 47) in heaven. But in most of the passages in question, something in the context indicates that hell is also being understood parodically as the seat of Satan's (or the devils') rule or lack of rule:[35] in l. 25 the poet says that the devils 'established a home in hell' (in helle hām staðeledon) in consequence of seeking to be themselves the 'rulers of glory' (wuldres waldend 24); in l. 38 Satan contrasts the devils' 'gloomy home' (ðēostræ hām) with their former 'glory of angels' (engla ðrym 36); in ll. 88 and 92 Satan has 'led home to hell' or 'led home to fetters' (tō helle hām gelēdde 88, tō hæftum hām gefærde 92) his followers, as the unexpected consequence of seeking to have in his possession all 'dominion over the [heavenly] strongholds' (burga gewald 86); 'this terrible home' (ðes atola hām) of l. 96 and 'this woeful home' (ðæs wālica hām) of l. 100 is contrasted by Satan with a 'wine-hall of exultant ones' (wloncra wīnsele 94) which is non-existent in hell;[36] when in ll. 110–11 Satan says that he has led the multitude of devils 'to this dim home' (tō ðissum dimman hām) he is contrasting it with his alleged former 'dominion over all glory' (gewald ealles wuldres 107); when in l. 138 Satan says that he is not allowed to enjoy a 'more hope-filled home' (hihtlicran hāmes) than hell, he has just called it 'this windy hall' (þes windiga sele 136), using the word sele, which is one of the favourite words for a lord's hall in heroic contexts,[37] and a like identification of 'the dim home' which the devils possess with 'the accursed hall' which they inhabit is found in ll. 337 (þone dimman hām) and 332 (þone werigan sele); even in l. 178,[38] Satan recognizes that his banishment to his infernal home is the result of his having tried to 'dethrone' (of selde ... adrīfan) Christ and usurp his rule (ll. 173–5). In sum, the overall impression left by the *Christ and Satan* references to hell as a hām is a diffuse version of the irony tersely expressed in *Genesis* 28–37; both of the discernible heroic meanings 'lord's seat' and 'lord's gift' are reflected, and both ironically.[39]

All the nine occurrences of hām in *Christ and Satan* which have not yet been examined (ll. 215, 276, 278, 294, 345, 362, 504, 552, and 658) refer to heaven. The universal human feeling of attachment to one's home seems to be a prominent part of the meaning of almost all of them, but the heroic sense of 'lord's gift' seems to be discernible in each to a greater or lesser degree. It is strongest in the passage (ll. 277–9) in which Satan or the devils ask themselves whether the Eternal will ever 'grant' (alēfan) them a 'home in the heavenly kingdom' (on heofona rīce hām) as before, and weakest perhaps in ll. 276 and 345 where reference is made to a time when Satan or the devils 'firmly occupied a home in heaven' (on heofonum hām staðelode/on). In the remaining six, heaven is the home of human souls, and in each of them Christ or the Father is somehow presented as an active agent comparable to a generous earthly lord. This is least clear in ll. 215–16, which merely tells of the 'more hope-filled home, in the heavenly kingdom, of those pleasing to Christ' (hyhtlicra hām in heofonrīce Crīste gecwēmra). In l. 294, however, we are told that the Resplendent One (Christ) 'will show us' (tæceð ūs) 'a firmly established home' (trumlicne hām); in ll. 359–62 the Father of mankind 'will lead' (lædað) the souls of the blessed to light, where they will have a 'home on high' (ūplicne hām); in ll. 504–6 and ll. 552–4, with much parallelism of wording, it is Christ who 'should lead' or who 'led' (gelædde) human souls 'home' (hām) out of fetters and up to their eard or ēðel; and finally in ll. 656–8 the martyrs and patriarchs address Christ as the one who 'didst lead up' (ūp gelæddest) the progeny of earth 'to this blessed home' (tō þissum ēadigan hām). The kind and degree of heroic resonance felt in these passages could hardly correspond more closely to that in *Guthlac A* 9–10, 96–8, *Guthlac B* 833–5, *Andreas* 102–5, *The Dream of the Rood* 147–8, *The Phoenix* 591–4, *The Seafarer* 117–20, *The Paris Psalter* 106. 35, *The Metrical Preface of Wærferth's Translation of Gregory's Dialogues* 5, and *Instructions for Christians* 262.[40]

The 'lord's place' sense of eard is not to be felt as identical with that of hām, because in certain passages eard refers more distinctly than hām ever does to a 'lord's domain,' that is, the entire territory ruled over by a king or lesser lord, as opposed to a 'lord's seat' such as a burg, heall, or sele. Thus in *The Battle of Maldon* when Byrhtnoth tells the Viking invaders that he and his troop will defend 'Aethelred's homeland' (Æþelrēdes eard 53) he means Aethelred's kingdom; five lines later, indeed, he is voicing his indignation that the invaders should already have come so far 'into *our* land' (on ūrne eard). The use of eard in this latter passage to represent a territory inhabited by a people strongly resembles that in the closing lines of *The Battle of Brunnanburh*, which recall the time when the Angles and Saxons 'got a homeland' (eard begēaton 73) by the conquest of Britain. Other uses of eard in tenth-century and eleventh-century Chronicle poetry show the same meaning of 'territory inhabited by a people' but not identified as the 'kingdom' of a named or clearly implied monarch: in *The Death of Edgar* (975) 24–8 Oslac is said to have been 'driven ... from the country' (adrǣfed ... of earde 24–5) into exile beyond the sea; and in *The Death of Alfred* (1036) the poet says that 'no bloodier deed had been done in this country since the coming of the Danes' (ne wearð drēorlicre dǣd gedōn on þison earde, syððan Dene cōmon 11–12) than the cruel punishments inflicted by Godwine on the eleventh-century prince Alfred and his supporters.[41] Presumably Scyld's eard in *Beowulf* 56, Beowulf's eard as king of Geatland in *Beowulf* 2736, and Nabochodonossor's eard in *Daniel* 637 are to be understood in the same manner as Æþelrēdes eard in *The Battle of Maldon* 53. In *Beowulf* 2198, where Hygelac and Beowulf alike are said to have an eard in the country of the Geats, the eard which is Hygelac's is identical with the 'spacious kingdom' (sīde rīce 2199), Geatland, which he rules. The eard which is Beowulf's is likewise his whole domain, the 'land' (lond) of l. 2197, probably not to be equated with the 'building and chieftainly seat' (bold ond bregostōl 2196) of the preceding sentence. In *Beowulf* 1726–7, when Hrothgar moralizes about the spiritual danger confronting a man to whom God has given 'wisdom ... a domain, and noble rank' (snyttru ... eard ond eorlscipe), the eard need not be any more clearly equated with the 'stronghold of men' (hlēoburh wera) of l. 1731 than with the 'spacious kingdom' (sīde rīce) of l. 1733, since both are in the following sentence. (Of course in *Beowulf* 2198 and 1727 a sense of 'lord's gift' or 'the Lord's gift' co-exists with the sense of 'lord's domain.') In *The Paris Psalter* 134.12.1 it is the 'land' (eardland) of Og and other kings that is given to the people of Israel; the joining of a second constituent land to eard in this compound makes it clear that the reference can only be to the entire kingdom. In other passages in the scriptural poetry, when God or Christ is represented as dwelling in heaven, by the use of either the noun eard or the verb eardian, the reference must be to his whole domain: examples are *The Lord's Prayer I* 1, *The Paris Psalter* 112.5.3 (on heofonrīce 2) and 135.27.2, and *The Seasons for Fasting* 31–4.

Yet the more specific sense of 'lord's seat,' though less characteristic, does occur, in the reference in *Juliana* to the 'dwelling place' (eard 20) possessed by the heathen lord Heliseus 'in the city Commedia' (in þǣre ceastre Commedia 21) and his 'treasure hoard' (hordgestrēon 22) there, and in various references, using either the noun eard or the verb eardian, to the Lord as dwelling in Jerusalem (*The Advent, Crist I* 63), in Zion (*The Paris Psalter* 73.3.3, 75.2.2, 131.14.2, and 124.22.5), or in his own house (*The Paris Psalter* 77.60.2). In two of the *Beowulf* passages mentioned earlier (2198 and 1727) the narrower sense of 'lord's seat' is introduced in a neighbouring sentence alongside the broader sense of 'lord's domain.' In *The Ascension* (*Crist II*), finally, Christ is said to 'mount up to his dwelling place' (eard gestīgan 514), which is 'the Father's royal seat' (Fæder ēþelstōll 516), as the 'Chief of princes' (æþelinga Ord 515), 'Ruler of all peoples' (ealra folca Fruma 516), 'with this dryht of angels' (mid þās engla gedryht 515); we may think of the Father's royal seat as the throne where Christ sits at the Father's right hand.

In *Christ and Satan*, however, there are only two occurrences of eard in which even a hint of the sense 'the Lord's seat' or 'the Lord's domain' can be discerned, in co-existence with other senses. In ll. 457–8 it is the company of souls delivered in the Harrowing of hell that rises 'up to the dwelling place, and the Eternal with them, the Lord of mankind, into the glorious city' (ūp tō earde, ond se Ēca mid him, Meotod mancynnes in þā mǣran burh). According to the sentence structure, the dwelling place is in the first instance that of the souls, but also, in the section introduced by ond, that of Christ: his domain, but also in a narrower sense the seat of his rule, as specified by burh. In ll. 504–5a, when Christ speaks of leading the souls home, 'up to the dwelling place' (ūp tō earde), from their bondage in hell, ll. 505b–508a develop the idea of the souls' enjoyment of *their* dwelling place in heaven, and only the fact that Christ is speaking suggests to us that the eard is also *his* domain.[42]

Of course an eard as a dwelling place is an appropriate and characteristic 'lord's gift' to a thane. Beowulf says in *Beowulf* 2493 that Hygelac gave him an eard, and the same implication is present in the reference in l. 2198 to the eard which Beowulf received from Hygelac and in l. 1727 to the eard which a fortunate man receives from God.[43] Yet we also find eard frequently occurring in the sense of 'dwelling place' with no overt suggestion in the context that the dwelling place was a lord's gift. Thus when Hengest remembers his eard in *Beowulf* 1129, we know he is homesick ('the exile, the stranger, was eager to leave the [Frisian] dwellings,' fundode wrecca, gist of geardum 1137–8), and if we choose we may introduce an inference that the eard was a gift from his lord, but such an inference is not prompted by the context and may be felt as intrusive. The situation is analogous with the dwelling place of Grendel and his mother in *Beowulf*: 'the dwelling of the monster brood' (fifelcynnes eard 104), 'you do not yet know the dwelling' (eard gīt ne const 1377), 'the dwelling of the alien creatures' (ælwihta eard 1500), 'the roomy dwellings' (ēacne eardas 1621). To be sure God had allotted this dwelling place to them, but after ll. 106–10 we are not again reminded of this. In *An Exhortation to Christian Living* 58–60 the hearer's eard and ēþel (60) are identical with the 'transitory abodes' (læne staþelas 59) which he is being admonished to understand that he must leave; that is, the hearer's eard is his earthly dwelling place, perhaps even his body as the earthly habitation of his soul, and any implication that it is 'the Lord's gift' is at best remote. The same is true in the continuation of the same passage when the hearer is warned 'no longer may you enjoy the possession of life, of a habitation in your homeland' (þū lengc ne mōst līfes brūcan, eardes on ēþle 62–3). Whenever a reference is made, literally or typologically, to heaven as the dwelling of angels or blessed souls, or to hell as the dwelling of devils or damned souls, the inference that these dwellings were bestowed by God is of course legitimate. These references are frequent in the Old English Christian poetry in general: Cynewulf alone says no less than four times (*The Fates of the Apostles* 93, 110, 113, and *Juliana* 701) that he does not know whether heaven or hell is to be his eard after death. *The Lord's Prayer 2* speaks of the same 'two dwellings' (twēgen eardas 97) as 'the mercy of the Lord or enslavement to the devil' (Drihtenes āre oððe dēofles þēowet 98).[44] In *Christ and Satan*, except for one passage that clearly refers to a dwelling in heaven as 'the Lord's gift' (Satan saying that he and the other devils cannot expect that the King of glory will ever 'grant them a dwelling place,' eard alēfan 116, as formerly), and one passage (l. 113) where the dwelling places are not specified as the gift of anyone whatever, all occurrences of eard or eardian are of this kind. Even in ll. 457–8 and 504–5a[45] it is primarily the souls that are rising or being led ūp tō earde in heaven. In l. 93 Satan has led his fellows home to bondage 'from [their heavenly] dwelling' (of earde); in l. 230 the fallen angels acknowledge that they sinned while 'in the dwelling on high' (uppe on earde); in l. 203 the poet exhorts his hearers to choose 'a dwelling in glory' (eard in wuldre); and in l. 592 heaven is characterized as the place where 'his [Christ's] retinue now dwells' (his hīred nū ... eardað). Even the dragons that 'dwell eternally' (æce ... eardigað 98) at hell's door have presumably been assigned that abode by Christ. To fit these Christian applications, the heroic senses of eard needed no adjustment at all.

The meaning of ēðel, unlike that of eard, includes or may include the feature that the property in question, whether a 'domain' or a 'gift,' is in some sense hereditary, a patrimony or birthright. The land whose possession is granted to Widsith as thane of Eadgils of the Myrgings in *Widsith* 93–6 is 'my [Widsith's] father's domain' (mīnes fæder ēþel 96); presumably the land had been held by Widsith's father, had formally reverted to his overlord Eadgils in the customary manner of a feudal estate on Widsith's father's death, and had then been formally reconferred upon Widsith by Eadgils in consideration of his continuing homage and service. In *Beowulf* 2884–8 Wiglaf, excoriating the cowardly Geatish thanes who did not help Beowulf in his last combat, tells them that 'all enjoyment of a holding of land' (eall ēðelwyn 2885) shall 'be forfeited' (alicgean 2886) by '[you and] your kin' (ēowrum cynne 2885). This passage gives almost exactly the same picture of inheritance by a thane as the *Widsith* passage, since only a right that exists can 'be forfeited,' that is, 'fail,' 'lapse,' or 'cease,' in consequence of misconduct. The ēðelriht or ēðelwyn which Beowulf receives from Hygelac in Geatland (*Beowulf* 2198, 2493) is naturally to be understood in the same way; and the fact that in *Beowulf* 2198 both Beowulf and Hygelac are said to have an ēðelriht in Geatland, Hygelac's being the 'great kingdom' (sīde rīce 2199) itself, reminds us that kingdoms also passed from ruler to successor by hereditary right, with whatever restrictions or exceptions. In fact a kingdom is sometimes explicitly called an ēðel, for example Heremod's in *Beowulf* 913, Offa's in *Beowulf* 1960, Nabochodonossor's in *Daniel* 637, and Edward the Confessor's in *The Death of Edward* (1065) 24.

An ēðel which from the sovereign's point of view is his 'domain' or 'kingdom' is from his people's point of view their 'homeland' or 'country.' When Breca returns to his 'own kingdom' (swæsne ēþel, *Beowulf* 520), the place to which he is returning is also the '(home)land of the Brondings' (lond Brondinga 521, compare *Widsith* 25); Byrhtnoth in *The Battle of Maldon* 51–3 says that he with his troop will defend 'this country, Aethelred's kingdom' (ēþel þysne, Æþelrēdes eard 52–3); in *Widsith* 109, Widsith tells of traversing 'the whole country of the Goths' (ealne ... ēþel Gotena) to seek out 'the hall-company [that is, the dryht] of Eormanric' (innweorud Earmanrīces 111); and in *Daniel* 68–78, after the people of Israel have been led into captivity in Babylon, Nabochodonossor sends Babylonian warriors to occupy the 'desolate country' (ēðne ēðel 78) from which the Israelites have been removed. No ruler of the 'country' is mentioned in this last passage, nor in *Andreas* 174–6 when the Lord bids Andreas go to the place where the 'cannibals ... have [their] country' (sylfætan ... ēðel healdaþ 175–6), nor in *The Death of Edgar* (975) 6, where 'on this country's turf' (in ðisse ēðeltyrf) simply means 'in England,' nor in *Aldhelm* 4 when Aldhelm is said to be exalted 'in the country of the Anglo-Saxons' (on æðele [ms æðel] Angolsexna).

The double aspect of an ēðel as a king's 'kingdom' and his people's 'country' is well illustrated by uses of the compound ēðelweard. Just as the verb weardian can mean either 'protect, govern' or 'occupy, inhabit,' so Hrothgar as king of the Danes in *Beowulf* is 'ruler of the kingdom' (ēþelweard 1702, compare 616), and Beowulf as king of the Geats likewise (2210), and on the other hand in *Judith* 319–21 Judith's '[fellow] country-men' (ēðelweardas 321) have overcome their enemies, and in *The Meters of Boethius* 1. 20–4, after the Emperor has fled from Rome to Constantinople, the ēþelweardas (24), that is, the inhabitants of Rome, reluctantly pay tribute to the Goths.[46]

Whether held as the patrimony of a lord or king on the one hand or of a thane on the other, an ēðel seems to be always understood as a substantial territory, a 'lord's domain'; a narrower meaning of 'lord's seat' is not attested in the poetry as far as can be ascertained from the Bessinger-Smith *Concordance*.[47] Such a meaning might conceivably be intended in *Beowulf* 1774–6 when Hrothgar says that 'in my [Hrothgar's] ēðel' (mē ... on ēþle 1774) a reversal of previous good fortune came when Grendel's cannibalistic raids began, but since there is no explicit indication that on ēþle means 'in Heorot,' it is best to understand it as 'in my kingdom,' especially since this also fits better with the immediately preceding context (1769–73). For precise localization of a 'lord's seat,' for example in a capital city, ēðel is compounded with a second constituent stōl meaning 'seat' or 'throne.' In *The Meters of Boethius* 9.10–11, the city of Rome is the 'royal city of his [Nero's] whole realm' (his rīces ... ealles ēðelstōl); in *Genesis* 1747–8 the city of Carran (Haran in the AV) is Abraham's 'father's chieftainly seat' (fæder ēðelstōl 1748). An ēðelstōl is just as much the precise locale of rule in a territory when that territory is viewed from its people's point of view as a 'country' as it is when it is viewed from its ruler's point of view as a 'kingdom' or 'domain.' Thus in *Widsith* 120–2, the Hrædas are said to have been accustomed, in a particular forested locality 'at Vistula Wood' (ymb Wistlawudu 121), to defend the 'old principal stronghold of [their] country' (ealdne ēþelstōl 122) against the people of Attila, and in *The Advent* (*Crist I*) 50–2 the poet apostrophizes Jerusalem as the 'capital city of the angels' homeland' (engla ēþelstōl 52).

The last example reminds us that it is not necessarily a human sovereign or a human people that rules or inhabits an ēðel. Not only is heaven the 'angels' country' (engla ēðel) in *Andreas* 525 and 642 and *The Ascension* (*Crist II*) 630; it is Christ's 'kingdom' (ēðel) as well in *Andreas* 226, *The Ascension* (*Crist II*) 741, *The Last Judgment* (*Crist III*) 1496,[48] and *The Creed* 37, and as such it confers sacramental solemnity on the closing lines of *The Dream of the Rood*, in which Christ with a host of souls delivered from infernal bondage is said to have entered into heaven 'where his kingdom was' (þær his ēðel wæs 156). This last passage, especially, is enriched for a reader by awareness of the 'birthright' sense of ēðel. Of course human souls too can have or obtain heaven as their 'homeland' (ēðel), their 'birthright' by divine grace, as in the same passage.[49] To it may be added at least the following: *The Fates of the Apostles* 112–14, where Cynewulf soberly reflects that the 'homeland' (ēðel 113) of himself and every man may be either heaven or hell; *The Advent* (*Crist I*) 434–6, where the poet says that the Saviour will reward the righteous man 'in that country where he never came before' (in þam ēðle þær hē ær ne cwōm 436); *The Last Judgment* (*Crist III*) 1336–46, where Christ is said to invite the blessed souls to 'enter into the country of the joy of angels' (on ēþel faran engla drēames 1342), and in direct address tells them 'Receive ... my Father's kingdom ... the bright splendor of [that] country' (Onfōð ... mīnes Fæder rīce ... beorht ēðles wlite 1344–6); *The Last Judgment* (*Crist III*) 1496, where Christ, speaking as judge to the souls of all mankind though using the second person singular (1377), says 'I was wretched in thy country so that thou mightest be blessed in mine' (earm ic wæs on ēðle þīnum þæt þū wurde [ms worde] ēadig on mīnum);[50] *The Last Judgment* (*Crist III*) 1639, where the kingdom of heaven is called 'the homeland that shall never perish' (se ēþel þe nō geendad weorþeð); *Guthlac A* 66–9, where the poet says that 'the [heavenly] homeland of all ... who serve the Lord shall endure through eternity' (se ēeðl [ms eleð] ēce bīdeð ealra ... þe geond middangeard

Dryhtne þēowiað 67–9); possibly *Guthlac A* 651–7, where Guthlac on his deathbed tells of his eagerness to go to the better home, the eternal dwelling where '[his] patrimonial country is beautiful and joyous in the Father's glory' (is ēþellond fæger ond gefēalic in Fæder wuldre 656–7);[51] *The Phoenix* 387–92, where the poet speaks of Christ's chosen thanes who while on earth lay up for themselves treasures of high glory 'in that country above' (in þām ūplican ēðle 392); and other similar references to 'that country above' or 'that kingdom above' in *An Exhortation to Christian Living* (þæs ūplican ēþelrīces 75), *The Creed* (ūplicne ēþel 32), and *The Seasons for Fasting* (þone ūplican æþel 151) as the homeland of souls.

Seven of the nine occurrences of ēðel in *Christ and Satan* refer directly or indirectly to heaven. Let us first consider four of the direct references. One of them represents heaven as Christ's kingdom only: Christ in his Incarnation came 'down from [his] kingdom' (ufan from ēðle 495). Three of them are more expressive if read with awareness of the double aspect of ēðel as a ruler's 'domain' and its inhabitants' 'homeland,' as Christ and delivered souls are represented as going together 'up to [his and their] ēðel' (ūp tō ēðle 402, 460, 553). It is not quite certain how strongly we should insist on a meaning of 'birthright homeland' in the three latter passages, and of 'birthright kingdom' in all four. Some scepticism about this is aroused by the fact that of two passages with closely parallel wording, ll. 504–507a and 552–5a, the former contains ūp tō earde in the place where the latter contains ūp tō ēðle, suggesting that the poet did not assign appreciably different meanings to the two words. Some countervailing points, however, are worth considering: (1) The holy prophets delivered from hell at the Harrowing, who on their hands bear Christ 'up to [his and their] [birthright?] kingdom' in l. 460, are 'the people of Abraham' (Abrahames cynn), and it is by a typological interpretation of God's covenant with Abraham that heaven is the birthright of human souls.[52] (2) The thematic significance of ll. 399–402, which together with ll. 190–3 constitute the central and unifying statement about the exaltation and abasement both of Christ and of Satan,[53] is heightened by the implication that the heavenly destination (ūp tō ēðle) of the human souls in l. 402 is their 'birthright' by divine grace. (3) The statement in l. 495 that Christ in his Incarnation came 'down from [his] kingdom' (ufan from ēðle) gains by the 'birthright kingdom' interpretation a solemnity comparable to that felt in the closing lines of *The Dream of the Rood*, where Christ is said, in a sort of combination of Harrowing of hell and Ascension, to have entered into heaven 'where his kingdom was' (þær his ēðel wæs 156).[54] By this reading l. 495 is reminiscent of the first part of the Philippians passage which so fully recounts the abasement and exaltation of Christ, 'who, being in the form of God, thought it not robbery to be equal with God: but made himself of no reputation, and took upon him the form of a servant, and was made in the likeness of men.'[55] Besides, a connection that reinforces the abasement-exaltation motif and the entire structure of the poem is thereby established between l. 495 and l. 402: Christ gave up his birthright kingdom in order to come back with a multitude of souls to heaven, his birthright kingdom and their birthright country by reason of his mercy.

Of the three remaining references to heaven, there is one in which Christ says that but for the Fall, Adam and Eve and their offspring could have lived many years in the 'patrimonial estate' (on ēðle 477), that is, Eden, which was their 'Lord's gift' and typologically refers to heaven. In the remaining two Satan is the speaker, and in both he speaks disconsolately of a 'domain' (æðel 117, ēðel [ms eðle] 279) in heaven which was formerly granted by God to him and his fellows, but which God will never again so 'grant' (alēfan 116, 278). One may well think of Wiglaf's commination of the cowardly thanes.[56] The other two occurrences of ēðel in *Christ and Satan* refer to hell, parodically, as Satan's 'horrible kingdom' (atolan æðele 108) or his thanes' 'horrible country' (atolan ēðles 327), both times in explicit contrast with the glory or joy of their forfeited estate in heaven;[57] here the double aspect of ēðel as 'kingdom' and 'country' again appears.

In sum, the uses of hām, eard, and ēðel in *Christ and Satan* reflect rather faithfully the shared meaning of all three words and the distinctive meaning of each as these can be observed in the heroic poetry and in secular contexts in general. They do so in much the same variety of ways as other Old English poems in the Christian tradition, though the range and diversity of use in this one poem is a bit less wide than in that whole body of poetry. Moreover, they do so without debasement of their meaning like the debasement to which the *Christ and Satan* poet subjected the words æht, āgan, gewald, and onwald.[58] Rather, hām, eard, and ēðel are freely used with strong favourable connotations wherever appropriate, and with correspondingly strong parodic irony to refer to hell.

Some words of the heroic vocabulary that can easily be applied to the heavenly city of Revelation 21, St Augustine's city of God, or the kingdom of heaven referred to in the gospels, such as burg 'stronghold, city,' cester 'city,' and rīce 'kingdom,' are used in *Christ and Satan* predominantly or exclusively of heaven, dwelling of God and angels, hope of righteous men, home of the heavenly dryht. Except for one literal reference (601) to cities of men on earth and one occurrence (686) in Satan's lying promise to Christ in the last temptation, burg (burh) alone or in compounds always means heaven, six times (214, 295, 363, 458, 560, 612) in reference to God or good men, three times (86, 139, 622) in other contexts, for instance when in 139 Satan laments its irretrievable loss. Of the three occurrences of cester, two (298, 655) refer to heaven as the dwelling of God and the blessed, and one (257) tells of the rebel angels' attempt to drive the 'King from [his] city' (Cyning of cestre). Except for one reference (499) to an earthly kingdom as the place of the Crucifixion and one occurrence (687) in Satan's lying promise to Christ in the last temptation, rīce in the remaining nine occurrences (260, 278, 308, 347, 368, 613, 617, 649, 692) makes a straightforward reference to heaven, and in 260 and 278 it is part of the vocabulary used by Satan and the other devils in lamenting their loss.

Occurrences in *Christ and Satan* of words that mean 'hero' or 'man' without explicit reference to the dryht relationship are sparse. The principal word of this kind, hæleð, cognate with German *Held*, which means 'hero' to this day, occurs six times; beorn, eorl, mecg, and secg once each. The reference of hæleð in five or probably all six of its occurrences, however, is not to heroes as such but to men, and not even specifically to males but inclusively to human beings and even sometimes to their souls, so that the original heroic sense shimmers through very palely if at all. In 194 every man (human being) on earth is exhorted not to offend the Son of God; in 581 Christ at the right hand of his Father bestows help and salvation every day upon human beings on earth; in 270 the devils are to roam through the lands of human beings on earth seeking to damn them by stirring up strife; in 399 Christ descends into hell for the sake of human beings, primarily those souls whom he delivers at the Harrowing, but with implicit reference to the rest of mankind since that time; and in 656 the patriarchs in heaven use the same word in reference to the souls of the blessed around the heavenly throne. Especially in view of this last reference it is probably best to suppose that Satan in 47 is using the word in the same way.[59]

The meaning of eorl in its one occurrence (477) is hardly distinguishable from that of hæleð: the eorlas who could long have dwelt in their homeland Eden except for the Fall are Adam and Eve and their offspring. The remaining three words all appear in disparaging contexts: mecg, used in a laudatory sense in *Guthlac B* 1219, *Andreas* 422, 1708, *Daniel* 264, and in the compound ōretmecg 'warrior' in *Beowulf* 332, 363, is in *Christ and Satan* 334 used of the devils who wail and gnash their teeth; secg, used of Beowulf no less than eight times, five of these (*Beowulf* 947, 1311, 1759, 1812, 2352) with an honorific modifier, is in *Christ and Satan* 497 used of those who plotted Christ's death; beorn, used of Beowulf three times

(*Beowulf* 1024, 2433, 2559) and of Aeschere twice (1299, 2121), is in *Christ and Satan* 509 used of those who pierced Christ (with nails and probably the spear as well) on the cross. Because of these three disparaging *Christ and Satan* passages, besides the implied likelihood that the hæleð in 270 can be successfully tempted to the deadly sin of ire, one might be inclined to think that the poet had a poor opinion of martial virtues (see p 75 above). This would be going rather far, and yet there is a conspicuous contrast, negatively at least, with *The Dream of the Rood*, where Christ himself is 'the Warrior'(se Beorn 42), the 'young Hero' (geong Hæleð 39), 'strong and resolute' (strang ond stīðmōd 40), 'courageous' (mōdig 41), hastening 'with great valour' (elne mycle 34) to mount on the cross. The *Christ and Satan* poet either fails to achieve striking effects like these with his 'hero' words, or else he does not desire them.

He observes a similar parsimony in the use of words directly expressive of combat, to a degree that is conspicuous in a poem whose whole overt subject matter is the archetypal struggle between Christ and Satan. The strongest verbs of this kind refer to the Harrowing of hell: Christ 'broke and overbore' (bræc ond bēgde 381) the gates of hell (the same expression is repeated in 467 with intensifying prefixes, forbræc ond forbēgde 'broke to pieces and crushed down'),[60] and 'after fettering the devils' (hæfde wītes clomma fēondum oðfæsted 443–4) 'shoved' (scēaf 444) them into yet lower depths where they were 'bent down in confinement' (nearwe gebēged 445); but the fettering and shoving down were done spiritually, 'by means of glory' (wuldre 443), and the engines of war that broke and flattened the gates of hell were 'light' (lēoht 388) and 'music of angels' (engla swēg 402) heard by the devils as 'din' (dyne 403) as Christ came to 'scatter like dust' (tōweorpan 392) the devils' torments 'through the power of his glory' (þurh his wuldres cræft 391). The same spiritual means are to be understood when the poet tells us that Christ had 'overcome' Satan (oferfohten 404), 'conquered' death (oferwunnen 461), 'put' Satan 'to flight' (geflēmed 462). In the casting of the rebel angels into hell after their revolt, Satan has been 'abased' (gehēned 190), but 'cannot tell how' (Ne mæg ic þæt gehicgan, hū 179) he has been 'driven out' (aworpen 181) of the shining world of heaven. In fact 'God alone knows how he had banished that guilty company' (God āna wāt hū hē þæt scyldige werud forscrifen hæfde 32–3). In passing moments of insight that lead nowhere, Satan recognizes that it is by his own 'sins' and 'stains' that he has been wounded (synnum forwundod 131, gewundod mid wommum 157): sin and its punishment are inseparable in God's universe. In the Temptation, the conflict to which our poet assigns climactic prominence, Christ's victory over Satan is effected by his word alone: when Christ reveals that he knows Satan (Sātānus seolf 'very Satan' 691), and reveals his own identity (þū wið God wunne 'you have fought with God' 704) and his 'incommensurate might' (þā hēhstan miht 693), Satan is vanquished and cannot but do as Christ commands (710–23).

In all these passages, and in Christ's strikingly passive account of his Crucifixion (508–12), Christ as victor in the struggle with Satan could hardly be more unlike the Christ of *The Dream of the Rood*. To be sure the kernel meaning is the same, Christ's Atonement for the sins of men by laying down his life, but in the imagery that surrounds and flavours the kernel the *Rood* poet makes Christ's Passion seem far more like an action. His Christ is 'the Warrior' (se Beorn 42), the 'young Hero' (geong Hæleð 39), 'strong and resolute' (strang ond stiðmōd 40), 'courageous in the sight of many' (mōdig on manigra gesyhðe 41), whom the cross has seen 'hastening with great valour' (efstan elne mycle 34) to mount upon it, and who 'stripped himself' (ongyrede hine 39) for the combat. Even the statements that he 'rested' (reste 64, 69), 'weary of limb' (limwērigne 63), 'tired after the great struggle' (mēðe æfter ðām miclan gewinne 65), make vivid the uttermost efforts of a mighty warrior. (The only gewinn in *Christ and Satan* is the dōmlēase gewinn 'strife without glory' 231 which the devils must endure.) Christ's passivity when crucified is transferred to the cross (Ealle ic mihte fēondas gefyllan, hwæðre ic fæste stōd 'I could have felled all the enemies, but I stood fast' 37–8; Ne dorste ic hira nænigum sceððan 'I dared not injure any of them' 47), even with erotic overtones (Bifode ic þā mē se Beorn ymbclypte 'I trembled when the Warrior embraced me' 42).[61] By such means the *Rood* poet created an unforgettable picture of Christ mighty in battle, but the *Christ and Satan* poet either does not achieve, or turns his back on, such arresting imagery.

One of the most praiseworthy qualities of a warrior in the heroic tradition was mægen 'strength, might.' It is ascribed to Beowulf no less than thirteen times, including two passages (670 and 1270) in which it is coupled with God's help or God's favour as the ground of his confidence when engaged in combat. The *Christ and Satan* poet, however, never ascribes mægen to a human being. In 518 he uses it of Christ's great might manifested in bursting forth from the tomb, and in 549 of the might of his spirit in mounting to the cross and shedding his blood. In 490 he fastidiously discriminates between the mægen of angels and the gemet of human beings. It is Christ alone who can save fallen mankind from the bondage of prison, not the good qualities of any lesser being such as monna gemet or mægen engla. In precise conformity with the etymological meaning of gemet as connected with metan 'to measure' and of mægen as connected with magan 'to be able,' he contrasts the 'capacity' of human beings, a measured amount of ability allotted to them as if by a system of rationing of a scarce commodity, with the more autonomous 'ability' or 'might' of angels, which is nevertheless not equal to Christ's. In this respect he appears to belong to a tradition that is observable also in *The Advent* (*Crist I*), *The Ascension* (*Crist II*), by Cynewulf, and *The Last Judgment* (*Crist III*). In *The Ascension*, mægen is used of human beings only in l. 748, where they are exhorted to go of mægne in mægen 'from strength to strength' in emulation of Christ; in l. 657 the reference is to heavenly powers above which Christ is raised, and in ll. 603, 787, and 832 to the might of Christ himself. In *The Advent*, mægen is used of human beings only in the idiomatic phrase ealle mægene 'with all one's might' (l. 382), but otherwise (ll. 145, 319) only with reference to Christ or God; the phrase gæstes mægne in the two latter passages refers to Christ's might in the Harrowing of hell and the Incarnation, two of the steps in his course of self-abasement, just as his gāstes mægen in *Christ and Satan* 549 refers to his might in another such step, the Crucifixion. In *The Last Judgment*, mægen is never used of human beings at all, but refers in its three occurrences (ll. 869, 956, 1018) only to might exceeding man's, as that of archangels or of the Last Judgment itself.

In summary we can see in the *Christ and Satan* poet's use of heroic imagery several related tendencies. He could float along the current of poetic tradition, as when he so far assents to the fading of the heroic sense of hæleð as to use it for human beings in general without reference to gender, or for their souls (p 105 above). He could use imagery that retains its heroic colouration but coincides with little or no adjustment with traditional Christian imagery, such as the 'song' and 'music' (sang and swēg) of an earthly dryht-hall or of the heavenly dryht, or phrases like weoroda Waldend or weoroda Drihten meaning 'Lord of hosts,' or for that matter the very word Drihten 'Lord' itself, or the 'dwelling place' words hām, eard, and ēðel (pp 89–90, 84–5, 76, 81–2, 92–104 above). He could mingle heroic with Christian imagery almost inextricably though always with a finally didactic purpose, as in a passage (650–62) about the rejoicing and praise of the heavenly dryht (pp 83–4 above), or with the heroic clearly subordinated to the Christian imagery which it strengthens, as when Christ's '(battle) blood' (swāt 544) is transfigured into 'baths of baptism' (fulwihtes bæðe 545), or when Peter addresses Christ between Harrowing and Ascension as 'adorned with glory' (dōme gewurðad 536) like a conquering hero returning to the royal hall because he has plumbed the depths of the abasement that shall lead to his exaltation, or in a clearly marked homiletic passage (216–23) with admixture of heroic diction (pp 79–81, 84 above). He could freely use heroic words that the poetic tradition had already made compatible with Christian doctrine by reinterpretation, such as dugan 'be strong,' strengðo 'strength,' dēman 'extol,' ēadig 'blessed,' blǣd 'splendour,' and a group of words occurring in 202–8 (pp 75–8 above). He could take a heroic word like mægen 'strength, might,' and apply it not to human beings but exclusively to angels or to Christ, and even to Christ in the Crucifixion (p 107 above). He could debase and repudiate some heroic words by using them to express Satanic self-exaltation, such as æht 'property,' āgan 'possess,' gewald 'dominion,' onwald 'rule,' and perhaps brytta 'dispenser, lord' (pp 16–18, 91 above). He could take words originally expressive of a lord's generosity to his dryht but already adopted (presumably by missionary clerics in the early stages of the Christianization of England) as the appropriate native words to express the central Christian concept of God's grace (ār, gifu, dǣlan, gedǣlan), and use them with his own particular emphasis to express the principle of charity which Christ embodies and which he carries to victory over Satan's covetousness in the cosmic struggle (pp 78–9, 90–1 above), even giving gedǣlan an apparently unique sense of 'bestow by creating' so as to represent the Creation itself as the primal act of Christ's charity. He could take the words aldor 'lord' and þegn 'thane,' central to the dryht relationship, and use them with great subtlety and power to express relations between God the Father and Christ, Christ and the rebel angels, and Satan and the rebel angels (now his fellow devils), in terms of the same cosmic struggle (pp 83, 86–7 above). This list of varieties of use is not exhaustive, nor are the varieties listed mutually exclusive. What we find is not just use of heroic diction as an organic feature of Old English Christian poetry, but a whole repertoire of such uses, a repertoire potentially limitless and potentially different for every poet and every poem.

In the course of our endeavour to place *Christ and Satan* appropriately within the whole body of Old English poetry, we have incidentally acquired an improved basis for an attempt to place it in relation specifically to the other three poems in Manuscript Junius 11. No matter how puzzling the 'Liber II' at the end of the manuscript may be and no matter how much the *Christ and Satan* part of the manuscript may differ physically from the rest, there can be no doubt that whereas *Genesis*, *Exodus*, and *Daniel* are based on the Old Testament, *Christ and Satan* is based on the New Testament and on early Christian tradition, and is an essential complement in that way to the three other poems, as the New Testament is the fulfillment of the Old (Matthew 5: 17). This remains true even if *Christ and Satan* was added to the manuscript with some delay or as an afterthought. *Genesis*, *Exodus*, and *Daniel* are bound together in thematic unity by the characteristically Old Testament concept of 'covenant,' expressed by several words of which the chief is wær. The relevant passages in *Genesis* include but are not limited to those telling of God's rainbow covenant with Noah (1542), God's covenant with Abraham whereby Abraham's descendants are to possess the Promised Land (2204), renewed and strengthened by the circumcision covenant (2309) and God's covenant with Isaac before his conception (2368), and the deeply moving near-sacrifice of Isaac by which Abraham proves that he will be faithful to his covenant with God even if it means killing, at God's command, the very son through whom God has said the covenant is to be fulfilled (2846–2936). In *Exodus* the Egyptian covenant-breakers (covenant-*devourers* 147, 140) are contrasted by implication with the Israelite covenant-keepers, and within the probably interpolated lines 362–446 (see pp 31–3 above), the poet says what the *Genesis* poet never said in so many words, that Abraham kept his covenant with God by his willingness to sacrifice Isaac (422); this links *Genesis* and *Exodus* more closely together. In *Daniel* the Israelites' well-being lasts as long as they keep their father's (Abraham's) covenant (10), and even in the Babylonian captivity the three Hebrew youths are called wærfæst 'covenant-keeping' in the same context in which they are called 'children of Abraham' (193–4).

By a typological interpretation at least as old as St Paul, God's covenant with Abraham and with Israel as a people foreshadows Christ's redemptive sacrifice of his life as Atonement for the sins of mankind. Thus in Paul's account of the institution of the sacrament of Communion at the Last Supper, Christ's words as he took the cup were 'This cup is the new covenant in my blood' (1 Corinthians 11: 25 Revised Standard Version). Paul uses the same word diathēkē that the Septuagint translators had used for the Old Testament covenants; and the idea of Christ's Atonement as a New Covenant foreshadowed by, fulfilling, and perfecting the Old is developed in great detail in the Epistle to the Hebrews, especially chapters 8–10.[62] As for *Christ and Satan*, it nowhere contains the word wær, but it is surely to be supposed that it contains some key word or determinate cluster of words as a counterpart thereto. Indeed it does contain such a word, miht, the 'incommensurate might' of Christ, appearing in significant contexts and related to other thematically important words in ways that clarify not only the relation of *Christ and Satan* to the three Old Testament poems but also the internal structure of *Christ and Satan* itself.

At the beginning Christ's miht (2, 6, 8, 13) is manifested in Creation seen unconventionally as the primal act of charity (19, and compare pp 90–1 above). At the end, in the Temptation, Satan questions Christ's miht (672), Christ enjoins Satan by the highest miht (693) to proclaim no hope but instead the greatest of sorrows to the hell-dwellers, and it is Christ as se Mihtiga 'the Mighty' (721) who makes tangible the victory of charity over cupidity by imposing the hell-measuring penalty on Satan.[63] Near the middle of the poem (399–400), Christ accomplishes in the Harrowing of hell the lowest point of his abasement 'for the sake of the children of men' (hæleða bearnum in the dative case of indirect object), and he does so with miht which will insure that his beneficent intention is effectual – the same miht that he showed in Creation. Then at the highest point of his exaltation (579–82) Christ at the right hand of the Father dispenses daily 'to the children of men' on earth (hæleþa bearnum again in the dative case of indirect object) 'help and salvation' (help ond hælo), implicitly though not explicitly with the same miht as at the Harrowing. This is the large-scale structure of *Christ and Satan*. No matter how imperfect the execution of the poem's details may be, it is a firm and shapely structure, and it is to *Christ and Satan* what wær and its associated words are to the three Old Testament poems.

Here we are, then, with our poem. It is a slashed and battered text, as if the jaws of oblivion from which it was snatched had already begun to mangle it or indeed had all but closed on it. Whoever pried it out and incorporated it, untidily enough, into the Junius Manuscript evidently did so because, though lacking the brilliance of a poem like *The Dream of the Rood*, it treated all the principal stages of the cosmic struggle between charity and cupidity embodied in Christ and Satan, from Creation to Last Judgment, within a structure that fully expressed its theme. That is to say, it must have been someone's choice as the poem which, whatever its shortcomings, most worthily presented the overt Christian message needed to complement the three Old Testament poems. If so, we have reason to respect his judgment.

# Appendix: Comparison of Sleeth's Text and Finnegan's Text

All the quotations in the body of this work, and all their line number references, are from my own text (see the microfiche). For the sake of convenience and accuracy, this appendix shows in detail the agreements and disagreements between my text, indicated by s, and Finnegan's, indicated by F. Because *o* predominates over *a* before nasals in the manuscript of *Christ and Satan*, I expand the invariable symbol 7 to *ond* instead of Finnegan's *and*; I read the prefix of verbs like arīsan 'arise' as *a-* instead of Finnegan's *ā-*; and I capitalize divine names though Finnegan does not. When a line of my text does not differ from the corresponding line of Finnegan's text except in one or more of these three ways, I do not print the line in this appendix.

Because a text like *Christ and Satan* has some value for the history of the language as well as for literature, it has seemed advisable to me to retain manuscript forms that appear likely to be genuine *late* Old English even if they are almost certainly not the poet's forms. Finnegan sometimes emends these, for example giving wuldres for ms wulres in l. 42. When my text differs from Finnegan's in this way, I print the line in this appendix, but without stating my reason for doing so.

No particular notice is taken of differences in punctuation unless they substantially affect the sense.

s 1–5 = F 1–5
s 6 as against F 6:
wæter ond wolcen     ðurh his wundra miht.
s 7–8 = F 7–8
s 9 as against F 9:

116 Appendix

Hē selfa mæg   sǣ geondwlītan
   As a Class 1 Strong verb, geondwlītan has a long root vowel.
S 10–18 = F 10–18
S 19 as against F 19:
Drēamas hē gedēlde,   duguðe ond geþēode,
   No emendation. The attestation elsewhere of a familiar collocation
duguð ond geoguð is not an argument for introducing it here, since a scribe is
more likely to substitute the familiar for the unfamiliar than the other way
round. A possible translation of the passage is suggested on pp 90–1 above.
S 20–30 = F 20–30
S 31 as against F 31:
niðær undær nessas   in ðone neowlan grund,
S 32 = F 32
S 33 as against F 33:
hū hē þæt scyldige werud   forscrifen hæfde.
S 34 = F 34
S 35 as against F 35:
wriceð wordcwedas   weregan reorde,
   For the short vowel of weregan, see p 39 above.
S 36–41 = F 36–41
S 42 as against F 42:
wēan ond wergu,   nalles wulres blǣd
   For the short vowel of wergu, see reference to l. 35 above.
S 43–5 = F 43–5
S 46 as against F 46:
þǣr nū ymb ðone Ǣcan   æðele stondað
S 47 = F 47
S 48–9 as against F 48–9:
wordun ond wercum,   ond ic in wīte sceal
bīdan in bendum,   ond mē bættran hām
S 50 = F 50
S 51–2 as against F 51–2:
Ða him ondsweradan   atole gāstas,
swarte ond synfulle,   sūsle begrorene:
   The ms has 7sweradan. The ms form begrorenne (accusative singular
masculine), on the other hand, is better emended to begrorene (nominative
plural masculine).
S 53–71 = F 53–71
S 72 as against F 72:
scinnan forscepene,   sceaðan hwearfdon,

s 73–9 = F 73–9
s 80 as against F 80:
ðonne hē in wītum    word in drāf:
s 81 = F 81
s 82 as against F 82:
Dryhtne dēore;    hefde mē drēam mid Gode,
s 83–4 = F 83–4
s 85 as against F 85:
þæt ic wolde tōwerpan    wulres Lēoman,
s 86–8 = F 86–8
s 89–90 as against F 89:
Wēne þæt tācen sutol    ond wærgðu...
þā ic of...    ...aseald wes,

This passage is certainly corrupt. Wülker 1894 assumes gaps after wærgðu and after of without attempting to fill them, and this probably runs less risk of distorting the original even more than the scribe has distorted it than any other treatment of the passage that has been proposed.
s 91 = F 90
s 92 as against F 91:
Nū ic ēow hebbe tō hæftum    hām gefærde

I take hebbe ... gefærde to mean 'have led.' The verb fēran is mostly intransitive, with meanings like 'go, journey,' but transitive use with a meaning 'lead' or 'bring' is attested in the Rushworth Gloss to Mark 1: 32. Indeed this is the etymologically original meaning, since it is the causative corresponding to faran 'go, come,' as German führen is the causative of fahren. Compare the use of fēran in s 110 (F 109).
s 93–107 = F 92–106
s 108 as against F 107:
ær ic mōste in ðeossum atolan    æðele gebīdan

I accept Ettmüller's emendation (1850) of ms þær to ær, in agreement with all subsequent editors except Clubb and Finnegan. By this reading ær introduces a subordinate clause, the preceding line being its main clause. Clubb's rendering of þær as 'whereas' is not well supported, and the time relation between s 107 and s 108–10a (F 106 and F 107–9a) makes ær thoroughly appropriate and will hardly accommodate þær in any sense.
s 109–16 = F 108–15
s 117–19 as against F 116–18:
æðel tō æhte,    swā hē ær dyde,
ēcne onwald;    āh him alles gewald,
wulres ond wīta,    Waldendes Sunu.

s 120–25 = F 119–24
s 126 as against F 125:
Swā se werega gāst   wordum sǣde
    See reference to l. 35 above.
s 127–32 = F 126–31
s 133 as against F 132:
hwīlum ic gehēre   helle scealcas,
    Since there is a space between helle and scealcas in the ms, and since the
genitive helle makes good sense here, there is no reason to read this
combination as a compound hellescealcas.
s 134–46 = F 133–45
s 147 as against F 146:
būtan þām ānum   þe hē tō āgan nyle;
    Without emendation it is possible to take āgan, in agreement with Grein
(*Sprachschatz*), as dative of an otherwise unrecorded weak feminine noun
āge 'property, possession,' corresponding in form and meaning to Old
Norse eiga.
s 148–51 = F 147–50
s 152–3 as against F 151–2:
wlite ond weorðmynt,   ful oft wuldres swēg
brōhton tō bearme,   bearn Hǣlendes,
    The word bearn unemended can be taken as nominative plural, and the
expression bearn Hǣlendes as referring to the angels. By this reading the
phrase bringan tō bearme 'offer' has no dative object, but neither does it
have one in s 357 (F 356).
s 154–9 = F 153–8
s 160 as against F 159:
Þā gȳt feola cwīðde   firna herede,
    See p 39 above.
s 161–71 = F 160–70
s 172–3 as against F 171–2:
þǣre byrhtestan   bēman stefne!
Ðæs ic wolde of selde   Sunu Meotodes,
    By my reading s 173–6 (F 172–5) are one sentence.
s 174 = F 173
s 175 as against F 174:
wuldres ond wynne,   mē þǣr wyrse gelamp
s 176 = F 175.
s 177 as against F 176:
Nū ic eom asceāden   fram þǣre scīran driht,

s 178–83 = F 177–82
s 184 as against F 183:
Meotode cwēman.   Ic þæt morðor sceal

Kock's emendation (1918) of the impossible dative morðre of the ms to accusative morðor, parallel in structure to the three accusative nouns in the next line, seems most likely to be a restoration of the original reading. The meaning of morðor here is 'torment,' as also in s 321 (F 320).
s 185–8 = F 184–7
s 189 as against F 188:
settan sorhgceari,   sīðas wīde.'

Finnegan does not accept Clubb's view that the final *g* of ms sorhgcearig was added by the Corrector.
s 190–1 = F 189–90
s 192 as against F 191:
gīfre ond grǣdige,   þā hig God bedrāf
s 193–8 = F 192–7
s 199–200 as against F 198–9:
upne ēcne gefēan,   engla Waldend.
Hē þæt gecȳdde,   þæt hē cræft hæfde,

The ms form upne can be accepted as the accusative singular masculine of an adjective up(p), of which the form uppe occurring in attributive position before godu in *The Paris Psalter* 81.6.1 seems to be a nominative plural example. Emendation of ms mægencræft to cræft seems advisable because the second constituent of a noun compound is subordinate to the first and usually does not bear the sole alliteration. Probably mægen was introduced as a gloss at some stage of ms transmission.
s 201–12 = F 200–11
s 213 as against F 212:
is wlitig ond wynsum,   wæstmas scīnað
s 214–22 = F 213–21
s 223–5 as against F 222–4:
geond ealra worulda woruld   mid Wuldorcyning.
    Ðā gēt ic furðor gefregen   fēonda ...
... ondetan;   wæs him eall ful strang

The preposition mid is found with the accusative in at least three other passages in this poem, and the meter is better without the final *-e* (probably added by the Corrector) of ms wuldorcyninge. Assumption of a short gap between fēonda and ondetan makes emendation unnecessary, but otherwise something must be emended, since the ic gefrægn formula is regularly followed by an infinitive accompanied by either an accusative subject or an accusative object or both, and neither accusative is present in the ms as it stands. In any case the sense is not hard to follow.

s 226 = F 225

s 227–8 as against F 226–7:

for oferhigdum    ān forlæten;
cwǣdon eft hraðe    ōðre worde:

The ms has a space between an and forlæten.

s 229–31 = F 228–30

s 232 as against F 231:

Hwæt, wē wuldres wlite    wunian mōston,

s 233–4 = F 232–3

s 235–43 as against F 234–42:

þūsendmǣlum.    Ðā wē þǣr wǣron,
wunodon on wynnum,    gehērdon wuldres swēg,
bēman stefne,    byrhtword arās
engla Ordfruma,    ond tō þǣm Æþelan
hnigan him sanctas.    Sigetorht arās
ēce Drihten,    ofer ūs gestōd
ond gebletsode    bilewitne hēap
dōgra gehwilcne,    ond his se dēora Sunu,
gāsta Scyppend.    God seolfa wæs

The proposal of Finnegan 1974b and 1977 to emend his in s 242 (F 241) to þes, and to supply mentally wæs before se, is not convincing. To call Christ 'Son' after all implies the Father, and since we cannot eliminate explicit reference to the Father in this particular passage except by rejecting what the manuscript says, we should refrain from doing so for fear of question-begging. The Christocentricity of the poem is still evident enough in any case. Besides, the poet implies by repeating arās that two persons rose up. If he had meant only one person, he could have said something like sigetorht Scyppend or sigetorht Ðēoden in s 239b (F 238b).

By my reading s 235b–239a (F 234b–238a) are a single sentence, of which ll. 237b–239a refer to Christ, and s 239b–243a (F 238b–242a) are another sentence, of which ll. 239b–242a refer to the Father, and 242b–243a to Christ. s 235b–237a (F 234b–236a) are a subordinate clause, hardly acceptable as a complete sentence, because in comparable passages in Old English poetry where two or more verbs occur with neither change nor repetition of subject they are usually best understood as being in parallel construction, not one in a subordinate clause and the other(s) in a main clause. Three examples occur within the first fifty lines of *Beowulf:* Oft

Scyld Scēfing ... monegum mǣgþum meodosetla oftēah, egsode eorl
(variously emended to eorlas or Eorle) 4–6; hē þæs frōfre gebād, wēox
under wolcnum, weorðmyndum þāh 7–8; hīe him asetton segen gyldenne
hēah ofer hēafod, lēton holm beran, gēafon on gārsecg 47–9. – Christ is the
byrhtword ... engla Ordfruma in s 237b–238a (F 236b–237a), just as the
Father is sigetorht ... ēce Drihten in s 239b–240a (F 238b–239a); these two
constructions, each subject of the same verb arās, may be supposed to
show as much parallelism as possible, and therefore byrhtword may be
taken as a compound word rather than two words, and if sigetorht is taken
as an adjective so may byrhtword be. However, Hill 1970 (who reads byrht
Word) is almost certainly right in seeing this epithet as an allusion to the
Word or Logos of John 1: 1–14; and Finnegan 1974b and 1977 (reading
byrhtword, which he calls a noun) adds confirmation and expressiveness to
Hill's reading by pointing out that John 1: 1–14 both word and light are
manifestations of Christ.

s 235b–243a (F 234b–242a) would then translate as follows: 'When we
were there, (when we) lived in joy (and) heard the music of glory, the voice
of the trumpet, the one whose word is light arose, the Creator (or Chief) of
angels, and to that Noble One the saints knelt. The one resplendent in
victory arose, the eternal Lord, stood over us and blessed the pure-hearted
host every day, and his dear Son (did likewise), the Creator of spirits.' The
Father and Son alike rise up, the Son first, and they stand over the kneeling
host of their obedient followers, including those who are soon to be
disobedient, and bless them every day. This is no less 'a most affecting
recollection of an almost liturgical ceremony in heaven' (Finnegan 1977:
100) than it is by Finnegan's reading.
s 244–9 = F 243–8
s 250 as against F 249:
gif gē willað mīre   mihte gelēfan.
s 251–72 = F 250–71
s 273–7 as against F 272–6:
Ic hēr geþolian sceal   þinga æghwylces –
bitres nīðæs   beala gnornian,
sīc ond sorhful –   þæs ic seolfa wēold,
þonne ic on heofonum   hām staðelode.
Hwæðer ūs se Ēca   æfre wille
The syntax proposed by Krapp 1931 and provisionally accepted by
Finnegan 1977 is forced and hardly yields intelligible sense. It is better,
following a suggestion of Clubb 1925, to take s 274–275a (F 273–274a) as

quasi-parenthetical. By this reading sceal goes with both geþolian and gnornian; beala is the accusative object of the otherwise intransitive gnornian, and bitres nīðæs a genitive dependent on beala; þinga æghwylces is the genitive object of geþolian in the sense 'forfeit, be deprived of' (amply attested for the simplex þolian) and the antecedent of the relative þæs. A new (interrogative) sentence begins with s 277 (F 276). s 273–5 (F 272–4) can then be translated thus: 'I must here forfeit each thing – (must), sick at heart and sorrowful, lament the harm of (= inflicted by) cruel enmity – which I myself possessed.' A like difficult syntactic pattern, with the beginning of a sentence being grammatically continued in different directions in a quasi-parenthetical expression and in the sentence segment immediately following it, occurs elsewhere in Old English verse, for example *Beowulf* 3054b–3056 nefne God sylfa, sigora Sōðcyning, sealde þām ðe hē wolde – hē is manna gehyld – hord openian 'unless God himself, the true King of victories, granted it to whomsoever he would – he is the protector of men – to open the hoard,' where God is antecedent of hē in the quasiparenthetical clause, and hord openian is functionally the direct object of sealde. Compare *Beowulf* 1661–4, 2864–72.

In his treatment of the key words of this passage in his Glossary, Finnegan 1977 seems to be following the syntax here indicated, though in his note (p 103) and his punctuation of the text he follows Krapp 1931.

s 278–319 = F 277–318

s 320–3 as against F 319–22:

wīde geond windsele   wēa cwānedon,

mān ond morður.   Wæs menego þǣr

swylce onæled;   wæs þæt eall full strong.

Ðonne wæs heora aldor,   þe ðǣr ǣrest cōm

The scribe wrote winsele, but the Corrector changed it to windsele, which is not attested anywhere outside of *Christ and Satan*. Since corruption of a text is more likely to change the unfamiliar to the familiar than the other way round, it is best to assume that in this instance the Corrector was right. If we do not make this assumption here, we risk committing verbicide! The close resemblance of windsele to the familiar wīnsele suggests that bitterly ironical word play was intended.

s 321b (F 320b) reads in the ms wæs ðær menego þær. Perhaps the simplest solution of the textual problem is to assume that the þær after menego was in the original poem but that the ðær before menego was not, having been introduced only later by a scribe's erroneous anticipation of the þær after menego. By this reading as by Finnegan's, menego is the subject of the sentence. It does not have to be accompanied by a form of the demonstrative se; in both its occurrences in *Beowulf* (ll. 41, 2143) it appears with no demonstrative. To be sure, in both instances the reference is to a multitude of inanimate objects; but for an example of a noun designating a group of persons and appearing without a demonstrative, see *Beowulf* 2254 duguð ellor sceōc.

Since s 322b (F 321b) appears to be a 'recapitulating or explanatory' remark of the kind that Klaeber (*Beowulf*, 3rd edition, 1936, p lxi) finds to be frequent in *Beowulf*, for example þæt wæs geōmuru ides (1075), and since in s 323a (F 322a) wæs immediately follows þonne and precedes its subject, it seems best to take þonne as introducing a new sentence rather than a subordinate clause attached to the preceding lines. Finnegan appears to agree with this reading by glossing þonne as the adverb meaning 'then' rather than the conjunction meaning 'when,' but he does not punctuate accordingly.

s 324–30 = F 323–9

s 331–2 as against F 330–1:

gōda lēase    nymþe gryndes.

Wunian mōten    þone werigan sele

This reading makes sense, and unusual but probably acceptable meter, with a minimum of tampering with the manuscript. The only emendation is the elimination of the symbol 7 for 'and' which occurs in the ms before þone, since the ah before nymþe is in the ms already underlined for cancellation.

For werigan, see reference to l. 35 above.

s 333–39 = F 332–8

s 340–42 as against F 339–41:

hlūde ond geōmre.    Godes andsacan

hweorfan geond helle    hāte onǣled

ufan ond ūtan    (him wæs ǣghwǣr wā),

s 343–51 = F 342–50.

s 352 as against F 351:

hū sunnu þǣr    scīneð ymbūtan

By a rather serious oversight, Finnegan represents the ms as having scir between hu and sunnu, which is not the case. Instead, insertion of scīr is an emendation proposed by Grein 1857a and has little to recommend it. The ms reading sunnu looks for all the world like the product of fusion or confusion in someone's mind, the poet's or a scribe's, between sunne 'sun' and sunu 'son.' If we accept sunnu as an erratic spelling of sunne, and if we accept this line as one of the lines in this poem that lack alliteration, the line makes excellent sense without emendation: 'how the sun [?with a hint at a second meaning 'the Son'] shines thereabout,' this 'sun' being explained three lines farther on by the half-line (emended in agreement with Clubb 1925 and Finnegan) þæt is se seolfa God 'that is God himself.' The imagery approximates that of Revelation 21: 23: *Et civitas non eget sole neque luna, ut luceant in ea: nam claritas Dei illuminavit eam, et lucerna ejus est Agnus* 'And the city had no need of the sun, neither of the moon, to shine in it: for the glory of God did lighten it, and the Lamb is the light thereof' (so Clubb 1925).

s 353–7 = F 352–6

s 358 as against F 357:

wyrta wynsume;   þæt synd word Godes.

s 359–67 = F 358–66

s 368–9 as against F 367–8:

on geārdagum   in Godes rīce.

Ðā hē in wuldre   wrōht onstalde,

s 370 = F 369

s 371 as against F 370:

Sātānus   swearte geþōhte

s 372–3 = F 371–2

s 374 as against F 373:

yfeles ordfruma.   Him þæt eft gehrēaw,

 The ms has yfeles.

s 375 = F 374

s 376 as against F 375:

ond his hīred mid hine,   in hīnðo geglīdan,

Clubb's reconstruction of the process of corruption in the second half-line is the most convincing, and entails acceptance of the vowel ī rather than ȳ or ē in hīnðo. The spelling ī for the *i*-umlaut of *ēa* is rather rare, but this text contains at least one example of it in līge, s 325 (F 324).

s 377–84 = F 376–83.

s 385–6 as against F 384–5:

wīde geond windsele   wordum mǣndon:

'Ðis is stronglic,   nū þes storm becōm,

 For windsele, see reference to s 320 (F 319) above.

 In s 386 (F 385), Finnegan's punctuation does not correspond to his reading (and mine) of nū as a subordinating conjunction meaning 'now that.'

s 387–92 = F 386–91

s 393–4 as against F 392–3:

dyne for Drihtne,    sceal þes drēorga hēap
ungeāra nū    atol þrōwian.

Finnegan glosses the nū in s 392 (F 391) as a subordinating conjunction meaning 'now that,' and so do I; but by this reading Drihtne in s 393 (F 392) should be followed by a comma and not a semicolon.

s 395–421 = F 394–420
s 422 as against F 421:
for þān hīrede    þe ðū hider lǣddest,
   Finnegan's hīerde is a misprint.
s 423–8 = F 422–7
s 429 as against F 428:
Segde ūs tō sōðe    þætte seolfa God

Eve's words (s 409–35 and 438–41, F 408–34 and 437–40) are addressed to Christ, and this consideration may have caused the ms segdest to be introduced erroneously at some stage of the transmission of the text in place of segde, which fits in this narrative segment (s 425–35, F 424–34) of her speech. By this reading the unexpressed subject of segde is the þegen Hǣlendes of s 425 (F 424). That Eve should interrupt the narrative to represent herself as addressing two lines to the þegen Hǣlendes (probably Judas), as Clubb 1925 and Finnegan maintain, is too incongruous to accept.

s 430–33 = F 429–32
s 434 as against F 433:
fægen in firnum    þæt Frēodrihten
s 435–7 = F 434–6
s 438 as against F 437:
'Hwæt, þū fram mīre dohtor,    Drihten, onwōce
s 439–58 = F 438–57
s 459–60 as against F 458–9:
Hōfon hine mid handum    hālige wītigan
ūp tō ēðle,    Abrahames cynn.

In s 459 (F 458) the ms has him between mid and handum. But mid him is so familiar a combination, besides having occurred only two lines earlier, that a careless scribe could easily add the him erroneously when his original had mid followed by a word with initial h. Omission of him, proposed by Ettmüller 1850 and accepted by Holthausen 1894b, Graz 1895, and Wieners 1913, at once solves all problems of sense, grammar, scansion, and alliteration in these two lines. Besides, ūp tō ēðle occurs as a formula filling a half-line in s 402a and 553a (F 401a and 552a), and resembles the formulas ūp tō englum in s 288 and 623 (F 287 and 623) and ūp tō earde in s 457 and 505 (F 456 and 504).

s 461–2 = F 460–61
s 463 as against F 462:
wītegan sǣdon    þæt hē swā wolde.
s 464–74 = F 463–73
s 475 as against F 474:
on middangeard    menio onwōcon;

If the original had þonon on, it is easy to see how a scribe could inadvertently reduce the three consecutive occurrences of the letter sequence *on* to two. Accordingly Ettmüller 1850 supplied on, and this emendation has been accepted by Grein 1857a, Klaeber 1913a, Clubb 1925, and Krapp 1931. The construction onwæcnan plus preposition plus accusative middangeard is paralleled above in s 438–9 (F 437–8) onwōce in middangeard.

s 476–7 = F 475–6
s 478–9 as against F 477–8:
       þæt hē afyrde eft
fēond in firenum.    Fāh is æghwǣr.

My reading is identical with Finnegan's except that he takes this triplet of half-lines to consist of a matched pair of half-lines followed by a single half-line, whereas I prefer to take it to consist of a single half-line followed by a matched pair of half-lines, to avoid assigning to the half-line which has two occurrences of the alliterating *f* a position as a second half-line. In any case the *f* alliteration continues throughout the triplet.

s 480–87 = F 479–86
s 488–9 as against F 487–8:
Ðā mē gehrēaw    þæt mīn handgeweorc
carcernes    clom ðrōwade.
s 490–98 = F 489–97
s 499 as against F 498:
rīces boran,    refnan mihten.

The ms boran is tentatively accepted, with a meaning like 'rulers,' even though bora is not known elsewhere except as the second constituent of compound nouns.

The ms hrefnan appears to be a reverse spelling by a scribe who was shaky about his initial *h*'s. This ms has forms without initial *h* where the *h* is both justified by etymology and needed for alliteration, in the following places: hnīgan for ms nigan s 207 (F 206), hinsīðgryre for ms in sið gryre s 455 (F 454), gehrēaw for ms gereaw s 488 (F 487), and hrēam for ms ream s 715 (F 715).

s 500–504 = F 499–503
s 505 as against F 504:

ūp tō earde,    þæt hēo āgan
s 506–9 = F 505–8
s 510–11 as against F 509–10:
gārum on galgum.    Hēow se giunga þǣr,
ond ic eft ūp becōm    ēce drēamas
s 512–20 = F 511–19
s 521–2 as against F 520–1:
englas eallbeorhte    ondleofan gingran,
ond hūru secgan hēt    Sīmon Petre

I expand ms 7leofan to ondleofan, consistently with my expansion of 7 to ond when it stands for the conjunction meaning 'and.'

Petre may be supposed to have a short *e* where the Greek has epsilon.
s 523–6 = F 522–5
s 527 as against F 526:
hāligne Godes Sunu,

The combination of this half-line and the preceding line makes sense as a triplet, and the three half-lines are bound together by *g*-alliteration. Neither emendation nor assumption of a gap is necessary. The gāstes blēd 'spiritual splendour' which the disciples had may be viewed as either inspired by the hāligne Godes Sunu 'holy Son of God' or as a variational reference to the hāligne Godes Sunu himself; by either interpretation both phrases are co-ordinate objects of hæfdon. (See p 79 above.) The asyndeton is demanding, especially by the former interpretation, but not more so than *Beowulf* 719 heardran hǣle, healðegnas fand '[Grendel never before] met harder luck, (stronger) hall-thanes.'
s 528–34 = F 527–33
s 535 as against F 534:
Ðā sōna sprǣc    Sīmon Petrus:

See reference to s 522 (F 521) above.
s 536–40 = F 535–9
s 541–2 as against F 540–1:
Sume hīe ne mihton    mōd' oncnāwan
þæt wæs se Dēora    (Didimus wæs hāten)

Sume hīe is so to speak an apposition of part to whole, and means 'some of them.' The same construction in the form hīe sume is found in the *Parker Chronicle* entry for 867, and in the form sume hī three times in *The Death of Alfred* (1036) 8–9.

Elision of the final *e* of instrumental dative mōde before a following initial vowel is assumed.

It is doubtful whether we have reason to attribute the logical and syntactical incoherence of these lines to anyone but the poet. He seems to have based the beginning of his sentence on the statement in Matthew 28: 17 that 'some doubted' (*quidam ... dubitaverunt*) and shifted abruptly to the account in John 20: 24–9, in which only one of the disciples, Thomas called Didymus, is identified as a doubter. The shift occurs in s 542b (F 541b), which by this reading must be taken as a parenthetical remark. In this parenthetical remark itself, and in the remainder of the sentence, the poet apparently forgets that he has started the sentence in the plural, and continues his sentence in a form that refers to Thomas alone. (So Clubb 1925, p 118.) The statement of Gregory the Great that Thomas's doubt was divinely ordained in order to dispel our doubts of the Resurrection does not give us sufficient reason to suppose that the poet would single out Thomas from among the disciples as pre-eminently 'the dear one.' On the other hand we know that he has called Christ se dēora Sunu 'the dear Son' in s 242 (F 241). s 542a (F 541a) is to be understood as an elliptical equivalent of þæt þæt wæs se Dēora or þæt hit wæs se Dēora 'that that (*or* it) was the Dear One,' that is, Christ.

s 543–52 = F 542–51

s 553 as against F 552:

ūp tō ēðle,    þær wē āgan

   See reference to s 505 (F 504) above.

s 554 = F 553.

s 555 as against F 554–5:

ond wē in wynnum wunian mōton.    Ūs is wuldres lēoht

   The parallelism between s 504–7 and s 552–5 (F 503–6 and F 551–5) is suggestive. In s 555a (F 554 entire), as in s 507a (F 506a), the poet could have had a normal first half-line wuniað in wynnum, alliterating with a second half-line containing the word wuldres, but on the evidence of our text he has not done so. His purpose in expanding the wording so as to repeat wē seems to be to drive home the point that not only the souls freed at the Harrowing of hell, but we too, may dwell in joy. The best way to express this is perhaps to follow the example of Bouterwek 1848, Grein 1857a, Wülker 1894, and Clubb 1925 in taking ond wē in wynnum wunian mōton as a single extended half-line, and Ūs is wuldres lēoht as the normal second half-line that goes with it.

s 556–63 = F 556–63

s 564–6 as against F 564–5:

hālig of heofonum.    Mid wæs hond Godes,
onfēng Frēodrihten,    ond hine forð lædde

s 566 = F 566.

s 567 as against F 567:

Him ymb flugon    engla þrēatas

Both the alliteration and an accent mark in the ms indicate that ýmb is stressed. Therefore it must be a postposed preposition rather than a verbal prefix. This is the justification for accepting Grein 1857a's reading of the ms, which has a slight space between ýmb and flugon, as ýmb flugon, which was also accepted by Wülker 1894.

s 568 = F 568.

s 569–70 as against F 569–70:
þā gȳt nergende Crīst ...
þæt hē þæs ymb tēne niht   twelf apostolas

s 571–86 = F 571–86

s 587–8 as against F 587–8:
his seolfes seld   sweglbetalden.
Leaðað ūs þider tō lēohte   þurh his læcedōm,

The ms has swegl betalden, altered to swegl behealden, probably by the Corrector. Finnegan, in agreement with Clubb 1925 and Krapp 1931, emends betalden to betolden, past participle of a Class III Strong verb beteldan 'surround, cover'; but the vowel need not be changed, since the *a* of betalden could be an instance of Anglian unrounding (see p 36 above and c s156). Also in agreement with Clubb and Krapp, Finnegan retains the word division of the ms, interpreting swegl as an uninflected instrumental; but perhaps it is better to emend to sweglbetalden, despite the infrequency of adjective compounds with a past participle as the final constituent.

s 589–94 = F 589–94

s 595 as against F 595:
Crīste cwēmæn.   þær is cūðre līf

s 596–607 = F 596–607

s 608 as against F 608:
Wile þonne gesceādan   wlitige ond unclæne

The ms gesceawian (for gescēawian) is metrically dubious, because when the second stressed syllable of a Type A half-line is long it is rarely if ever followed by more than one unstressed syllable. It seems best to emend to gesceādan, following Thorpe 1832, Bouterwek 1848, Graz 1895, and Krapp 1931. This also improves the sense by bringing it closer to that of Matthew 25: 32.

s 609–23 = F 609–23

s 624 as against F 624:
ah him bið reordende

s 625–7 = F 625–7

s 628 as against F 628:
Sōna æfter þǣm wordum   werige gāstas,
   See reference to l. 35 above.

s 629–37 = F 629–37

s 638 as against F 638:

swarte sūslbonan,  ... stǣleð

In agreement with Clubb 1925, Finnegan inserts after stǣleð a word fēondas which is not in the ms; but this does not yield acceptable alliteration, since *st* alliterates only with another *st* in this poem, and in Old English verse generally. On the other hand, insertion before stǣleð of a word beginning with *s*, such as Sātān (Holthausen 1894b) or synna (Cosijn 1896), would yield an acceptable line with an alliterative pattern like that of *Beowulf* 411: secgað sǣlīðend þæt þæs sele stande. Perhaps sāre, which apparently no one has suggested, might be even better. If the metrical gap is left unfilled, or filled by a word like synna or sāre, we should take stǣleð as plural; its subject is then hīe (l. 637), with its appositional variant swarte sūslbonan (l. 638).

s 639–42 = F 639–42

s 643 as against F 643:

þæt wē Hǣlende  hēran onginnen,

With this punctuation, gemunan in l. 644 is probably to be taken as an infinitive in parallel construction with geþencan in l. 642.

s 644–5 = F 644–5

s 646 as against F 646:

selfe mid swegle,  sunu Hǣlendes!

The word torht, which in the ms stands before sunu, has never been accounted for by any editor in a way that does not leave some problem of grammar or sense unsolved. It is probably best to regard it as an erroneous scribal insertion and omit it, as Clubb 1925 and Krapp 1931 have done, following the example of C.W.M. Grein, *Sprachschatz der angelsächsischen Dichter* 2. 504 (Cassel & Göttingen 1864), at the entry svegl. By this reading sunu is nominative plural, in apposition with ēadige in l. 645, and refers to the souls of the blessed in heaven.

s 647–59 = F 647–59

s 660–1 as against F 660–1:

þegnas ymb Þēoden.  Þǣr is þrym micel,

sang æt selde;  is sylf Cyning,

s 662–6 = F 662–6

s 667 as against F 667:

Þā gewearð þone weregan,  þe ǣr aworpen wæs

See reference to l. 35 above.

s 668–75 = F 668–75

s 676 as against F 676:

'...                              ...

ac geseted hafast,    sigores Āgend,

There must be something missing before the adversative ac, but it is not at all certain that ll. 676–8 are misplaced. On the reasonable assumption that what is missing before ac may have included Satan's second temptation of Christ, as in Matthew 4: 5–6, and the first part of Christ's answer, it is not hard to imagine that answer's being couched in such terms that ll. 676–8 would be a fitting close for it. For instance Christ, in rejecting Satan's suggestion that he test God's providence by throwing himself down from the pinnacle of the temple, may have addressed to God the Father a prayer of thanksgiving for his true providence in offering to men not preservation of life in this temporal world but salvation throughout eternity. On this hypothesis no gap need be assumed after l. 678. In fact ll. 678–9 are probably best taken as a triplet with *h*-alliteration.

s 677 = F 677

s 678–9 as against F 678–9:

on heofenrīce    hālige drēamas.'

   Đā hē mid hondum genōm

 See note on s 676.

s 680–98 = F 680–98

s 699 as against F 699:

helhēoðo drēorig,    ond mid hondum amet.

If the second constituent of helhēoðo is etymologically connected with Greek kytos 'hollow, jar, hold of a ship,' as suggested by Dietrich 1856, the *eo* of ms heoðo would necessarily be the long diphthong ēo, which is the Old English representative of the Indo-European normal ablaut grade *eu*, as the *y* of kytos is the Greek representative of the Indo-European reduced ablaut grade *u*. With its final *-o* taken as a variant of *-u*, hēoðo might be a feminine of the Germanic ō-declension like lufu 'love,' a neuter plural of the Germanic *a*-declension like hofu, plural of hof 'dwelling,' or a noun of any gender of the Germanic *u*-declension like sunu 'son' or duru 'door.' In all these declensional classes, however, the final *-u* or *-o* is regularly lost after a long syllable, so that we would expect *hēoð rather than hēoðo. Loss of the final *-u* of *u*-declension nominative singulars after long vowels in Old English is believed by some authorities (including Eduard Sievers, *An Old English grammar*, 2nd ed., translated and edited by Albert S. Cook, Boston 1895, s273 n 4) to have occurred late enough for instances of this *-u* to survive in early texts such as the Epinal and Erfurt Glosses and the Franks Casket (but see C s346, who denies this). Thus it seems perhaps best to consider -hēoðo as a *u*-declension noun, and if it is, numerical probabilities favor the supposition that it was masculine. If the retention of the final vowel seems to point to an earlier date than we would assign to *Christ and Satan* on any other ground, we can still conjecture that hēoðo, as an archaic word confined to poetry, was not subject to the same changes as other words of its declensional class.

s 700–9 = F 700–9

s 710 as against F 710:

Đā þām werga wearð   wrece getenge.

   See reference to l. 35 above, and pp 40–1 and 43 above.

s 711–19 = F 711–19

s 720 as against F 720:

tō helle duru   hund þūsenda

   See reference to s 133 (F 132) above. The space between helle and duru is minimal, but the same is true of adjacent words elsewhere on this page, such as he and licgan in l. 714.

s 721–2 = F 721–2

s 723 as against F 723:

Đā hē gemunde   þā hē on grunde stōd.

   Without emending, it is possible to take ðā as the accusative plural of the demonstrative pronoun and as the object of gemunde. Its antecedent is then the whole of ll. 719–22. Line 723 would then mean 'He was mindful of these things, when he stood on the bottom.'

s 724–6 = F 724–6

   It may be noted that ll, 712, 717, 723, and 726 have regular scansion and no alliteration. If this was a liberty the poet occasionally permitted himself, then he may have purposely increased the frequency of it in this closing section, using cacophony for rhetorical effect. See p 26 above.

s 727 as against F 727–8:

Wordum in wītum ongunnon   þā werigan gāstas reordian ond cweðan:

   See reference to l. 35 above.

s 728 = F 729.

   The scribe's indication of the end of the work is approximately as follows:

FINIT LIBER.II'AMEN.

# Abbreviations

ab. = about
acc. = accusative
Angl. = Anglian
*Angl. = Anglia*
*Arch. = Archaeologia*
*ASNS = Archiv für das Studium der neueren Sprachen*
ᴀᴠ = Authorized Version
*Beibl. = Beiblatt*
*Beitr. = Beiträge zur Geschichte der deutschen Sprache und Literatur*
ᴄ = A. Campbell, *Old English Grammar* (Oxford 1959)
*C & S = Christ and Satan*
Corr. = Corrector
dat. = dative
e = early
*ELN = English Language Notes*
*ES = Englische Studien*
*f* = folio
gen. = genitive
*Germ. = Germania. Vierteljahrsschrift für deutsche Altertumskunde*
Grimm = Conrad Grimm, *Glossar zum Vespasian-Psalter und den Hymnen* (Heidelberg 1906)
*IF = Indogermanische Forschungen*
indic. = indicative
*Ist. = Istituto Orientale di Napoli, Annali, Sezione Germanica*
*JEGP = Journal of English and Germanic Philology*
Kt. = Kentish
l = late
*LUÅ. = Lunds Universitets Årsskrift*

m., masc. = masculine
ME = Middle English
Merc. = Mercian
*MLN = Modern Language Notes*
n. = neuter, note
*Neo. = Neophilologus*
Nhb. = Northumbrian
*NM = Neuphilologische Mitteilungen*
nom. = nominative
*NS = Die neueren Sprachen*
OE = Old English
par. = paragraph
part. = participle
pers. = person
PG = Proto-Germanic
*PG* = J.P. Migne, *Patrologia Graeca*
*PL* = J.P. Migne, *Patrologia Latina*
*PMLA = Publications of the Modern Language Association of America*
*PQ = Philological Quarterly*
pres. = present
*Proc. Brit. Ac. = Proceedings of the British Academy*
*RES = Review of English Studies*
Ru.[1] = The Rushworth Gloss to the Gospel of Matthew
sg. = singular
*Spec. = Speculum*
*Sprachschatz* = C.W.M. Grein, *Sprachschatz der angelsächsischen
Dichter* (as revised by Ferdinand Holthausen and J.J. Köhler, Heidelberg
1912, unless otherwise indicated)
subj. = subjunctive
*TPS = Transactions of the Philological Society*
VP = The Vespasian Psalter Gloss
WG = West Germanic
wk = weak
WS = West Saxon
*ZfdA. = Zeitschrift für deutsches Altertum*
*ZfdPh. = Zeitschrift für deutsche Philologie*
* = reconstructed linguistic form
< = coming from
> = becoming

# Bibliography



THE MANUSCRIPT, A TRANSCRIPT, REPRODUCTIONS

*The Manuscript*

Manuscript Junius 11, Bodleian Library, Oxford, pages 213–29

*A Complete Indirect Transcript and a Complete Reproduction*

– Grimm 1817. A transcript of the Göttingen copy of Junius 1655, made
  by Jacob Grimm in 1817, now in the Stiftung Preussischer Kultur-
  besitz Staatsbibliothek, Marburg an der Lahn. Reported by Merrel D.
  Clubb, 'Grimm's Transcript of Caedmon,' *PQ* 44. 152–72 (1965). See
  also Clubb 1966, p 70
– Gollancz 1927. Sir Israel Gollancz, The Caedmon manuscript of Anglo-
  Saxon biblical poetry, Junius 11 in the Bodleian Library, with introduction. Oxford University Press 1927

*A Partial Reproduction*

– Bouterwek 1848 (see Editions: Complete). A facsimile of the first
  eight lines of p 213 of MS Junius 11, facing p 96

EDITIONS

*Complete*

Junius 1655. Franciscus Junius, Caedmonis Monachi Paraphrasis poetica
  Genesios ac praecipuarum Sacrae paginae Historiarum, abhinc annos

M.LXX. Anglo-Saxonicè conscripta, & nunc primum edita. Amsterdam: Apud Christophorum Cunradi 1655

Thorpe 1832. Benjamin Thorpe, Caedmon's Metrical paraphrase of parts of the Holy Scriptures, in Anglo-Saxon; with an English translation, notes, and a verbal index. London: Published by the Society of Antiquaries of London 1832

Bouterwek 1848, 1851. Karl W. Bouterwek, Caedmon's des Angelsachsen biblische Dichtungen. Erster Theil. Gütersloh: C. Bertelsmann 1854. (Der ersten Abtheilung zweite Hälfte. Elberfeld: Sam. Lucas 1848.) Zweiter Theil: Ein angelsächsisches Glossar. Elberfeld: Julius Bädeker 1851

Grein 1857a, 1858. C.W.M. Grein, Bibliothek der angelsächsischen Poesie in kritisch bearbeiteten Texten und mit vollständigem Glossar herausgegeben. Vols I & II. Göttingen: Georg H. Wigand 1857, 1858

Wülker 1894. Richard Paul Wülker, Bibliothek der angelsächsischen Poesie begründet von Christian W.M. Grein. Neu bearbeitet, vermehrt und nach neuen Lesungen der Handschriften herausgegeben. Vol. 2. Leipzig: Georg H. Wigand's Verlag 1894

Clubb 1925. Merrel Dare Clubb, Christ and Satan. An Old English poem edited with introduction, notes and glossary. New Haven: Yale University Press 1925

Krapp 1931. George Philip Krapp, The Junius manuscript. New York: Columbia University Press 1931

Finnegan 1977. Robert Emmett Finnegan, Jr, Christ and Satan. A critical edition. Waterloo, Ontario: Wilfrid Laurier University Press 1977

*Partial*

Ettmüller 1850. Ludwig Ettmüller, Engla and Seaxna scôpas and bôceras. Anglosaxonum poëtae atque scriptores prosaici, quorum partim integra opera, partim loca selecta collegit, correxit, edidit Ludovicus Ettmüllerus. Quedlinburg and Leipzig: Gottfr. Basse 1850 (Ll. 1–223, 336–512)

Rieger 1861. Max Rieger, Alt-und angelsächsisches Lesebuch nebst altfriesischen Stücken mit einem Wörterbuche. Giessen: J. Ricker'sche Buchhandlung 1861 (Ll. 160–89)

Williams 1909. O.T. Williams, Short extracts from Old English poetry chiefly for unseen translation. Bangor [Wales]: Jarvis & Foster 1909 (Ll. 19–64, 75–125, 384–435, 679–722)

Klaeber 1913a. Fr. Klaeber, The Later Genesis and other Old English and Old Saxon texts relating to the fall of man. Heidelberg 1913 (New edition, with supplement. Heidelberg: Carl Winters Universitäts-buchhandlung 1931) (Ll. 409–20, 469–93)

Craigie 1923. W.A. Craigie, Specimens of Anglo-Saxon poetry selected and edited. I. Biblical and classical themes. Edinburgh: I.B. Hutchen 1923 (Ll. 1–74)

Craigie 1926. W.A. Craigie, Specimens of Anglo-Saxon poetry. II. Early Christian lore and legend. Edinburgh: I.B. Hutchen 1926 (Ll. 384–424, 665–709)

Kaiser 1954. Rolf Kaiser, Alt-und mittelenglische Anthologie. Berlin-Wilmersdorf 1954 (Ll. 34–43, 51–69, 160–78, 190–7, 316–48)

TRANSLATIONS

*Complete*

Thorpe 1832. See Editions: Complete
Bouterwek 1848. See Editions: Complete
Grein 1857b. Dichtungen der Angelsachsen stabreimend übersetzt. Vol. I. Göttingen 1857 (Second edition. Cassel and Göttingen 1863)
Kennedy 1916. Charles W. Kennedy, The Caedmon poems translated into English prose. London: George Routledge & Sons Limited 1916
Finnegan 1969. See Philological and Critical Works

*Partial*

Gordon 1934. Robert Kay Gordon, Anglo-Saxon poetry. Selected and translated. New York: E.P. Dutton & Co. 1934 (Ll. 1–223, 366–468)
Kennedy 1952. Charles W. Kennedy, Early English Christian poetry translated into alliterative verse. London: Hollis & Carter 1952 (Ll. 1–365, 698–707a)
Kennedy 1960. Charles W. Kennedy, An anthology of Old English poetry. Translated into alliterative verse. New York: Oxford University Press 1960 (Ll. 34–50, 81–106, 130–78)

TEXTUAL STUDIES

Dietrich 1856. Franz Dietrich, 'Zu Cädmon,' *ZfdA*. 10.310–67 (1856)
Grein 1865. C.W.M. Grein, 'Zur Textkritik der angelsächsischen Dichter,' *Germ*. 10.416–29 (1865)

Sievers 1872. Eduard Sievers, 'Collationen angelsächsischer Gedichte,' *ZfdA*. 15.456–67 (1872)

Sievers 1885a. Eduard Sievers, 'Zur Rhythmik des germanischen Alliterationsverses,' *Beitr*. 10.209–314, 451–545 (1885)

Sievers 1887. Eduard Sievers, 'Zur Rhythmik des germanischen Alliterationsverses,' *Beitr*. 12.454–82 (1887)

Holthausen 1894a. Ferdinand Holthausen, 'Beiträge zur Erklärung und Textkritik altenglischer Dichtungen,' *IF* 4.379–88 (1894)

Holthausen 1894b. Ferdinand Holthausen, *Angl., Beibl.* 5.193–8, 225–34 (1894). (A review of the appropriate part of Wülker 1894)

Graz 1895. Friedrich Graz, 'Beiträge zur Textkritik der sogenannten Cädmon'schen Dichtungen. I,' *ES* 21.1–27 (1895)

Cosijn 1896. Peter J. Cosijn, 'Anglosaxonica. III,' *Beitr*. 21.8–26 (1896)

Bright 1903. James W. Bright, 'Jottings on the Caedmonian *Christ and Satan*,' *MLN* 18.129–31 (1903)

Kock 1904. Ernst A. Kock, 'Interpretations and emendations of early English texts. III,' *Angl*. 27.218–37 (1904)

Holthausen 1907. Ferdinand Holthausen, 'Zur Textkritik altenglischer Dichtungen,' *ES* 37.198–211 (1907)

Frings and Unwerth 1910. Theodor Frings and Wolf von Unwerth, 'Miscellen zur ags. Grammatik,' *Beitr*. 36.559–62 (1910)

Sievers 1912. Eduard Sievers, 'Zu Satan 42,' *Beitr*. 37.339–40 (1912)

Sperber 1912. Hans Sperber, 'Exegetische Miszellen,' *Beitr*. 37.148–56 (1912)

Klaeber 1913b. Fr. Klaeber, 'Notes on Old English poems,' *JEGP* 12.252–61 (1913).

Holthausen 1917. Ferdinand Holthausen, 'Zu altenglischen Denkmälern,' *ES* 51.180–8 (1917)

Kock 1918. Ernst A. Kock, 'Jubilee jaunts and jottings. 250 contributions to the interpretation and prosody of old West Teutonic alliterative poetry.' *LUÅ*., Ny Följd, Avdelning 1, Bind 14, Nr. 26 (1918)

Holthausen 1919. Ferdinand Holthausen, *Angl., Beibl.* 30.1–5 (1919) (A review of Kock 1918)

Kock 1919a. Ernst A. Kock, 'Interpretations and emendations of early English texts. V,' *Angl*. 43.298–312 (1919)

Kock 1919b. Ernst A. Kock, 'Kontinentalgermanische Streifzüge,' *LUÅ*., Ny Följd, Avdelning 1, Bind 15, Nr. 3 (1919)

Holthausen 1920. Ferdinand Holthausen, 'Zu altenglischen Dichtungen,' *Angl*. 44.346–56 (1920)

Kock 1920. Ernst A. Kock, 'Interpretations and emendations of early

English texts. VI,' *Angl.* 44. 97–114, and 'Interpretations and emendations of early English texts. VII,' *Angl.* 44.245–60 (1920)

Kock 1921. Ernst A. Kock, 'Interpretations and emendations of early English texts. VIII,' *Angl.* 45.105–31 (1921)

Kock 1922a. Ernst A. Kock, 'Interpretations and emendations of early English texts. IX,' *Angl.* 46.63–96, and 'Interpretations and emendations of early English texts. X,' *Angl.* 46.173–90 (1922)

Kock 1922b. Ernst A. Kock, 'Plain points and puzzles. 60 notes on Old English poetry,' *LUÅ.*, Ny Följd, Avdelning 1, Bind 17, Nr. 7 (1922)

Klaeber 1927. Fr. Klaeber, 'Weitere Randglossen zu Texterklärungen,' *Angl., Beibl.* 38.354–60 (1927)

Clarke 1931. Daisy E. Martin Clarke, *The year's work in English studies* 12.75 (1931) (Commenting on Malone 1931)

Malone 1931. Kemp Malone, 'Ealhhild,' *Angl.* 55.266–72 (1931)

Hulbert 1938. J.R. Hulbert, 'On the text of the Junius Manuscript,' *JEGP* 37.533–6 (1938)

Meroney 1942. Howard Meroney, 'Old English ðær "if",' *JEGP* 41.201–9 (1942)

Malone 1943. Kemp Malone, 'Plurilinear units in Old English poetry,' *RES* 19.201–4 (1943)

Manganella 1964. G. Manganella, 'Cristo e Satana,' *Ist.* 7.273–81 (1964)

Clubb 1966. Merrel D. Clubb, 'Junius, Marshall, Madden, Thorpe – and Harvard,' *Studies in language and literature in honour of Margaret Schlauch*, ed. Mieczysław Brahmer, Stanisław Helsztyński, and Julian Krzyżanowski, Warsaw: Państwowe Wydawnictwo Naukowe 1966, pp 55–70

Robinson 1966. Fred C. Robinson, 'Notes and emendations to Old English poetic texts,' *NM* 67.356–64 (1966)

Finnegan 1970. Robert E. Finnegan, 'Two notes on MS Junius XI *Christ and Satan*: lines 19–20; lines 319 and 384,' *PQ* 49.558–61 (1970)

Bliss 1971. A.J. Bliss, 'Single half-lines in Old English poetry,' *Notes and Queries*, New Series 18.442–9 (1971)

Stanley 1971. E.G. Stanley, 'Studies in the prosaic vocabulary of Old English verse,' *NM* 72.385–418 (1971)

## PHILOLOGICAL AND CRITICAL WORKS

Hickes 1705. George Hickes, Linguarum Vett. Septentrionalium Thesaurus grammatico-criticus et archaeologicus. Vol. I (pp 133–4). Oxford: E Theatro Sheldoniano 1705

Conybeare 1826. John Josias Conybeare, Illustrations of Anglo-Saxon poetry. London: Harding and Lepard 1826

Ellis 1832. Henry Ellis, 'Account of Caedmon's metrical paraphrase of scripture history, an illuminated manuscript of the tenth century, preserved in the Bodleian Library at Oxford,' *Arch.* 24.329–40 plus 53 plates (1832)

Bouterwek 1845a. Karl W. Bouterwek, Ueber Caedmon, den ältesten angelsächsischen Dichter, und desselben metrische Paraphrase der heiligen Schrift. Elberfeld: Sam. Lucas 1845

Bouterwek 1845b. Karl W. Bouterwek, De Cedmone poëta Anglo-Saxonum vetustissimo brevis dissertatio. Elberfeld: Julius Baedeker 1845

Bouterwek 1854. Karl W. Bouterwek, Caedmon's des Angelsachsen biblische Dichtungen. Erster Theil. Gütersloh: C. Bertelsmann 1854

Sandras 1859. S.G. Sandras, De carminibus Anglo-Saxonicis Caedmoni adjudicatis disquisitio. Paris: A. Durand 1859

Götzinger 1860. Ernst Götzinger, Ueber die Dichtungen des Angelsachsen Caedmon und deren Verfasser. (PHD dissertation.) Göttingen: Dieterichsche Universitäts-Buchdruckerei 1860

Wülcker 1872. Richard Paul Wülcker, Das Evangelium Nicodemi in der abendländischen Literatur. (PHD dissertation, Marburg.) Paderborn-Marburg 1872

Hammerich 1874. Frederik Hammerich, Aelteste christliche Epik der Angelsachsen, Deutschen, und Nordländer. Ein Beitrag zur Kirchengeschichte. (Translation by Al. Michelsen.) Gütersloh: C. Bertelsmann 1874

Watson 1875. Robert Spence Watson, Caedmon, the first English poet. London: Longmans, Green, and Co. 1875

Rieger 1876. Max Rieger, 'Die alt- und angelsächsische Verskunst,' *ZfdPh.* 7.1–64 (1876)

ten Brink 1877. Bernhard ten Brink, Geschichte der englischen Litteratur. Erster Band: Bis zu Wiclifs Auftreten. Strassburg: Karl J. Trübner 1877

Balg 1882. Hugo Balg, Der Dichter Caedmon und seine Werke. (PHD dissertation.) Bonn: Universitäts-Buchdruckerei von Carl Georgi 1882

ten Brink 1883. Bernhard ten Brink, Early English literature (to Wiclif). Translated from the German by Horace M. Kennedy. New York: Henry Holt and Company 1883

Groschopp 1883. Friedrich Groschopp, Das angelsächsische Gedicht 'Crist und Satan.' (PHD dissertation, Leipzig.) Halle: E. Karras 1883

Kühn 1883. Albin Kühn, Ueber die angelsächsischen Gedichte von Christ und Satan. (PHD dissertation, Jena.) Halle: E. Karras 1883

Ziegler 1883. Heinrich Ziegler, Der poetische Sprachgebrauch in den sogenannten Caedmonschen Dichtungen. (PHD dissertation.) Münster: E.C. Brunn'sche Buchdruckerei 1883

Hofer 1884. Oscar Hofer, 'Der syntaktische Gebrauch des Dativs und Instrumentals in den Caedmon beigelegten Dichtungen,' *Angl.* 7.355–404 (1884)

Sievers 1885b. Eduard Sievers, 'Zu Codex Jun. XI,' *Beitr.* 10.195–9 (1885)

Wülker 1885. Richard Paul Wülker, Grundriss zur Geschichte der angelsächsischen Litteratur. Leipzig: Verlag von Veit & Comp. 1885

Stoddard 1887. F.H. Stoddard, 'The Caedmon poems in MS Junius XI,' *Angl.* 10.157–67 (1887)

Morley, 1888. Henry Morley, English writers: an attempt towards a history of English literature. Vol. II. From Caedmon to the Conquest. London: Cassell & Company 1888

Deering 1890. Robert Waller Deering, The Anglosaxon poets on the Judgment Day. Halle: Ehrhardt Karras 1890

Ungemach 1890. Heinrich Ungemach, Die Quellen der fünf ersten Chester Plays. Erlangen and Leipzig: A. Deichert'sche Verlagsbuchhandlung Nachfolger (Georg Böhme) 1890

Brooke 1892. Stopford A. Brooke, The history of early English literature, being the history of English poetry from its beginnings to the accession of King Aelfred. London: Macmillan and Co. 1892

Lawrence 1893. John Lawrence, Chapters on alliterative verse. London: Henry Frowde 1893

Graz 1894. Friedrich Graz, Die Metrik der sogenannten Caedmonschen Dichtungen mit Berücksichtigung der Verfasserfrage. Weimar: Verlag von Emil Felber 1894

Wülker 1896, 1907. Richard Paul Wülker, Geschichte der englischen Litteratur von den ältesten Zeiten bis zur Gegenwart. Leipzig and Vienna: Bibliographisches Institut 1896. Second edition 1907

Cramer 1897. Julius Cramer, 'Quelle, Verfasser, und Text des altenglischen Gedichtes "Christi Höllenfahrt",' *Angl.* 19.137–74 (1897)

Becker 1899. Ernest J. Becker, A contribution to the comparative study of the medieval visions of heaven and hell, with special reference to the Middle-English versions. (PHD dissertation, Johns Hopkins University.) Baltimore: John Murphy Company 1899

Barnouw 1902. Adriaan Jacob Barnouw, Textkritische Untersuchungen nach dem Gebrauch des bestimmten Artikels und des schwachen Adjectivs in der altenglischen Poesie. Leiden: E.J. Brill 1902

Gaskin 1902. Robert Tate Gaskin, Caedmon, the first English poet. Third edition. London: Society for Promoting Christian Knowledge 1902

Abbetmeyer 1903. Charles D.A.F. Abbetmeyer, Old English poetical motives derived from the doctrine of sin. (PHD dissertation, University of Minnesota.) Minneapolis: The H.W. Wilson Company 1903.

Brown 1904. Carleton F. Brown, *MLN* 19.221–3 (1904) (A review of Abbetmeyer 1903)

Grüters 1905. Otto Grüters, Ueber einige Beziehungen zwischen altsächsischer und altenglischer Dichtung (Bonner Beiträge zur Anglistik 17) Bonn: P. Hanstein's Verlag 1905

Förster 1906. Max Förster, 'Altenglische Predigtquellen. I,' *ASNS* 116.301–14 (1906)

Blackburn 1907. Francis A. Blackburn (ed.), Exodus and Daniel. Two Old English poems preserved in MS Junius 11 in the Bodleian Library of the University of Oxford, England. Boston: D.C. Heath and Co. 1907

Meyer 1907. Ernst Meyer, Darstellung der syntaktischen Erscheinungen in dem angelsächsischen Gedicht 'Christ und Satan.' Rostock: Buchdruckerei von Eichemeyer & Fett, G.m.b.H. 1907

Smith 1907. M. Bentinck Smith, in A.W. Ward and A.R. Waller (eds.), The Cambridge history of English literature. Vol. 1: From the beginnings to the cycles of romance. New York and London: G.P. Putnam's Sons 1907

Walter 1907. Ludwig Walter, Der syntaktische Gebrauch des Verbums in dem angelsächsischen Gedichte 'Christ und Satan.' (PHD dissertation, Rostock.) Rostock: Buchdruckerei von Eichemeyer & Fett, G.m.b.H. 1907

Brandl 1908. Alois Brandl, 'Englische Literatur,' in Herman Paul (ed.), Grundriss der germanischen Philologie, Second edition, Band 2, Abteilung 1, pp 941–1134. Strassburg: Karl J. Trübner 1908

Grau 1908. Gustav Grau, Quellen und Verwandtschaften der älteren germanischen Darstellungen des Jüngsten Gerichtes. Halle: Max Niemeyer 1908

Richter 1910. Carl Richter, Chronologische Studien zur angelsächsischen Literatur auf Grund sprachlichmetrischer Kriterien. Halle: Verlag von Max Niemeyer 1910

Schmitz 1910. Theodor Schmitz, 'Die Sechstakter in der altenglischen Dichtung,' *Angl.* 33.1–76, 172–218 (1910)

Gajšek 1911. Stephanie von Gajšek, Milton und Caedmon. Vienna and Leipzig: Wilhelm Braumüller 1911

Frings 1913. Theodor Frings, 'Christ und Satan,' *ZfdPh.* 45.216–36 (1913)

Sarrazin 1913. Gregor Sarrazin, Von Kädmon bis Kynewulf. Eine litterarhistorische Studie. Berlin: Mayer & Müller 1913

Wieners 1913. Reinhold Wieners, Zur Metrik des Codex Junius XI. Köln 1913

Barnouw 1914. Adriaan Jacob Barnouw, Anglo-Saxon Christian poetry. (Translation by Louise Dudley.) The Hague: Martinus Nijhoff 1914

Bradley 1915. Henry Bradley, 'The numbered sections in Old English poetical MSS,' *Proc. Brit. Ac.* 7.165–87 (1915–16)

Strauss 1925. Otto Strauss, 'Beiträge zur Syntax der im Codex Junius enthaltenen altenglischen Dichtungen,' *NS*, 6. Beiheft, 172–82 (1925)

Crawford 1926. S.J. Crawford, 'The Caedmon poems,' *Angl.* 49.279–84 (1926)

Merwe Scholz 1927. Hendrik van der Merwe Scholtz, The kenning in Anglo-Saxon and Old Norse poetry. Utrecht: N.V. Dekker & van de Vegt 1927

Clubb 1928. Merrel Dare Clubb, 'The second book of the "Caedmonian" manuscript,' *MLN* 43.304–6 (1928)

Greene 1928. Richard L. Greene, 'A re-arrangement of *Christ and Satan*,' *MLN* 43.108–10 (1928)

Ricci 1929a. Aldo Ricci, 'The Anglo-Saxon eleventh-century crisis,' *RES* 5.1–11 (1929)

Ricci 1929b. Aldo Ricci, 'The chronology of Anglo-Saxon poetry,' *RES* 5.257–66 (1929)

Dustoor 1930. P.E. Dustoor, 'Legends of Lucifer in Early English and in Milton,' *Angl.* 54.213–68 (1930)

Bartlett 1935. Adeline Courtney Bartlett, The larger rhetorical patterns in Anglo-Saxon poetry. New York: Columbia University Press 1935

Bracher 1937. F. Bracher, 'Understatement in Old English poetry,' *PMLA* 52.915–34 (1937)

Schirmer 1937, 1954. Walter F. Schirmer, Geschichte der englischen Literatur von den Anfängen bis zur Gegenwart. Halle 1937. (Second, revised edition Tübingen: Max Niemeyer Verlag 1954)

Crotty 1939. Genevieve Crotty, 'The Exeter *Harrowing of Hell*: a reinterpretation,' *PMLA* 54.349–58 (1939)

Renwick and Orton 1939, 1966. W.L. Renwick and Harold Orton, The beginnings of English literature to Skelton 1509. London: The Cresset Press 1939. (Third edition, revised by Martyn F. Wakelin, London: The Cresset Press 1966)

Williams 1940. Margaret Williams, Word-Hoard: passages from Old English literature from the sixth to the eleventh centuries, translated and arranged. New York: Sheed & Ward 1940

Kennedy 1943. Charles W. Kennedy, The earliest English poetry: a critical survey of the poetry written before the Norman Conquest with illustrative translations. New York: Oxford University Press 1943

Schirmer 1945. Walter F. Schirmer, Kurze Geschichte der englischen Literatur von den Anfängen bis zur Gegenwart. Halle 1945

Lohr 1946. Evelyn Lohr, Patristic demonology in Old English literature. (PHD dissertation, New York University 1946)

Malone 1948. Kemp Malone, 'The Old English period (to 1100),' in Albert C. Baugh (ed.), A literary history of England. New York: Appleton-Century-Crofts 1948

Anderson 1949. George K. Anderson, The literature of the Anglo-Saxons. Princeton University Press 1949

Anderson 1950. George K. Anderson, in Hardin Craig (ed.), A history of English literature. Oxford University Press 1950

Timmer 1951. B.J. Timmer, 'Expanded lines in Old English poetry,' *Neo*. 35.226–30 (1951)

Hodgkin 1952. R.H. Hodgkin, A history of the Anglo-Saxons. Third edition. Oxford University Press 1952

Slay 1952. D. Slay, 'Some aspects of the technique of composition of Old English verse,' *TPS*, 1952, 1–14

Magoun 1953. Francis P. Magoun, Jr, 'Oral-formulaic character of Anglo-Saxon narrative poetry,' *Spec*. 28.446–67 (1953)

Schubel 1953. Friedrich Schubel, 'Zur Bedeutungskunde altenglischer Wörter mit christlichem Sinngehalt,' *ASNS* 189.289–303 (1953)

Woolf 1953. R.E. Woolf, 'The devil in Old English poetry,' *RES*, New Series, 4.1–12 (1953)

Schubel 1954. Friedrich Schubel, Englische Literaturgeschichte. I. Die alt- und mittelenglische Periode. (Sammlung Göschen 1114.) Berlin: W. de Gruyter 1954

Greenfield 1955. Stanley B. Greenfield, 'The formulaic expression of the theme of "exile" in Anglo-Saxon poetry,' *Spec*. 30.200–6 (1955)

Blair 1956. Peter Hunter Blair, An introduction to Anglo-Saxon England. Cambridge University Press 1956

Schaar 1956. Claes Schaar, 'On a new theory of Old English poetic diction,' *Neo.* 40.301–5 (1956)

Schlauch 1956. Margaret Schlauch, English medieval literature and its social foundations. Warsaw: Państwowe Wydawnictwo Naukowe 1956

Ker 1957. N.R. Ker, Catalogue of manuscripts containing Anglo-Saxon. Oxford University Press 1957

Workman 1958. Rhea Thomas Workman, The concept of hell in Anglo-Saxon poetry before A.D. 850. (PHD dissertation, University of South Carolina 1958.)

Huppé 1959. Bernard F. Huppé, Doctrine and poetry: Augustine's influence on Old English poetry. State University of New York Press 1959

Young 1959. Jean I. Young, 'Two notes on the *Later Genesis*,' in Peter Clemoes (ed.), The Anglo-Saxons: Studies in some aspects of their history and culture presented to Bruce Dickins. London: Bowes & Bowes 1959

White 1960. W.D. White, The descent of Christ into hell: a study in Old English literature. (PHD dissertation, University of Texas 1960)

Benning 1961. Helmut A. Benning, 'Welt' und 'Mensch' in der altenglischen Dichtung. Bedeutungsgeschichtliche Untersuchungen zum germanisch-altenglischen Wortschatz. Bochum-Langendreer: Verlag Heinr. Pöppinghaus Ohg. 1961

Zesmer 1961. David M. Zesmer, Guide to English literature. From *Beowulf* through Chaucer and medieval drama. With bibliographies by Stanley B. Greenfield. New York: Barnes & Noble, Inc. 1961

Anderson 1962. George K. Anderson, Old and Middle English literature from the beginnings to 1485. New York: Collier Books 1962. (A reprint with some revision of Anderson 1950)

Dubois 1962. Marguerite-Marie Dubois, La littérature anglaise du Moyen Age (500–1500). Paris: Presses Universitaires de France 1962

Bloomfield 1963. Morton W. Bloomfield, 'Patristics and Old English literature: notes on some poems,' in Stanley B. Greenfield (ed.), Studies in Old English literature in honor of Arthur G. Brodeur. Eugene: University of Oregon Press 1963

Frey 1963. Leonard H. Frey, 'Exile and elegy in Anglo-Saxon Christian epic poetry,' *JEGP* 62.293–302 (1963)

Greenfield 1965. Stanley B. Greenfield, A critical history of Old English literature. New York University Press 1965

Morrell 1965. Minnie Cate Morrell, A manual of Old English biblical materials. Knoxville: The University of Tennessee Press 1965

Shepherd 1966. Geoffrey Shepherd, 'Scriptural poetry,' in Eric Gerald Stanley (ed.), Continuations and beginnings. Studies in Old English literature. London and Edinburgh: Nelson 1966

Standop and Mertner 1967. Ewald Standop and Edgar Mertner, Englische Literaturgeschichte. Heidelberg: Quelle und Meyer Verlag 1967. (Identical in second edition, 1971)

Whitbread 1967. L. Whitbread, 'The doomsday theme in Old English poetry,' *Beitr.* (Halle) 89.452–81 (1967)

Wrenn 1967. C.L. Wrenn, A study of Old English literature. New York: W.W. Norton & Company, Inc. 1967

Isaacs 1968. Neil D. Isaacs, Structural principles in Old English poetry. Knoxville: The University of Tennessee Press 1968

Robinson 1968. Fred C. Robinson, 'Some uses of name-meanings in Old English poetry,' *NM* 69.161–71 (1968)

Finnegan 1969. Robert Emmett Finnegan, Jr, MS Junius XI *Christ and Satan* and the Latin and vernacular prose homiletic traditions. (PHD dissertation, University of Notre Dame 1969)

Hill 1969. Thomas D. Hill, 'Apocryphal cosmography and the "stream uton sǽ": a note on *Christ and Satan*, lines 4–12,' *PQ* 48.550–4 (1969)

Hill 1970. Thomas D. Hill, '"Byrht Word" and "Hǽlendes heafod": Christological allusion in the Old English *Christ and Satan*,' *ELN* 8.6–9 (1970)

Keenan 1970. Hugh T. Keenan, '*Exodus* 312: "the green street of paradise",' *NM* 71.455–60 (1970)

Benskin 1971. Michael Benskin, 'An argument for an interpolation in the Old English *Later Genesis*,' *NM* 72.224–45 (1971)

Clemoes 1971. Peter Clemoes, "Cynewulf's image of the Ascension,' in Peter Clemoes and Kathleen Hughes (editors), England before the Conquest: Studies in primary sources presented to Dorothy Whitelock, Cambridge: At the University Press 1971, pp 293–304 (especially pp 299–300)

Hill 1971. Thomas D. Hill, '"Hwyrftum scriþað": *Beowulf* l. 163,' *Mediaeval Studies* 33.379–81 (1971)

Finnegan 1972. Robert Emmett Finnegan, '*Christ and Satan*, 63–64,' *The Explicator* 31 no. 2, item 10 (1972)

Hill 1972. Thomas D. Hill, 'Satan's fiery speech: *Christ and Satan* 78–9,' *Notes and Queries*, New Series 19.2–4 (1972)

Lee 1972. Alvin A. Lee, The guest-hall of Eden: four essays on the design of Old English poetry. New Haven and London: Yale University Press 1972

Ohlgren 1972. Thomas H. Ohlgren, 'Five new drawings in the *MS Junius 11*: their iconography and thematic significance,' *Spec.* 47.227–33 (1972)

Shippey 1972. T.A. Shippey, Old English verse. London: Hutchinson University Library 1972

Brown 1973. Alan K. Brown, 'Neorxnawang,' *NM* 74.610–23 (1973)

Doane 1973. A.N. Doane, '"The green street of paradise": a note on lexis and meaning in Old English poetry,' *NM* 74.456–65 (1973)

Grose and McKenna 1973. M.W. Grose and Deirdre McKenna, Old English literature. Totowa, New Jersey: Rowman and Littlefield 1973 (pp 80, 85)

Hall 1973. James R. Hall, The Old English book of salvation history: three studies on the unity of MS Junius 11. (PHD dissertation, University of Notre Dame 1973)

Kuznets 1973. Lois Rostow Kuznets, Point of view in Old English Christological poetry. (PHD dissertation, Indiana University 1973)

Wentersdorf 1973. Karl P. Wentersdorf, 'On the meaning of O.E. *dreorig* in *Brunanburh* 54,' *NM* 74.232–7 (1973)

Finnegan 1974a. Robert Emmett Finnegan, '*Christ and Satan*: structure and theme,' *Classica et Mediaevalia* 30.490–551 (1969, actually published 1974). (A publication, with additions and revisions, of major sections of his dissertation of 1969, especially Chapters 1 and 2 and the last part of Chapter 4)

Finnegan 1974b. Robert Emmett Finnegan, 'Three notes on the Junius XI *Christ and Satan*: lines 78–79: lines 236–42; lines 435–38,' *Modern Philology* 72.175–81 (1974)

Hume 1974. Kathryn Hume, 'The concept of the hall in Old English poetry,' *Anglo-Saxon England* 3.63–74 (1974)

Keenan 1974. Hugh T. Keenan, 'Satan speaks in sparks: *Christ and Satan* 78–79a, 161b–162b, and the *Life of St Anthony*,' *Notes and Queries*, New Series 21.283–4 (1974)

Rendall 1974. Thomas N. Rendall, 'Bondage and freeing from bondage in Old English religious poetry,' *JEGP* 73.497–512 (1974)

Cosmos 1975. Spencer Cosmos, 'Old English "limwæstm" ("Christ and Satan" 129),' *Notes and Queries*, New Series 22.196–8 (1975)

Gardner 1975. John Champlin Gardner, The construction of Christian poetry in Old English. Carbondale and Edwardsville: Southern Illinois University Press 1975

# Notes



1 Different editors have reached different conclusions about line division and line numbering; my own (in the appendix and the microfiche text) do not quite agree with anyone else's, but since the differences are slight I abstain from double numbering, and will use my own line numbering consistently, in references to the work of earlier scholars as well as my own.
2 P 189
3 Pp viii–xi, xv, vii
4 P 135
5 P 194
6 Esp. pp 83 and 86
7 P 6
8 Pp 109–11
9 Esp. p 7
10 Esp. pp 12, 41
11 P 10
12 Pp 16–34
13 Pp 93, 96–8
14 P 115
15 P 16, in contrast to his uncertain
acceptance in 1943 (pp 188–90) of a unity developing from theological rather than literary roots
16 P 56
17 Pp 33, 35
18 Pp 98–9
19 P 68
20 Pp 70–3
21 Pp 101–8
22 P 235
23 Pp 236, 217
24 Pp 1045–6
25 P xlvii
26 Pp l–liii
27 Pp xlviii–xlix
28 P cv
29 Pp xxxiv–xxxv
30 Pp 68, 69
31 Pp 227–31, esp. pp 227, 230
32 Pp 232–4; see also Finnegan 1974a: 530–2, and Finnegan 1977: 26
33 Pp 13–19
34 P 231
35 P 128
36 P 144

37 P 66; see also Finnegan 1974a: 540–2, 550–1, and Finnegan 1977: 32

38 Pp 21–68, esp. pp 21–47; see also Finnegan 1974a: 503–42, esp. pp 503–24, and Finnegan 1977: 17–36, esp. pp 17–22

39 Pp 54–62; see also Finnegan 1974a: 530–8, and Finnegan 1977: 26–30

40 Pp 62–7, esp. p 62; see also Finnegan 1977: 30–3, esp. p 31

41 Pp 13–19

42 P 5 above

43 Clubb 1925n

44 P xlix

45 Ten Brink 1877: 110 had already called attention to the depiction of Christ in Part I as Creator, principal target of the revolt of the angels, and punisher of that revolt, without seeing it as an argument for the unity of the work.

46 Compare l. 86 where Bearn Hēlendes necessarily means that the Son but just as inescapably Hēlend must mean the Father.

47 Clubb 1925, pp xlix, 48

48 Pp 227–8

49 P 48

50 Karl August Eckhardt, ed., *Leges Anglo-Saxonum 601–925* (Göttingen: Musterschmidt-Verlag 1958) 72

51 'Hymnum diebus dominicis,' *The Vespasian Psalter*, ed. Sherman M. Kuhn (Ann Arbor: The University of Michigan Press 1965) 159–60, with its English interlinear gloss written at Lichfield in the early ninth century, according to Kuhn pp v–vi.

52 See pp 7–8 above.

53 Finnegan 1969: 93–102; see also Finnegan 1977: 48–9

54 The pervading importance of this doctrine in much mediaeval English thought and writing has been made clearer and clearer in the last few decades in an imposing body of work by such scholars as Huppé and Robertson. The fruitfulness of this approach has by no means been exhausted.

55 It seems likely that Grein may have traveled some indeterminable distance along this mental path or a similar one when he decided to treat Book Two of MS Junius 11 as a single work and to name it *Christ and Satan*.

56 See the page references under 'might of God (Christ)' in the index.

57 Further, on pp 109–11 below, I argue that the 'abasement-exaltation' motif together with its everywhere supportive 'might' motif constitutes a complex theme which is in some way a counterpart to the 'covenant' theme of the other three poems in MS Junius 11.

58 This matter is considered at greater length on pp 50–67 below (especially pp 54–60); and then on pp 68–70 I argue that the evidence of sources and analogues suggests that the poem as a whole evolved out of Part II, which is firmly located within a certain homiletic tradition.

59 Paul uses the same verb tapeinoûn, 'to humble, abase' as do Luke and Matthew, and changes Luke and

Matthew's verb hypsoûn 'to exalt' by adding the intensive prefix hypér to it: thus hyperypsoûn 'to exalt highly.' In the Vulgate the two verbs are identical in all the passages: *humiliare* and *exaltare*. Both the gospel passages and the Philippians passage, moreover, sound like developments of the words 'he hath ... exalted them of low degree' which are part of the Virgin Mary's hymn called the Magnificat (Luke 1: 52 AV: Greek hýpsōse tapeinoús, Latin *exaltavit humiles*).

60 In fact both the poet and the homiletic tradition which he was following narrate the post-Crucifixion life of Christ from the Harrowing of hell to the Last Judgment as an interconnected whole. See pp 54–60 below.

61 Pp 135, 136

62 For a possible implication that the heavenly destination of the human souls is their 'birthright' by divine grace, see pp 103–4 below.

63 Finnegan 1977: 41

64 The English translation of the clauses of the Creed is from Philip Schaff, *The Creeds of Christendom with a History and Critical Notes* (New York: Harper & Brothers 1878) 2.69.

65 Clubb 1925: pp 131–2 rejects this reading on the ground that these lines are misplaced.

66 See also pp 65–6 below.

CHAPTER 2: DATE AND DIALECT

1 A notable exception is Abbetmeyer 1903, who on pp 18–19 ascribes some sections of Part I to the beginning of the eighth century and the rest of the work to a later date.

2 See p 5 above.

3 P 112

4 Pp 56, 59

5 Pp 112, 110

6 Pp 80, 79

7 P 326

8 Pp 24–7

9 P 5

10 Pp 19–20

11 Pp 8, 35, 37

12 P 95

13 Pp 53–4

14 Pp xiii, 194–7

15 P lx

16 P xxxvi

17 Pp 920–1

18 P 21

19 P 195

20 P 69

21 P 144

22 Pp 211–12

23 P 477

24 P 101

25 Finnegan 1977: pp 60–3

26 Excepting Ricci 1929a (see p 28 above)

27 See also pp 60–4 below.

28 Vol. I, p 133

29 See p 28 above.

30 Pp 101–8

31 P 230

32 P 1046

33 Pp 3–5, 34–5, 92–3, and esp. 100–1

34 P 233

35 See above.

36 See p 5 above.

37 Max Kaluza, *Der altenglische Vers: Eine metrische Untersuchung* (Berlin: Verlag von Emil Felber 1894)

38 John C. Pope, *The Rhythm of Beowulf* (New Haven and London: Yale University Press 1942, rev. ed. 1966)

39 Marjorie Anderson and Blanche Colton Williams, *Old English Handbook* (Boston: Houghton Mifflin Company 1935)

40 Henry Sweet, *An Anglo-Saxon Reader* (9th ed. rev. by C.T. Onions [Oxford: The Clarendon Press 1922])

41 *Proc. Brit. Ac.* 18.304–8 (1933)

42 *Studies in the History of Old English Literature* (Oxford: The Clarendon Press 1953) 119–39

43 Pp 232–3

44 Pp 223–36

45 A. Campbell, *Old English Grammar* (Oxford: The Clarendon Press 1959, 1969 printing). Hereafter cited as C.

46 Hereafter cited as Ru.[1].

47 Hereafter cited as VP.

48 Conrad Grimm, *Glossar zum Vespasian-Psalter und den Hymnen* (Heidelberg: Carl Winter's Universitätsbuchhandlung 1906). Hereafter cited as Grimm.

49 P lix

50 Henry Sweet, *A Second Anglo-Saxon Reader: Archaic and Dialectal* (Oxford: The Clarendon Press 1887)

51 For a strong and well-defended statement in favour of this latter possibility, see Sisam, *Studies in the History of Old English Literature* (1953) 123–6.

52 J.M. Hart, *MLN* 22.220–2 (1907)

53 F. Klaeber, ed., *Beowulf and the Fight at Finnsburg*, 3rd ed. (Boston: D.C. Heath and Company 1936) 133, note to l. 133.

54 P 50

55 See also Richard Jordan, *Eigentümlichkeiten des anglischen Wortschatzes* (Heidelberg: Carl Winter's Universitätsbuchhandlung 1906) 62–5, 46–8.

56 Sherman M. Kuhn, ed., *The Vespasian Psalter* (Ann Arbor: The University of Michigan Press 1965) v–vi

57 Karl D. Bülbring, *Altenglisches Elementarbuch. Erster Teil: Lautlehre* (Heidelberg: Carl Winter's Universitätsbuchhandlung 1902) 10.

58 See p 54 below.

59 See pp 57–8 below.

60 See pp 58–9 below.

61 See pp 66–7 below.

62 See p 47 above.

CHAPTER 3: SOURCES, INFLUENCES, TRADITIONS

1 Pp 37–9

2 Finnegan 1977: 39–42

3 See Shepherd 1966: 26

4 Finnegan 1977: 42–4

5 P 42

6 Pp 44–7

7 P 65

8  Pp 48–9

9  Pp 13–20 above.

10  Pp 48–9

11  *Œuvres complètes de Saint Avit...*, ed. Ulysse Chevalier (Lyon: Librairie Générale Catholique et Classique 1890)

12  *PG* 43.481–4

13  P 51 above

14  *Aldhelmi Opera*, ed. Rudolfus Ehwald (Berlin: Weidmann 1919)

15  *The Riddles of Aldhelm*, ed. and tr. James Hall Pitman (New Haven: Yale University Press 1925)

16  Pp xxvii–xxviii

17  Barnouw 1914: 25

18  Ten Brink 1877: 110

19  Pp. 93–8; considerably abridged in Finnegan 1977: 48–9

20  *PL* 76.1246–59

21  *The Apocryphal New Testament ...*, tr. M.R. James (Oxford: 1924) 94–5, 117–46

22  Pp 133–4

23  P 111

24  Ed. R. Morris, Early English Text Society, Original Series, Nos 58, 63, 73, the homily in question being in No. 63 (London 1876) 82–97

25  P 111

26  See also p 60 below.

27  Morris's edition, p 89, ll. 19–20

28  Morris 85/3 to 89/32

29  Morris 91/11–29

30  Morris 91/29 to 95/11

31  Morris 95/11–23

32  Morris 95/23 to 97/6

33  Pp 180, 194–6, XIII

34  This homily has been edited in part by C. Hofmann, *Gelehrte Anzeigen* der königlichen bayerischen Akademie der Wissenschaften 50.349–55 (Munich 1860).

35  P 195

36  Pp 301–7

37  At this point the words Næs hē mid nænigum nēde gebæded, ac hē mid his sylfes willan ... lēt his līchoman on rōde mid næglum gefæstnian correspond to the words *Nulla necessitate, sed propria voluntate in ligno se suspendi permisit, clavis corpus suum perforari non renuit* of Pseudo-Augustine 160, par. 1 l. 13 (*PL* 39.2059)

38  At this point *Blickling Homily* 7 has as the closing sentence of a prayer of the delivered souls Gecȳþ nū middangearde blisse þæt on þinum ūpstige geblissian & gehyhton ealle þīne gecorenan, corresponding to *redde jam laetitiam mundo. Jucundentur in ascensu tuo fideles tui ...* of Pseudo-Augustine 160, par. 5 ll. 8–10 (*PL* 39.2061).

39  Morris 87/25 to 89/32

40  See pp 55–6 above.

41  Pp 301–7

42  A.B. Kuypers, ed., *The Prayer Book of Aedeluald the Bishop Commonly Called the Book of Cerne...* (Cambridge University Press 1902) xi–xiv

43  Kuypers, pp 196–8

44  Kuypers, p 196

45  L. 5

46  Ll. 11–12

47  *PL* 39.2061

48  Morris 87/8–9

49 L. 16
50 Ll. 6–9
51 Par. 5, ll. 3–6
52 *F* 99*a*, ll. 10–13
53 Par. 5, ll. 7–10
54 See p 58 above.
55 *F* 99*a*, ll. 13–14
56 Morris 87/25–6
57 *F* 99*a*, ll. 14–15
58 *F* 99*b*, ll. 12–13
59 Morris 87/26–7
60 Morris 89/4–5
61 *F* 99*b*, l. 13
62 Morris 89/5–6
63 Ll. 14–19
64 Morris 89/6–7
65 Morris 89/12
66 Morris 89/13–28
67 Morris 89/28–32
68 Morris 89/17–22
69 Ll. 438–9
70 See p 56 above.
71 Par. 5, ll. 11–12
72 Morris 89/32–4
73 Pseudo-Augustine 160, par. 5,
   ll. 24–6
74 Morris 91/9–10
75 Par. 5, ll. 14–16
76 *PL* 39. 2060–1
77 See p 54 above.
78 M.R. James's translation, pp 135–9
79 6.1
80 Clubb 1925: pp xxx–xlii
81 Pp xxxi–xxxii
82 Pp xxxvii–xl
83 P xxvi n 35
84 Pp xl–xli
85 Grüters 1905: 36–41 and Clubb
   1925: 109
86 See p 61 above.

87 See also pp 28–9 above.
88 P xli
89 Finnegan 1969: 141–6; see also Finnegan 1974a: 542ff., and Finnegan
   1977: 33
90 Finnegan 1977: 33–6
91 *Ibid* 35
92 *Ibid*
93 *Ibid* 36
94 To paraphrase Huppé 1959, p 227
95 See pp 25–6 above.

CHAPTER 4: AN HYPOTHESIS
ABOUT THE GENESIS OF THE
WORK

1 Pp liv–lvi
2 See pp 14–15 above.
3 P 109
4 1883 translation, p 86

CHAPTER 5: CHRIST AND
SATAN IN THE TRADITION OF
OLD ENGLISH POETRY

1 (Boston: D.C. Heath & Co. 1922)
  xlviii–liii
2 *Proc. Brit. Ac.* 22.245–95 (1936)
3 Lee 1972: 3
4 R.W. Chambers, *Beowulf: An Introduction…*, 3rd ed. with a supplement by C.L. Wrenn (Cambridge
  University Press 1967)
5 Lee 1972: 15–16
6 *Ibid* 109, 171
7 Compare Lee 1972: 182
8 Lee 1972: 13
9 *Ibid* 13–14
10 The point of view is that of Satan or
   his followers in ll. 36–7, 42–8,
   81–3, 93–6, 115–23, 138–45, 150–6,
   164–78 (note in l. 177 asceāden

fram þǣre scīran driht 'parted from that shining dryht'), 232–45, 277–9, 327–30; that of the poet in ll. 198–9, 202–8, 216–23, 287–98, 309–15, 351–65, 552–6, 588–96, 642–62; and that of Christ in ll. 504–8, echoed by the poet 552–5.

11 Lee 1972: 14
12 *Ibid*
13 See p 105 below.
14 See also pp 105–6 below.
15 Here and elsewhere, quotations from *Beowulf* are in no way meant to suggest that *Beowulf* is a source of *Christ and Satan*; rather, they are parallel examples of phraseology characteristic of the traditional poetic style as a whole. Other Old English poems are frequently quoted for the same purpose.
16 Lee 1972: 15
17 *A Concordance to the Anglo-Saxon Poetic Records*, ed. J.B. Bessinger, jr, programmed by Philip H. Smith, jr, with an index of compounds compiled by Michael W. Twomey (Ithaca and London: Cornell University Press 1978)
18 Compare p 12 above.
19 See n 17 above.
20 *Ibid*
21 In yet another passage, *The Phoenix* 124, and swegl occur together (swinsað ond singeð swegle tōgēanes), but with no clear evocation of minstrelsy in a dryht-hall.
22 See p 87 n 17 above.
23 This has been treated on pp 16–18 above.
24 The following examples are the re-

sults of a very incomplete search: *Christ and Satan* 116 eard alēfan, 278 hām alēfan; *Christ and Satan* 402, 460, 553 ūp tō ēðle, 457, 505 ūp tō earde; *Christ and Satan* 96 ðes atola hām, 108 in ðeossum atolan ǣðele, 327 atolan ēðles; *Christ and Satan* 362 ūplicne hām, *Instructions for Christians* 262 tō þām ūplican hāme, *An Exhortation to Christian Living* 78 þā ūplican eardwīc, *The Creed* 37 þone ūplican ēðel, *The Seasons for Fasting* 151 þone ūplican æþel, *The Phoenix* 392 in þām ūplican ēðle, *The Creed* 32 ūplicne ēþel, *Andreas* 119–20 to þām ūplican ēðelrīce, *An Exhortation to Christian Living* 75 wið þæs ūplican eþel-rīces; *The Ascension* (*Crist II*) 646, *Vainglory* 74, *Riddle 66* 8 engla eard, *Andreas* 525, 642 engla ēðel, *The Ascension* (*Crist II*) 630 engla ēþel.
25 The ms has him, but the emendation is beyond cavil.
26 The readings feohgestealda and bēorsetle are derived by emendation, unobjectionably, from ms feoh ge stealde and beor sele.
27 Some additional examples (though less illuminating for our purpose) of hām as 'lord's seat' are *Widsith* 7, *Beowulf* 1147, 1156, *Andreas* 227 (?), 978 (?), *The Battle of Maldon* 292, *The Advent* (*Crist I*) 350, *The Ascension* (*Crist II*) 647, *The Paris Psalter* 102.18.1, 122.1.2(?), and *The Meters of Boethius* 9.18.

28 See p 96 below.

29 On ēadig see p 77 above; on eorl, p 105 below.

30 See pp 92–3 above.

31 John Howard Payne, 'Home, Sweet Home'

32 To be sure, it is a dwelling place without ār: see p 78 above.

33 This interpretation of the passage is probably better than the rival interpretation suggested on p 103 below.

34 See p 74 and n 10 above.

35 Ll. 148, 425–30, and 503 are perhaps the only exceptions.

36 See p 88 above.

37 See pp 88–9 above.

38 See p 95 above.

39 See pp 92–3 above.

40 See pp 94–5 above.

41 A similar development of meaning of ēðel is attested by a larger number of examples, some of them earlier. See pp 100–1 below.

42 See also p 98 above.

43 See pp 97–8 above.

44 See p 78 above for the Christian use of ār to mean 'divine grace or mercy' as a development from the heroic sense of 'lordly generosity.' For other uses of eard or its derivatives or compounds in reference to heaven as the dwelling of angels or blessed souls, see for example *Solomon and Saturn* 504, *The Judgment Day 2* 304, and *An Exhortation to Christian Living* 78.

45 See pp 98–9 above.

46 See pp 97–8 above.

47 See n 17 above.

48 See below.

49 If we may read any intimation of the 'birthright' sense in this and *some* other references to heaven as the ēðel of human souls, we may suppose that such passages to that extent reflect the doctrine expressed by St Paul in his Epistle to the Galatians 4: 1–7, especially 6–7 (AV): 'And because ye are sons, God hath sent forth the Spirit of his Son into your hearts, crying Abba, Father. Wherefore thou art no more a servant, but a son; and if a son, then an heir of God through Christ.'

50 See above.

51 The rival interpretation given on p 95 above is probably better.

52 See p 96 above; also, for the importance of the covenant motif in MS Junius 11 as a whole, pp 109–11 below.

53 See pp 18–19 above.

54 See p 102 above.

55 Philippians 2: 6–7 (AV): see pp 14–15 above.

56 See p 100 above.

57 In this respect the *Christ and Satan* poet is at least slightly innovative, for uses of ēðel to refer to hell are surprisingly rare in the rest of the Old English Christian poetry. In *Genesis* the fallen world as the 'domain' (ēðel 927, ēðyl 962) which Adam and Eve are condemned to occupy after the Fall is typologically hell; so, in *Andreas*, is the cannibals' country (ēðel 176);

Cynewulf in *The Fates of the Apostles* speaks of the unknown ēðel (113) which will be allotted to him and all men after death, which may be hell or heaven: and in *Solomon and Saturn* hell is characterized as 'the narrowest country' (ðæs ængestan ēðelrīces 106). Other examples appear to be lacking.

58 See above, p 92 and pp 16–18.

59 This supposition agrees with the view of Clubb (1925: 55–6) that Satan's words have a timeless reference as spoken in eternity and are not to be taken as anachronistic because they precede the Fall of man. However, Finnegan (1977: 93) holds the contrary view that 'for the creature, as opposed to the Creator, events, even in eternity, must be described linearly,' and that the word here can only apply to the angels.

60 This combination is formulaic at least to the extent of being used in reference to the Harrowing of hell in one other poem, *The Descent into Hell* 35 (forbrecan ond forbȳgan).

61 To be sure, one warrior may embrace and kiss another, as Hrothgar embraces and kisses Beowulf in *Beowulf* 1870–2a, but this consideration hardly accounts for the trembling in the *Rood* passage.

62 See A. Yonick, in the *New Catholic Encyclopedia* (New York: McGraw-Hill Book Company 1967) 4.404–5.

63 Incidentally we expose our own limitations if we allude to the 'hundred thousand miles' of 720–1 with an air of superiority as if the poet were less sophisticated than we just because he lacked the concept of light years; it is his hyperbolical way of making concrete the breadth and length and depth and height of Satan's presumption, mirror-imaging the exaltation of Christ at the right hand of the Father as well as 'the breadth, and length, and depth, and height' of the love of Christ, Ephesians 3: 18.

# Index

The Old English words entered in this index are only a selection from among those mentioned or discussed in the book.

Caedmon 3, 27–30, 33, 62; Caedmon's
  *Hymn* 29, 33
Cain 85
Campbell, A. 35–46, 129, 131
cannibals 101, 104n57
cantos 8
caritas (charity) 8, 13–26, 51, 55–6, 63,
  69, 81, 91, 109–11
Carran 102
Celestial Kingdom, the 73–4, 79
cempa 94
cester 81, 93, 98, 104–5
Chambers, R.W. 72
charity. See caritas
Chevalier, U. 52n11
Christ as Creator 9n45, 11–12, 15,
  20–2, 24, 48, 52, 63, 66–7, 73, 77, 80,
  86, 90–1, 109, 111, 120–1; as punisher of the rebel angels 9–11, 15–
  16, 19, 50–1; as target of the angels'
  revolt 9–11, 50–1, 73
Christocentricity 7, 9–13, 19–22, 29,
  120–1
Chronicle. See *Anglo-Saxon Chronicle*
Clark Hall, J.R. See Hall
clomm 106
Clubb, M.D. 6, 9, 11 and n47, 23,
  25n65, 28–9, 35, 40, 43, 51–3, 60–4,
  68, 105n59, 117, 119, 121–2, 124–6,
  128–30
Colossians (Epistle to the) 11, 20
comitatus 6, 12, 73–4, 78, 87. See
  also dryht
Commedia 98
Communion 110
*Concordance to the Anglo-Saxon
  Poetic Records, A* 82n17, 89, 91,
  101
Constantine 77, 83, 91
Constantinople 101

Conybeare, J.J. 3
Cook, A.S. 131
copyist(s). See scribe(s)
Corinthians (First Epistle to the) 22,
  110
Corrector 5, 34, 36, 40, 43, 45–6, 89,
  119, 122, 129
Cosijn, P.J. 130
covenant. See wǣr
covetousness. See cupiditas
creation 20–2, 24, 52, 71, 73–4, 77,
  86, 91, 109, 111. See also Christ as
  Creator
Creed: (Athanasian) 15, 24; (Nicene)
  12, 20, 24
*Creed, The* (poem) 92n24, 102–3
*Crist* 29. See also *Advent, Ascension,
  Last Judgment*, and Cynewulf
Crucifixion (of Christ) 15, 24, 26, 54–5,
  57, 60, 63, 66, 71, 79–80, 82–3, 105,
  107–9. See also Passion
cupiditas (covetousness, cupidity)
  13–26, 53, 69, 81, 92, 109, 111
Cynewulf 28–34, 60–4; *The Ascension (Crist II)* 30–2, 61–2, 72,
  92n24, 93n27, 98, 102, 108; *Elene*
  30–2, 61, 72, 77, 83, 91, 95; *The
  Fates of the Apostles* 31–2, 72, 94,
  99, 102, 104n57; *Juliana* 12, 30–2,
  61, 72, 92, 95, 98–9
cyning 76, 81, 84, 86, 93, 95, 105. See
  also wuldorcyning, heofoncyning
cȳþan 77

dǣd 78
dǣlan 79, 90–1, 109
damned, damned souls 18, 24, 51, 57,
  63, 74–5, 79, 81–2, 89, 99
Dane(s), Danish 29, 78, 84, 93, 97,
  101

# McMaster Old English Studies and Texts